Indian Society and Culture

Indian Society and Culture

Padma Charan Dhal
Kalyani Jena
Nalini Prava Mohanty

ATLANTIC
PUBLISHERS & DISTRIBUTORS (P) LTD

Published by

ATLANTIC

PUBLISHERS & DISTRIBUTORS (P) LTD

7/22, Ansari Road, Darya Ganj, New Delhi-110002
Phones : +91-11-40775252, 23273880, 23275880, 23280451
Fax : +91-11-23285873
Web : www.atlanticbooks.com
E-mail : orders@atlanticbooks.com

Branch Office
5, Nallathambi Street, Wallajah Road, Chennai-600002
Phones : +91-44-64611085, 32413319
E-mail : chennai@atlanticbooks.com

Printed in India at Nice Printing Press, A-33/3A, Site-IV, Industrial Area, Sahibabad, Ghaziabad, U.P.

Preface

Nowadays India is at a threshold of socio-economic revolution whereby the country's prosperity and power are on high growth trajectories. The implications of this are more than obvious, as each and every sector is developing at such a rapid pace that, change is the only thing that seems to be permanent. In such a scenario, the society and culture in India are witnessing a sea change. Needless to say that Indian society and culture have influenced the societies and cultures of different countries in the world. The society and culture in India may exhibit diverse and pervasive characteristics, still our country has maintained secularism and integrity. The unique features of Indian way of life have attracted the attention of scholars, academicians and researches since long. Hence, it is quite desirable to have a glance at the Indian society and culture and note its various facets and aspects.

With the passage of time Indian society and culture have undergone metamorphic changes with the basic tenets remaining constant. The present book entitled *Indian Society and Culture* is attempt to acquaint the readers with the society and culture in India so that they have a sound idea about its typicalities.

Encouraged by the widespread response and the warm welcome given to my previous works by the student community as well as teacher fraternity of different universities and institutions of higher learning with which I am associated, I have the pleasure in presenting this book along with the active support and cooperation of my co-authors Mrs. Kalyani Jena and Mrs. Nalini Prava Mohanty. I owe my deep sense of gratitude and indebtedness to them.

This book has been organized into five chapters, Chapter 1 describes the origin and composition of Indian society. Chapter 2 deals with social change witnessed in India over the years. Chapter 3 takes up the process of socioculture change in India. Chapter 4 throws light on different aspects of Indian culture, including religious movements, social reform, art and architecture. Chapter 5 focuses on growth of nationalism in India. We hope that it will appeal to the readers interested in knowing about various aspects of Indian society and culture.

No writer of a book of this dimension can isolate himself. We owe our intellectual debts to many and are deeply indebated to the authors of various books on this subject both Indian and foreign which we have freely drawn upon. Critical comments and suggestions for the improvement of the book are most welcome.

Padma Charan Dhal
Kalyani Jena
Nalini Prava Mohanty

Acknowledgements

The present book has been brought to fruition through the help of following distinguished scholars who willingly formed a support system which was always available to us. They are Dr. Kumar B. Das, Professor of Analytical and Applied Economics, Utkal University; Professor (Dr.) S.C. Kumar, Reader in Economics, P.N. College, Khurda; Professor Sudhakar Dhal, Principal, Kharasrota Mahavidyalaya, Singhpur; Professor Upendranath Dhal, Principal, S.G. College, Kanikapada, Jajpur; Professor (Dr.) Sudhakar Patra, Department of Economics, Ravenshaw University, Cuttack; Ms. Ifat Nawaj; Professor K.C. Patra, Principal, Pattamundai College Pattamundai; Chief Librarian Harekrishna Mahtab, State Library, Bhubaneswar and members of the staff of Kharasrota Mahavidyalaya, Singhpur, Jajpur.

Special mention may be made of the members of our families who have extended their whole-hearted support from initiation till completion of this work.

Last but not least, we are thankful to Mr. Harjeet Singh, Publication Co-ordinator, Atlantic Publishers & Distributors (P) Ltd., for his personal efforts in bringing out the book in a short time.

Padma Charan Dhal
Kalyani Jena
Nalini Prava Mohanty

Contents

Indian Society: Origin and Composition

1

1.1 Nature of the Indian Society

Indian society is complex, plural, diverse and pervasive in nature. Its social mosaic consists of multiple races, language groups, religious faiths, castes and tribes. History reveals that there are as many as 4,635 communities in India. The nature of Indian society can be studied with reference to three important factors such as space, time and population. In terms of space, India is the seventh largest country in the world. It covers nearly 3.7 million kms. In terms of time, it has a splendid past covering a span of 5000 years, further in terms of population; it is the second largest populated country in the world next to China. The heterogeneity of India makes it a land of diversity or a land of contradictions. The most important thing is that in spite of manifold diversity, there exists a thread of unity.

India is a vast peninsula. It owes its name to the mighty river Sindu. The early people called this country Bharat, a legendary king of great fame. The Muslim rulers called the country Hindustan and the British called it India.

Indian society has an inherent compactness unity. The bond of unity is called Indian culture. Indian culture is quite old. It has grown since the dawn of civilization. Indian culture is reflected in many splendors. The unity in diversity in Indian culture is unique. As W.G. Hegel remarks, "The Rome is the land of empire, Persia is the land of knowledge, Greece is the land of grace and India is a land of dream."

1.2 Composition of Indian Society

Indian culture may be studied under the following heads:

(a) Geographical Composition

India has its geographical identity. It is a vast subcontinent comprising the Himalayas in the north, Indian Ocean in the south, Bay of Bengal in the east and Arbian Sea in the west. There are perennial rivers like the Ganga, the Brahmaputra, the Narmada, the Krishna and the Kaveri. These rivers have made the country prosperous. They enjoy social respect for their contribution to human civilization. The people inhabiting in this country are proud of the resources both existing and potential. India is our matrubhumi. The people are very much proud of their motherland.

(b) Indian Culture

Indian culture is very old. The uniqueness of Indian culture lies in her wonderful power of accommodation and synthesis. The land is culturally fertile as it has manifested so many cultures all down the ages. Each culture has contributed something to the social fabric so that it has become vibrant. Indian culture is very ancient tradition which is nearly 5000 years old. It consists of literature, religion, language, dress and custom, dance and music, food and drinks, fairs and festivals, ethnic variations and social features. Indian culture has passed through many phases of evolution. It has produced religious thinkers, philosophers, prophets, saints and sages who have contributed a lot to the Indian culture.

(c) Religious Composition

India is a storehouse of all religions of the world. In India, there are Hindus, Muslims, Christians, Buddhists, Jains, Sikhs and Zorastrians. They all have a place in India to flourish. Each of the religions has a number of seats of its own. Hinduism is the religion of majority of people in India. It is an amalgamation of Indo-Aryan, Dravidian and pre-Dravidian religious elements. Hinduism have a number of seats such as the lingayat, the Kabirpanthi, the Sakta, the Radhaswamy and the Satnami, etc. It is the major religion in India and it provides a basis for national unity. Islam as a religion of Muslims entered into India at the end of the 12th century A.D. and thrived under political patronage of the Muslim rulers. India has a large Muslim population. Islam has two sects—the Sunni and the Shia. Christianity as a religion prevails mostly in the southern part of India. This religion has spread sporadically and is confined to certain sections of the tribal population. Christianity has three sects such as Romo Syrians, Roman Catholics and Protestants. Sikhism as a religion was founded by Guru Nanak in the 16th century A.D. They concentrate in the Punjab region, Tarai region of Uttarakhand and in Delhi. Buddhism originated in India during the 6th century B.C. It was founded by Goutam Buddha. This religion has two sects—Hinayana and Mahayana. This religion is prominent in Maharashtra. Jainism as a religion was established in 6th century B.C. Its founder was Mahavir. People belonging to this religion are found in Punjab, Uttar Pradesh, Rajasthan, Gujarat and Maharashtra. Jainism has three sects—the Digambars, the Svetambaars and the Phundias. Zorastrianism as a religion developed in India in the 7th century A.D. people of this religion are mostly found in Mumbai.

In India, religious affiliations seem to be overemphasized. The religious diversity has been a factor and source of disunity and disharmony in the country, but in spite of diversities, there are a few basic common points which unite all religions together. Faith in divinity, sympathy for the fellowmen, keenness for salvations and better life after death, faith in karma and rebirth, ethical principles and a life of purity and simplicity are some basic issues which unite the Indians.

(d) Political Unity

The culture and religious unity of India have created the motive force for political unity. The political thinkers and writers of ancient India always stressed the importance of establishing an all India empire. The term Chakravarti, Samrat, Ekrat, etc. signify the importance of political unity of ancient times. Ashok, Akbar and the British have succeeded in unifying India under their rule. Thus, politics has given a sense of unity in India.

(e) Racial Composition

Indian people represent many rules. India is a museum of races. Sir Herbert Risley has classified Indian population into seven races such as Terko Iranian, Indo-Aryan, Seytho-Dravidian,

Aryo-Dravidian, Mongolo-Dravidian, Mongoloid and Dravidian. A.C. Haddon has classified Indian population into five distinct races such as the pre-Dravidian, the Dravidian, the Indo-Aryan, the Indo Alpine and the Monogolian, etc. B.S. Guha has classified Indian races into six categories such as Negrito, Proto Australaid, Mongoloid, Mediterranean, Western Brachyaphals and Nordic, etc. This seems to be the most authoritative and widely accepted classification. People belonging to all these races fall into four categories—the Aryans, the Sakas, the Huns, and the Greeks, etc. They have settled down permanently and absorbed by Indian. They have no separate racial identify. The process of assimilation has resulted in making them one nationality, i.e. Indian. Thus, the bonds of unity in India are stronger than the causes of its diversity.

1.3 Origin of the Caste System in India

The word 'Caste' is used in everyday life and we use it to distinguish one person from another. We say that such and such a person belong to a particular caste. In this way caste is a hereditary group. Caste may be defined as a hereditary endogamous group which decides the individual's status in the social stratification and his profession, etc.

Thus, caste is a system of social stratification which lies at the very root of Indian social structure. The word caste is derived from the Portuguese word 'caste' which means lineage. Among the Europeans who come to India in 15th-16th centuries, the Portuguese appear to have understood the Indian system correctly and applied the appropriate word caste. In Hinduism, caste is referred to as varna meaning colour.

It is very difficult to determine the origin of the caste system. Modern thinkers consider it best to enumerate the features of caste in defining it. Prof. Rapson is of the opinion that varna is the root cause of caste system. Varna means colour and it was originally used to refer to the distinction between Das and Arya in ancient India. In its very early stages the Indo Aryans had no social or professional groups. They lived as one homogeneous people. In the Rig Vedic age, there were only two classes of people in the society, the Aryans and the non-Aryans or the fair skinned and the dark coloured aborigines. Thus, the Aryan society was divided on the basis of varna or colour.

1.4 Characteristics of Caste System

Hutton, Ghurye and Duti have discussed the following predominant characteristics of caste system:

(a) Determination by Birth

The membership of caste is determined by birth. A person remains the member of the caste into which he is born and his membership does not undergo any change even if changes take place in his status, occupations, education and wealth, etc.

(b) Rules and Regulations Concerning Food

Each individual caste has its own laws which govern the food habits of its members. Generally, there are no restrictions against fruit, milk, butter, dry fruit, etc., but kachcha food (bread, etc.) can be accepted only from a member of one's own or of a higher caste.

(c) Definite Occupations

In the Hindu scriptures, there is a mention of the occupation of all varnas. According to Manu, the functions of the Brahmin, Kshatriya, Vaishya and Shudras were definite. The functions of the Brahmin were to study, teach, guide and perform religious rituals and to give and receive alms, that of the Kshatriya to study, perform religious rituals, give alms, punish the evil and go to war, that of the Vaishya to study, perform religions rituals, give alms, work in agriculture trade and animal husbandry, that of the Shudra to do mental work for all the other Varnas. Having developed from varna system the occupations in caste system are definite. In Hindu society even today in most cases the son of a black smith pursues the occupation of his father the son of carpenter becomes a carpenter while the son of a shoe maker becomes a shoe maker.

(d) Endogamous Group

The majority of persons marry only within their own caste. Brahmin, Kshatriya, Shudra and Vaishya all marry within their respective castes. Waster Marck has considered this to be the chief characteristic of the caste system. Hindu community does not sanctify inter-caste marriage even now.

(e) Rules Concerning Status and Touchability

The various castes in the Hindu social organization are divided into a hierarchy of ascent and descent one above the other. In this hierarchy, the Brahmins have the highest and the untouchables the lowest position. To the sense of superiority among the Brahmins is also conjoined the law of untouchability. This sense of superiority is much exaggerated and manifests in the south. The very touch and sometimes even the shadow of a member of lower caste is enough to defile an individual of a high caste. In Kerala, the Namboodari Brahmin is defiled by the touch of a Nayar, but in the case of a member of Tiya caste a distance of 36 feet must be kept to avoid being defiled and in the case of a member of the pulayana caste the distance must be 96 feet. The stringent observation of the system of untouchability has resulted in some low castes of the Hindu society being called untouchables who were consequently forbidden to make use of places of worship, cremation grounds, educational institutions, public roads and hotels, etc., and were disallowed from living in the cities. These characteristics of the caste system as mentioned above do not take into account all the numerous variations presently taking place in the caste system. Actually, it is difficult to formulate a definite and permanent definition of caste. The most that can be done is to describe the features of the caste system in a particular contest, since the caste system is undergoing considerable transformation and modification. It would not be surprising if castes were eventually reduced to a word signifying merely a group since inter-caste marriages are increasing and the restrictions on mutual behaviour, exchange of goodwill and conduct are breaking. Some people are changing their caste on the strength of their monetary wealth. The occupations of various castes are no longer fixed, a member of any caste takes to any profession that he desires, the Brahmins have been deprived of much of their past glory and respect. Very few caste Panchayats are to be seen and even they have no control whatsoever over other members. Many people have even started excluding their caste name from the name they use. In this way caste is continually taking on the shape of class and casteism is growing in the form of classicism. On the one hand some candidates are favouring its existence, while on the other they are unfavourable.

1.5 Conditions Favouring the Caste System

The conditions favouring the caste system are too numerous. However, the most important conditions are as follows:

(a) Geographical Isolation

Geographical isolation has a larger part to play in rendering a society static and powerless. The absence of adequate means of transport leads to the geographical isolation from others of people who inhabit distantly situated areas and this fosters old customs, mores, traditions and superstitions all of which encourage the caste system.

(b) Static Society

Hindu society is not sufficiently dynamic. There has never been any stupendous change in its political circumstances and economic conditions. Its social mores, customs and traditions have failed to change over the ages as times have marched along. But this does not mean that Hindu society has not changed at all. To say that it is static of changeless is only to indicate the extremely slow rate at which changes and modifications are instituted in it. As a general rule, the caste system was most acceptable in India in those days when the dynamic elements were at low ebb in the society. Thus, the comparatively static nature of society is a favourable condition to the continued existence of the caste system.

(c) Foreign Aggression

A further contribution to the desirability and utility of the caste system was made by foreign aggression. Many scholars hold that the caste system started in India when the Aryans invaded the country. The Aryans were fair skinned and victors. The natives of India were 6 lakh skinned and the victims. Hence, the society was divided into two classes; the members of the Victorian class considered themselves superior to the victimized class and thought it below their dignity to associate themselves with it and to marry into it. Therefore, strict laws regarding conduct, diet, marriage, etc., were formulated. These were the fundamental constituents of the caste system.

(d) Rural Social Structure

As compared with the urban social structure, the rural social structure is usually respected in it. As the rural structure weakens, or as urbanization in the country increases, the caste system also becomes progressively weaker.

(e) Influence of Religion

The influence of religion is the most important factor contributing to the continuation of the caste system. The Hindu caste system is looked upon as a divine ordained institution. People who violate it are considered sinners and it is believed that God will punish them. But to this reason, people do not have that courage to violate the laws of the caste system.

(f) Difference of Races

The existence of many races in the country led to the formulation of many strict laws concerning discrimination since each race endeavoured to maintain its purity. In the medieval period of Indian history, stringent laws concerning caste were laid down to protect Hindu society from the Muslims.

(g) Lack of Education

Lack of education occupies an important position among the factors which gave encouraged the existence of caste system in Hindu society. An illiterate community is usually static and orthodox. Superstitions, traditions and mores play an important role among uneducated people. In this way lack of education is a condition which favours the caste system.

1.6 Conditions Unfavourable to Caste System

The following conditions are unfavourale to the caste system:

(a) Modern System of Education

The modern system of education plays an important part in weakening the caste system. Modern education is negative as regards religion. It emphasizes on democratic values such as liberty, equality and fraternity. Modern education bears the stamp of the scientific and independent thinking in the west. It has laid much stress upon the importance of man. Thus, the progress of modern education is proportionately diminishing the ties of caste, etc. Education has encouraged inter-caste marriage. The feelings of superiority and untouchability are being gradually eliminated from the mind of younger generation as children of all castes study in the same school.

(b) Industrialization

Industrialization also has led to a decrease in the intensity of caste fervour because persons from all castes and from all classes sought and obtained employment in factories. According to A.W. Green, although the Brahmin has to take a prolonged religious both in order to purify himself against the defilement caused by the mere shadow of Shudras in the crowded lanes of city and the busy office. As a result of industrialization, individuals of all castes came into mutual contact in factories, hotels, markets, trains, trams and buses, etc., and the observance of laws concerning touchability became impossible.

(c) Increase in the Importance of Wealth

In the modern age, wealth is replacing caste as the basis of social prestige. Nowadays a person adopts that occupation which appears to him to be the most profitable. The consideration in the choice of a profession is no longer caste but individual capability and the facility in earning wealth. A wealthy Shudra is more respected than a poor Brahmin. For this reason, the ties of the caste are being loosened in the frantic race after wealth.

(d) Movements to Social Emancipation

As a result of the influence of modern education there has been a veritable flood of movements for social emancipation.

(e) Means of Communication

Along with the progress of industrialization in India means of communication also developed. This put an end to geographical isolation and thought, customs, etc., of different places that influenced each other. It became difficult to maintain the rigidity of caste in the whirl wind of communication set into motion by industrialization through such means as buses, trains, trams and cars, etc. In this connection Riley has pointed out that it is not possible to enquire the caste of the seller while purchasing something from him.

(f) Political Agitation

An important part of the aims of national agitation for a political awakening of the people in India was to end the discriminatory practices on the basis of the caste system. The objective of this national movement was the establishment of a democratic pattern of a democratic pattern of society in India. For this reason, it made efforts towards weakening the caste consciousness in the people.

(g) New Legal Machinery

In the new legal machinery of the British government the members of all castes were similarly punished for the same offence, the establishment of judicial courts deprived the caste Panchayats of their power and they no larger retained the authority to punish a criminal. In this way, the restrictions upon the opponents of the caste system were removed and gradually its laws also lost their meaning and significance.

(h) Emergence of New Social Class

At present new classes are appearing in Indian society. These social classes are replacing the castes. The organization of castes is vertical while that of classes is horizontal. Therefore as the class consciousness is increasing the caste consciousness is decreasing.

(i) Norms of Democracy

The most severe shock to the caste system was the establishment of a free democracy in India. Para 15(2) of the constitution of Indian republic declared all citizens to be equal. The fortress of caste system collapsed when foreign rule come to an end. According to the untouchability crime act of 1955 it is a crime to prevent any one from using a public place. The respect one accorded to the caste dwindled through the means of transport, educational facilities, industrialization, the democratic method of Government, etc.

In spite of the presence of so many adverse circumstances the caste system continues to exist in an aggravated condition in the country and though being identified with political interests it has become even more strong at some places. Much in the way of a combined effort must be done to eliminate it from the country. The disorganization of the caste system leads people to infer that the caste system will cease to exist in the future. But some scholars have dissolved this doubt. According to G.S. Ghurye, there is no fear of the extinction of the caste system in the near future due to the following conditions:

(1) Election

Due to the establishment of a democracy in India, the administrative machinery is operated by representatives elected by the people. The method of election has done much to encourage the caste system because the candidates want to achieve their support by drumming the cause of casteism among the voters. In this way, people are asked to vote for their caste candidate and this casteism is maintained by the elected leaders after the elections are over. Political parties also sponsor only that candidate for election in a particular area which caste is most numerous in that area.

(2) Protection of Backward Classes

The Indian constitution has provided for the protection of the backward and scheduled castes. Some posts are reserved for them in government services. Some seats are also retained for them in the legislative assemblies. They are given all types of facilities and special scholarships for education. All these special rights have encouraged casteism in the backward castes since the caste is proving very beneficial to them because of these prerogatives.

1.7 Progress of Class Consciousness and Casteism

Class is a status group. The consideration of the class as a status group renders it possible to apply it to any society which has many strata. Wherever a status group has a particular position in a hierarchy of ascent and descent the status group can be called social classes. This not only separates the members of social groups manifestly, but the sense of social status separates them mentally. Social class is a group of people who possess a particular social status or position by virtue of which they possess some privileges, responsibilities and powers. In each class there is class consciousness and a specific culture.

In India, on the one hand, the caste is becoming weaker due to the influence of such factors as industrialization, increase in the means of transportation, popularity of English education, political and social awakening, democratic government and laws abolishing untouchability, etc., and on the other, such new organization, as labour unions, etc., on the basis of occupation, post, capacity, etc., are being established. Due to an increase in the desire for more brought by the influence of materialistic tendencies, superiority or inferiority is now based on wealth and social power rather than on caste. Thus, the caste consciousness is being replaced by class consciousness. In view of these changes it is believed that the caste system will generally take on the form of a class system. It is very much contradictory that while on the one hand class consciousness seems to be progressing, on the other progress of casteism is observed, casteism is blind group loyalty towards one's caste or sub-caste which does not care for the interests of other castes and seeks to realize the social, economic, political and other interests of its own group. For people who are specially gifted in a particular occupation, other occupations are very limited in India and the paths to those that are available are closed. Children of these parents who have a small income or who have no wealth only look out for service. It is very common in big business institution and sometimes even in educational institution that the persons belonging to the castes of the proprietors, organizers and senior officials mostly get employment. Casteism of a similar type prevails in government services and political elections. Hence, it cannot be inferred that in the present context the caste is being destroyed and classicism is increasing. Actually in India, casteism is being transformed into classicism.

1.8 Recent Changes in the Caste System

In recent years the caste system has undergone radical transformation due to the impact of industrialization, urbanization, secularization, modernization spread of transport and communication and the change in the pattern and system of education, etc. As M.N. Srinivas states "Caste is taking on a new AVATAR or incarnation." Following are the most important changes taking place in the caste system:

(a) Erosion of the Supremacy of the Brahmins

In the early times Brahmins occupied a superior position in the society. Now there has been a sharp decline in the domination of the Brahmins. Their dominance has been restricted to only ritual activities.

(b) Change in the Lifestyle

At present the lifestyle of people has been changed into a considerable extent. In the past, every caste had its own lifestyle. The difference in the style of life diffentiated a man from lower caste from a man from higher caste. At present, the people of lower castes are adopting the lifestyles of higher castes and thereby claiming higher status in the society. This kind of change is known as sanskritization.

(c) Change in the Concept of Purity and Pollution

The concept of purity and pollution has undergone drastic change with the passage of time. People of different castes mix freely in public places, workplace, offices and in educational institutions. They travel in the same vehicle. The concept of purity and pollution are no where there because the people of high castes and touching the untouchables. This kind of change is known as de-sanskritization.

(d) Change in Commensality

Due to the spread of modern system of education, commensality has been changed. People of both higher caste and lower caste are eating together. Even the Brahmins do not hesitate to interline with untouchables due to the fulfillment of their political ends and self-interests.

(e) Change in Endogamous Rules

The rules relating to endogamy have become outlived after the enactment of the Hindu marriage act 1955. The incidence of inter-caste marriages is increasing day by day.

(f) Change in the Power of Caste Councils

Caste council is the legislative and judicial body of a particular caste which is authorized to frame rules and regulations for the welfare of the caste. But nowadays, such caste council is deprived of its power of rendering justice in any matter.

(g) Change in Inter-Caste Relations

In earlier times inter-caste relations involved traditionally prescribed and clear cut rights, obligation, authority and subordination. But nowadays, members of the lower caste are not obliged to carry out the orders of the members of higher castes. They hesitate to perform forced labour for upper caste people. They even resist to carry on their traditionally prescribed occupations such as removing of dead animals, beating of drums at the festivals of village God's and removing of leaf plates on which people belonging to the caste dine. As a result the natural rights and obligations have crumbled down.

(h) Change in Philosophy

Previously people had the idea that the law of karma determines the caste in which a man is born. The lower castes look upon their caste status as something for which they are responsible by their own acts in the past lives. Each member used to perform the caste rule and it was believed that violation of the caste discipline was a sin. This type of attitude is quite absent nowadays. They claim for equal right and equal opportunities.

(i) Change in Power and Domination

Under the prevailing caste system, the people belonging to the higher strata of society used to enjoy decisive power and domination. But now, power and domination is moving away from the higher strata to the lower strata. It is due to social mobility of labour, proletarianization and bourgeoisification. A person from a lower caste is becoming the representative of people by winning election. Certain electoral constitutions are reserved for them. Once elected they enjoy the status and dignity and forget their duties and responsibilities to the people belonging to the upper strata. This is social mobility of labour. The process of proletarianization refers to the lowering position of higher castes and bourgeoisification means mobility of people from lower starta to that of the higher enjoying economic status, social prestige and power.

(j) Change from a Closed System to an Open System

Caste is changing from a closed to an open system. This implies that mobility has then place within the caste system. This is due to Sanskritization and westernization. Sanskritization is a process where a low Hindu caste changes its customs, rites, rituals, ideology and way of life in the direction of a high twice born caste. This has simplified the process of mobility to take place within the caste system. Further westernization is a process of change in ideology values, institution and technology of a non-western society as a result of cultural contact with the western society for a long time.

1.9 Future of Caste System in India

It is difficult to make an unqualified statement concerning the future of the caste system. It is certainly true that the restrictions on marriage, diet, mode of life, etc., based on the caste system are breaking down. In spite of the spread of modern education, adoption of westernization and sanskritization casteism is increasing and caste system is being encouraged by the method of election and the protection of the government to backward classes. Actually, it seems more or less definite that there is no possibility of the caste system being eliminated from the Indian society in the near future. The root of the caste system goes deep in Hindu society and at its base are the important and beneficial principles of division of labour, specialization in occupation, etc. Foreign invaders made their best efforts to wipe out the Hindu region. In spite of all the efforts of the Muslims and the Christians no appreciable change could be brought in the caste system. It has been definitely affected somewhat by the influence of western education and its form has undergone a vast change. There is no room for doubt that this form of caste system will change further in future, it may even change beyond recognition. It will also be influenced by the development of the sense of democracy and nationalism, industrial progress and by new political and economic movements.

1.10 Tribe and Its Origin

Tribe is a spatial group which is constituted because of spatial congruity of its members. The term 'tribe' is derived from the Latin word 'tribus' which means differently in different countries. For Greek, the word meant fraternities, for the Roman it meant political divisions and the Irish history used it to refer to communities having a common surname. Defining the tribe in *Dictionary of Sociology*, George Peter Murdock has stated that it is a social group in which there are many clans, nomadic bands, villages or other sub-groups which usually have a definite geographical area, a separate language, a singular and distinct culture and either a common political organization of at least a feeling of common determination against strangers.

The *Dictionary of Anthropology* defines it as "a social group, usually with a definite area, dialect, cultural homogeneity and unifying social organization". According to Bogadus, "the tribal groups was based on the need for protections, on ties of blood relationships and on the strength of common religion".

Andre Beteille writes, "A tribe is a society with a political, linguistic and a defined cultural boundary. Further it is a society based upon kinship where social stratifications is absent".

According to another view, two essential elements of the tribe are a common dialect and a common topography. In short, the tribe is a group of persons having a common definite territory, common dialect, common name, common religion and a common culture in whom there is blood relationship and consequently a feeling of unity, who have a peculiar political organization and who generally marry within their own group.

India is unique in the tribal map of the world because of its high concentration of tribal population. As per the census of 1991, there are 67.76 million tribal people in India constituting 8.08 per cent of the total population. In India, tribe has a unique connotation referring to the bodering and enchanting group of people. In India, they are known by different names such as Janajati, Vanyajati, Vanavasi, Pahari, Adimjati, Adivasi and Anusuchitjati, etc. G.S. Ghurye call them backward tribes. They were called scheduled tribes after 1950.

1.11 Characteristics of Tribe

The following characteristics of the tribe emerge from its various definitions:

(a) Definite Common Topography

The tribe inhabits and remains within a definite and common topography. In the absence of a common topography the tribe would also lose its other characteristic features as community sentiments common language, etc. For this reason, a common habitat is essential for a tribe.

(b) Consciousness of Unity

A group of people living in particular area and possessing a consciousness of mutual unity can be called a tribe. This psychological element is an invariable and essential characteristic of the tribe.

(c) Common Language

The members of a tribe are required to speak a common language. This will help to generate and evolve a sense of communal unity among them.

(d) Endogamous Group

The members of a tribe generally marry into their own group but now due to increased contact with other tribes, the consequence of an increase in the means of transportations, the system of marrying within the tribe is also changing.

(e) Ties of Blood Relationship

A major cause of the sense of communal unity in the tribe is the tie of blood relationships between its members. The members of the tribe have faith in their having descended from a common, real or mythical ancestor and hence believe in blood relationships with the other members.

(f) Experience of Need for Protection

The members of a tribe very much experience the need for protection. Keeping this need in view, a political organization of the tribe is established and all authority for administration is vested in one person. This leader employs his mental power and skill in protecting the entire tribe. A tribal committee is formed to render assistance in the form of advice to the tribal chief. As a general rule, the tribal chief accedes to the wishes of the committee. The tribe is divided into numerous small groups each of which has its own chief. These chiefs solve the problem of their own groups and act according to the directives of the tribe.

(g) Political Organization

In this way each tribe has its own political organization which maintains harmony and avoids notes of discord among its members and protects them.

(h) Importance of Religion

Religion assumes much prominence in the tribe. The tribal political and social organization is based on religion because social and political laws become inviolable once they are granted religions sanctity and recognition. In the form of ancestor worship, tribal religion has rendered important service in developing the habits of obedience. The authority of a common religion is an important characteristic of a tribe.

(i) Common Name

The tribe has a common name.

(j) Common Culture

Resulting from a feeling of unity, common language, common religion, common political organization, etc., a common culture is found to exist in a tribe.

(k) Organization of Clans

A tribe is constituted of many clans. There exists laws of mutual reciprocity among its members.

1.12 Classification of Tribes

Sociologists have classified tribes into four categories on the basis of area of concentration, race, language and the nature of their profession, etc.

(a) Geographical Classification

Considering the widespread concentration and distribution of tribes in India, tribal population may be classified into five regions such as:

(i) Himalayan region (with tribes like Gaddi and Naga, etc.)

(ii) Middle India (Munda and Santal)

(iii) Western India (Bhil and Grasia)

(iv) South India (Toda and Chenchu)

(v) Island region (Onge and Minicoyans)

(b) Racial Classification

Anthropologists have classified tribes into three categories on the basis of race. They are:

(i) The proto Australoids (Mundas, Has, Oraons and Khonds).

(ii) The mongoloids with light skin, straight hair, flat nose, medium stature distribute all from the sub-Himalayan region.

(iii) The Negrito group is characterized by dark skin, round head, wide nose and frizzle hair (Kerala and Andaman).

(c) Linguistic Classification

On the basis of language spoken, tribes are classified into four major families:

(i) Indo-European family

(ii) Austro-Asiatic family

(iii) Dravidian family

(iv) Tibet Chinese family

(d) Economic Classification

On the basis of nature of work and pattem of livelihood tribes are classified into seven groups:

(i) Food gatherers and hunters

(ii) Shifting cultivators

(iii) Settled agriculture

(iv) Artisans

(v) The pastoralists and cattle herders

(vi) The folk artists

(vii) The wage labourers

1.13 Distinction between Tribe and Horde

A nomadic horde is a group of a small number of people. Horde becomes a tribe when the members increase to a very sizeable figure. A very strong community feeling exists in both horde and tribe which differ from each other mainly in respect of size. In both, such economic activities as collections of fruit, animal hunting, animal husbandry, fishing, etc., are carried on. In both, a similarity of blood relations is to be found. In both there is a conglomeration of families. The chief of the group is well respected and obeyed in both. In spite of such a great extent of similarity, the horde and the tribe differ from each other in the following respects:

(a) In the tribal group the need of protection stands out more prominently, as compared to the horde.
(b) The tribe is bigger in size than the nomadic horde.
(c) In the tribe, religion is more developed than in the horde because in the former a greater solidarity and strength of political and social laws as to be expected.
(d) Being a larger and more cumbersome size the tribe possesses a weaker sense of unity than does the horde.
(e) The tribe is divided into many smaller groups but the horde has no such divisions.
(f) Agriculture occupations is an accepted mode of life in the tribe whereas in the horde agriculture is not indulged into a large extent.
(g) The tribe inhabits a definite locality. On the other hand, instead of staging at a definite place the horde wanders over a definite geographical area.

1.14 Distinction between Tribe and Caste

Both tribe and caste exhibit considerable similarity, yet they differ from each other in many respects. Marriages within the clan are for bidden both in the tribe as well as in the caste. Both generally condemn marriage outside the group. The modern development in the means of transport and communications has induced increased contact between members of various tribes and has weakened the laws of endogamy in both.

F.G. Bailey is of the opinion that "there is no single and accepted criterian by which we can distinguish a tribe from a caste: but scholars and researchers like G.S. Ghurye, T.B. Naik and Verrier Elwin have used different criteria like religion, geographical isolation, language, economic backwardness and political organization for distinguishing caste from tribe.

The distinction between tribe and caste may be discussed in the following manner:

(a) According to Risley, the conventions of edogamy are not rigidly enforced in tribe whereas such is the case in a caste. But this view is not universal because the law of endogamy is enforced with extreme rigidity in same tribes.

(b) According to Max Weber, when an Indian tribe loses its territorial significance, it assumes that form of a caste. In this way, the tribe is a local group whereas the caste is a social group.

(c) The caste was originated in ancient Hindu society, with a view to division of labour on the basis of profession and occupations. The tribe comes about because of the evolution of community feeling on a group inhabiting a definite geographical area.

(d) According to D.N. Majumdar, the tribe looks upon Hindu ritualism as foreign and extra religions even though indulging in the worship of gods and goddesses whereas in the caste these are necessary parts of religion. The tribes of Madhya Bharat which are called Hindu and Kshatriya tribes are better acquainted with their own Banga then with the Hindu gods.

(e) According to Max Weber, the status of all people is similar in the caste, whereas there is much difference of status and rank in the tribe. This view of Max Weber does not apply to all castes. Difference of rank and status can be found in many castes also.

(f) There is greater consciousness of differences in status and rank in the caste than in the tribe.

(g) Caste is never a political association whereas the tribe is a political association.

(h) The names of clans on castes are adopted from some seer or mystical savant such as Vashisht, Vishvamitra,

Bhardwaj, Kashyap, etc. In the tribe, thc clans are based on totem e.g. the clans in the Komti tribe of my sore are named after all kinds of fruits, vegetables, spices and food grains, etc. The list presented by Thurston castes and tribes of southern India seems to indicate that hardly any name in the animal and vegetable world remains to be used as the basis for a totem name among the tribes.

In the tribe, individuals generally pursue their own definite occupations because functions are divided under the caste system. In the tribe, individuals can indulge their families in whatever profession they please because there is no fixed relation between them and the occupations.

Nowadays the tribes are gradually being converted into castes. Risley has mentioned four processes in this transformation. They are:

(i) By changing one's lineage.

(ii) By accepting the principles of any school of Hindu religion.

(iii) By joining Hindu religion.

(iv) By entering into relations with Hindus without changing name.

According to D.N. Mazumdar, a tribe can enter Hindu society by adopting the clan and name of a caste. As a result of these changes the differences between tribe and caste are being continually reduced.

F.G. Bailey did not admit caste tribe dichotomy. He preferred caste tribe continuum with two ideal poles in the scale.

1.15 Major Religions

Indian peninsula is an epitome and storehouse of many religions. In this country we found the existence of all world religions namely Hinduism, Jainism, Buddhism, Islam, Christianity and Zorastrianism, of these religions Hinduism and Jainism are considered the three major religions:

(a) Hinduism and Its Evolution

Hinduism is the ancient religion of India. As Dr. S. Radhakrishna states, "Hinduism is more a way of life than a way of thought." This ancient religion has shaped the destiny of millions of lives from their evolution to decay. Considering its efficacy Mrs. Annie Besant has rightly remarked that "without Hinduism India has no future. Hinduism is the soil into which Indian roots are struck and torn out of that, she would inevitably wither as a tree torn out from its place". It is appropriately called 'Vedika Dharma' or 'Sanatan Dharma'.

With the advent of Aryans, India experienced Hinduism. When the Aryans reached Punjab, the hymns of *Rig Veda* had already been composed. These hymns symbolize the early form of Hinduism. In the passage of time, new thinking and philosophical interpretations led to the composition of early vedic literature. The *Sam Veda*, the *Yajur Veda*, the *Atharva Veda*, the *Upanishads*, the *Aranyakas* provide the details of Hinduism. Hinduism is an admixture of the elements of various isms. Hinduism exhibits the worship of so many gods and goddesses and the association of gods and goddesses with nature. The Aryans were fascinated by the natural phenomenon like the mountains and personified each of them as living beings are worshipped them as deities. Early vedic literature had 1028 hymns and these hymns were used in honour of each god and goddess. The Aryans conceived Heaven as father Dyaus who was considered as the father of all divinities. He was eclipsed by his son Indra, the rain god. The *Rig Veda* contains 250 hymns in his honour. The Aryans considered Agni as the second god. He represented purity. Varuna the god of nature was recognized as the third powerful god who upheld the balance of nature. The Aryans personified marut as the god of storm and soma as the god of plants. They used to worship mother goddess like Aditi and Usha. They used to offer prayers in their honour.

When civilization flourished, the Brahmanical religion made rapid strides. The Aryan gods and goddesses lest their importance and new gods and goddesses appeared to have gained prominence. In the later vedic period Prajapati, the god of creators, Rudra, the god of animals, Vishnu, the god of protections, Pushan, the god of the Sudra and the god of cattle assumed prominence. In this period people used to worship gods and goddesses for attaining material prosperity. The king or chieftain used to perform sacrifices for the welfare of his subjects. Sacrificial worship was the most popular form of religions activity. Animal sacrifice was very common. The persons belonging to the priestly class were performing the sacrificial rites for which they were getting Dakshinas. Religious rites become the monopoly of the priestly class, even they exercised control and influence on the kings. They propounded the philosophy of knowledge, i.e. soul, rebirth and the almighty God. Thus, there was a predominance of the priestly class. Later on, with the advent of Greeks and Persians the Brahmanical religion was called Hinduism and the followers were known as Hindus.

In this context, the statement given by A. Lyall is worth citing, he says, Hinduism as "the collection of rites, worships, beliefs, traditions and mythologies that are sanctioned by the sacred books and ordinances of Brahmans and are propagated by Brahmanic teaching".

(b) Cardinal Virtues of Hinduism

(i) An Ancient Religion

It has the distinction of being the ancient religion in the world. The doctrines of Hinduism are not embodied in one sacred book nor does Hinduism have a single historical founder. Though its origin is shrouded in mystery, yet it is universally accepted that it is the single oldest of all religions the world have ever seen.

(ii) A Way of Life

Hinduism is a tolerant religion based on belief. It does not believe in fanaticism. Any Hindu is free to choose his God, follows his spiritual calling and pursue the path of salvation. It is not a mere religion. It is a way of life of the masses.

(iii) Pre-Defined Objectives

Hinduism believes in an eternal and ultimate force called Brahman (the universal soul). There is a tangible relationship between Brahman and Atman (the individual soul). This is the main concern of Hinduism. The life of a Hindu involves the pursuit of four goods—Dharma, Artha, Kama and Moksha. Dharma and Artha symbolizes material pursuits. Kama symbolizes have and desire and Moksha symbolizes salvation. There are four stages of life for a Hindu, i.e. Brahmacharya, Grihasta, Vanaprastha and Sanyasa. There are four important obligations of a Hindu, i.e. obligations to sages, to the ancestors, to God and to human beings. The notions of Dharma and Karma and closely interlinked.

(iv) The Concept of Purusarthas

The concept of purusartha is central to Hindu view of life. It is the assimilation of the four gods of life, i.e. Dharma, Artha, Kama and Moksha. This can be achieved through the manifestation of Gunas inherent in human beings. There are three Gunas such as Satwa, Raja and Tama.

(v) Sacredness

Sacredness is the cardinal asset of Hinduism. It is related to purity. It permeates all areas of life and existence. There are sacred books, sacred prayers, sacred mantras, sacred rivers, sacred mountains, sacred places, sacred rites and sacred individuals, etc.

(vi) Catholicity

Hinduism is recognized for its broad outlook. It allows maximum freedom to its followers. There is no imposition at all. It believes that the essence of all religions is one, only their approaches are different. Hinduism cherishes the value of equal respect to all religions.

(vii) Synthesis of Many Sects

Hinduism is based on synthetic philosophy. It is not a uniform monolithic religion. It allows many sects within its fold. It is the amalgamation of Vaishnavism, Shaivism and Shaktism.

(viii) Emphasis on Nature Worship

Hinduism has an important facet of great significance. To a Hindu, the whole nature is divine. Among gods and goddesses, Hinduism includes animals and plants. Cow is considered as a sacred animal. Trees like Banana, Peepal, Bilwa and Tulsi are sacred. Hinduism has very cleverly associated Gods with plants, animals or birds. In Hinduism, tree cult is very popular. God Vishnu is worshipped with Tulsi leaves and his vehicle is royal bird Garuda. God Shiva is worshipped with Bilwa leaves and his vehicle is bull. Lord Ganesh has an elephant head and his vehicle is mouse. Further a grass called Kusa and Duba has great religions significance as they are used in rituals.

(ix) Value Themes

Puja and Bhakti are important aspects of Hinduism. Hinduism stresses on four values such as hierarchy, holism, karma and transcendence. The value themes find place in Geeta, Puranas, Vedas and Upanishads. Hierarchy implies ranking interims of high and low and thus denotes the notion of inequality.

For a devout Hindu, the value of inequality is comprehensive and also includes occupational life cycles such as Ashramas, the moral duties of dharma. Castes is also organized on the basis of inequality hierarchy. Holism is manifested in the relationship between individual and group. In Hindu society the individual is not autonomous. He is constrained by the norms and values of the society. Thus community dominates the individual karma is the most important element of Hinduism. The theory of rebirth explains the concept of karma. The doctrine of karma is one and unique philosophy of Hinduism. It provides a satisfactory meaning to ones suffering and the social inequality prevailing in the society. On the other hand, transcendence implies beyond the limit of possible experience and knowledge of the individual. According to the values can never challenged.

(x) Belief in God

Hinduism asserts that God is pervasive and easily accessible to the people in one form or the other. It stresses that God is the ultimate cause, the ultimate principle of morality and the ultimate aim of life. God is considered as nirguna nirakar (formless) and suguna sakara (having form). God manifests in three forms—Brahma, Vishnu and Maheswar—the creator, the sustainer and the destroyer.

(xi) Idol Worship

The most important feature of Hinduism is its belief in idol worship. The idols are worshipped in the temples. They vary according to the people and according to the self. In India, Rama, Krishna, Vishnu, Shiva, Hanuman, Kali and Laxmi are worshipped on separate occasions.

(xii) Purity and Pollution

The concept of purity and pollution constitute the essence of Hinduism. They pervade the whole of Hindu life. The rules of purity and pollution vary from region to region.

(xiii) Dynamism

Hinduism has universal applicability for its dynamism. Not only its modes of worship and religious practices but even the religious spirits have changed from time to time. The religious reformation movements in India have lead to its reinterpretation. The reformers have tried to interpret Hindu religion as the religion of Humanity, a brotherhood of religion, etc. Hindu religion bolds its sanctity and integrity for the creation of an ideal world of realization of human values.

Thus, Hinduism is more than a religion. It is a philosophy. It is based on justice and harmony.

1.16 Buddhism and Its Origin

Buddhism was one of the new religious movements in India which had its origin in the 6th century B.C. It is rooted in the traditional Indian religion called Sanatan Dharma. It is one of the three major forms of Indian religions, the other two being Hinduism and Jainism. It was founded by Goutam Buddha, son of Suddhodhan, the king of Kapilavastu from his very childhood he did not want to be confined in a family. He think that a family life had not freedom at all. He had a life of seclusion for long 24 years because his father did not want him to become a recluse. His father got him married to Yasodhara. He led a temporary family life and had a son. The family environment failed to tie him. He was fascinated by the life of a Sanyasi and he adopted the life of an ascetic leaving family comforts and wandered from place to place, in quest of knowledge. Ultimately he settled down at Gaya for meditation. He got enlightenment through deep meditation. The enlightenment gave him the answer for the questions he was wandering all through relating to life, its sufferings on account of old age, disease and death. According to him knowledge is Bodhi. After attainment of knowledge or Bodhi, he called himself Buddha, the enlightened one.

The deep meditation and introspection let him known that sufferings of human beings were caused by the desire. Sufferings could not end so long as there was no end to desire. In order to put an end to desire, man must lead a noble and truthful life. This discovery of knowledge made Buddha a unique person. He turned prophet releasing the wheel of law or Dharmachakra for the good of mankind. His action was known as Dharmachakra pravartana or propagation of Dharma. He preached Buddhism for long 45 years.

(a) Basic Tenets of Buddhism

The basic tenets of Buddhism are as follows:

(i) Triple Refuge or the Three Jewels

The Buddhist profession of faith is known as the "Triple Refuge" of the three Jewels—the Buddha, the Dharma and the Sangha. The Buddha is the enlightened teacher or the prophet. The Dharma is the doctrine given by the Buddha and the Sangha is the community of believers in the doctrine taught by the Buddha. Anybody can become a Buddhist by reciting the triple refuge three times—"I go for refuge to the Buddha I go for refuge to the Dharma and I go for refuge to the Sangha."

(ii) Interpretation of Dharma

In Buddhism Dharma has four meanings—(i) the absolute truth, (ii) right conduct, (iii) doctrine, and (iv) the ultimate constituent of experience. Buddhism has certain relationship with Hinduism.

(iii) Four Noble Truths

The Buddhists believe in four noble truths preached by the Buddha. The first noble truth is that there is suffering and it is inevitable. The second noble truth is that there is cause of each suffering. It is known as desire. Thus, desire is the cause of suffering. The third noble truth is that suffering can be removed. The fourth noble truth provides a detailed blue print for the removal of the cause of suffering.

(iv) Arya Astang Marg or the Eight-Fold Path

Buddhism prescribes the eight fold path popularly known as Arya Astang marg for the achievement of Nirvana which involves the end of all sufferings. They are right view, right aspiration, right speech, right action, right livelihood, right effort, right mindfulness and right meditations.

(v) Scriptures of Buddhism

Buddhism provides three basic scriptures known as *Vinay Pitaka* (book of discipline), *Sutta Pitak* (book of sermons) and *Abhidham Pitak* (book of doctrines).

(vi) Forms of Buddhism

There are four major forms of Buddhism. They are: (i) Therakad, (ii) Mahyan, (iii) Vajrayan or Tantra, and (iv) Sen.

(b) Teachings of Buddha

The gospel of Buddhism is known as Tripitak consisting of three Pitakas such as Suta, Vinaya and Abhidhamma. Tripitak provides the full version of Buddha's teachings. Buddha was well-versed with the philosophy of Hinduism and the prevailing socio-economic conditions. When Brahmanism was in full sway and exercised predominance on the society and people, Buddha preached his religions sermon as a reaction against Brahmanism. Buddha exposed the irrelevance of religions ceremonies and supper stations like idol worship and caste system. He denounced the supremacy of Vedas. Buddha was the exponent of social equality. His preaching centred round practical moralities.

Buddhist philosophy was very simple as a layman could understand. Explaining the nature of human life Buddha said that human life is full of sorrows and sufferings. These are quite inevitable because every human being aimed at materialistic pleasure and lack of it caused sufferings, when desire ends, suffering also ends. End of desire will lead to end of rebirth and end of rebirth means Nirvana brings eternal peace and happiness.

With a view to achieve Nirvana he recommended human beings to follow Arya Astang marg. Human beings living in the society can achieve Nirvana by following this noble path. He was aware of the fact that all cannot renunciate samsara. There is no need for meditation or penance. So he prescribed the middle path, the Arya Astang marg between complete renunciation and complete engrossment in materialism.

He did not believe in God and the rituals people observe. There was no role for the priestly class and no need for respecting the Vedas. He believed in Karma. Good Karma brings good results and evil Karma brings bad results. Depending upon one's Karma, a man takes birth again and again. Rebirth is very much associated with desire and Nirvana is the cessation of desire. The prime objective of human being shall to attain Nirvana. It includes non-violence, love, compassion and truth. In order to get Nirvana man should restrain from greed, lust, greed and immortal conduct.

He liked to maintain a simple life backed by finger sentiments. He taught his religions and philosophy through didactic fables which had lasting impression on the human being. He was of the view that there was no destination between king and his subjects. All are human beings and every body should aim at achieving Nirvana through good deeds to get eternal bliss of the divinity. His charming personality lucid style of presentation of his teachings appealed one and all as a result Buddhism become a world religion.

1.17 Jainism and Its Origin

Jainism was one of the most important religions movement appeared in India during the 6th century B.C. It was founded by Mahavir, the son of Siddhartha, the chief of the Jantrika clan. Propagation of Jainism by Mahavir was the result of the reaction against the predominance of the priestly class in the existing Hinduism. Being dissatisfied with worldly affairs Mahavir left home at the age of 30 in search of the spiritual goal. He was a wandering ascetic moving from place to place to find out truth of knowledge for a long 12 years. He found truth in 13th year. He called himself Mahavir Jain. The word Jain is derived from Jina which means the conqueror. He practiced deep penance and mediations, torturing himself by physical pain to find truth. He was an exponent of truth that is eternal.

He was the 24th tirthankar who had preached Jainism. The first tirthankar was Risabhdev and the 23rd tirthankar was Parsvanath whom Mahavir accepted the religious doctrines of Parsvanath. After sever asceticism, he attained supreme knowledge and means of moksha. Hence, he was called Mahavir (Great hero) and Jain (the conqueror). Those who adopted his religions were called Jain.

1.17.1 Philosophy of Jainism

Jainism derived the basic principles from Upanishad and denied the authenticity of the Vedas and the efficacy of the rites enumerated in them for the purpose of salvation. Jainism laid adequate emphasis upon a pure and moral life, specially non-injury to animate beings. The principle of non-violence was the foundation of Jainism.

The teachings of Jainism laid stress on the greater service to the case of humanity. According to Jainism, everything whether animate or inanimate has Jiva (a life force). The Jains believe in soul, theory of karma, the cycle of birth and death. Their quest is directed for achieving emancipation from worldly existence and the cycle of birth and death. Jainism stood for non-violence, truth, non-stealing and non-possession. Mahavir supplemented Brahmacharya as a new principle. He advised his followers to adopt right faith, right knowledge and right action. They were known as triratna or three gems. These are essential ingradients to lead a noble life and for the attainment of salvation. Salvation cannot be attained by mere worshiping gods and goddesses. Mahavir believed in karma, result of karma largely depended upon the nature of karma whether good or evil. Evil karma should be avoided as far as practicable as it would cause rebirth and suffering. In order to get moksha one need not pray God rather to engross upon right conduct and right action.

Jainism prescribed certain code of conduct for the Jains. Fasting and austerity were considered essential for self-purification. It laid stress on mental disciplines to obtain self-control, concentration in contemplations and purity of thought. It also laid emphasis on personal spiritual development for the welfare of the community. Altruism could be the source of positive social welfare. Jainism prescribed five-fold disciplines for the maximization of social welfare. They were Ahimsa (non-violence), Satya (truth), Astaya (not to steal), Aparigrha (non possession) and Brahmacharya (self-control).

Jainism in general and Mahavir in particular espoused the cause of Ahimsa or non-violence. He protested against the prevailing practice of animal sacrifice. According to Jain philosophy every life was sacred and destroying life was sin. Kindness was the cardinal virtue of human beings. Man must do good work to preserve life. Jainism did not allow even small insects to die. They used to cover there mouth and nostril not to kill small insects. They led a detached life. They were not in favour if material prosperity. Mind should be free from greed. They were strict vegetarians and tried to attain the status of kevlin with a view take through soul to Siddhasila which meant the abode of eternal bliss. Salvation or eternal bliss was the ultimate goal of Jainism.

1.17.2 Importance of Jainism

Jainism was propounded by a Kashtriya whose social status was next to the Brahmans in the prevailing society. He was qualified and exercised his intellect for the promotion of social welfare through eradication of evils from the society by imbibing a spirit of tolerance, non-violence and a broader outlook among human beings. He did so through his moral courage and personality. He was a free thinker who appeared the tradition and demanded its change. He created an ideology for new generations which become instrument in bringing great changes in the society. He propagated the religions in people's own language to get mass appeal. He was a social reformer who preached for social equality. The teachings of Jainism laid adequate stress with greater service to the case of humanity and rendered great service to the Indian society by giving a rude shock to the caste system.

Thus, Jainism heralded a new era in the religions of India

1.18. Sikhism and Its Origin

The term 'Sikh' was originated from the Sanskrit word Shishya which means disciple. Sikhism was founded by Guru Nanak 550 years ago. It is considered as the 51st largest religion in the world. In the Sikh faith reverence for the Guru is the cardinal quality and devotion to their teaching is a sacred duty. Thus, the followers of this ism were known as Sikhs. Sikhism preaches a message of devotions and remembrance of God at all times, truthful living and equality of mankind. It denounces superstitions and blind rituals.

There are ten religious teachers or Gurus of Sikhs. Guru Nanak was the first Guru and Guru Govind Singh was the tenth Guru. Arjun Dev was the fifth Guru who is credited for compiling the holy book of the Sikhs named *Guru Granth Sahib*. This Granth is an embodiment of hymns composed by the Sikh saints. The *Granth Sahib* is considered as the Guru eternal for the Sikh temple 'Gurudwara' is not a mere place of worship but also servers as a shelter for the homeless.

1.18.1 Basic Philosophy of Sikhism

Sikhism is considered as a reconciler of the two conflicting traditions such as Hinduism and Islam. Acordintg to Sikhism, God is monistic or non-dual. He is the creator of the universe. God is both Saguna (with attributes) and Nirguna (without attributes). He is known by several names such as Sat (truth), Sat Guru (true guru), Akal Purkh (timeless being), Kartar (creator) and Wahe Guru (praise to the God). Sikhism does not believe in the incarnation of God in human form. It disapproves asceticism and self-mortification as part to enlightenment. Like Buddhism and Jainism, Sikhism also believes in Salvation (Liberation or Mukti). This can be achieved by being God conscious (Gurmukh). Sikhism prescribes the recitation of hymns, devotional prayers or Kirtans singing the name of God (Nam Simran) to be nearer to God.

Sikhism rejects the orthodox Hindu concept of pollution. It rejects the caste name and all males have Singh (Lion) and all females Kaur (Princess) after their name. In Sikh marriages there is a great emphasis on simplicity and dowry is not a precondition. Sikhism condemns the caste system and lay emphasis on own egalitarian society. Baptized Sikhs have to adhere to five symbols such as Kesh (Unshaven hair), Kara (Iron bangle), Kirpan (Sword), Kanga (Comb) and Kachha (underwear).

1.18.2 Importance of Guru Granth Sahib

Guru Granth Sahib popularly known as the *Adi Granth* is the supreme spiritual authority of the Sikh religion. It is an embodiment of the spiritual works of Sikh Gurus. It contains 1430 pages. Each page is adorned with spiritual scriptures in the form of devotion songs and poetry. It also contains the guidelines to be followed by Sikhs for a healthy and peaceful living. It contains the code of conduct, moral and ethical rules for the development of the soul, spiritual salvation and unity with God.

1.19 Zoroastrianism and Its Essence

This is one of the oldest religions of the world. It was propounded by Zoroaster, a prophet in Persia more than 2500 years ago. It is also known as Parsism. It was originally a religion of nature worship. According to Zoroastrianism, all the natural objects such as fire, water, sun and air are sacred; more emphasis has been given on fire. The Zoroastrians are basically fire worshippers. The permanently burning fire shrine at Udwada is the brightest example of worshipping the fire, the son of God. They (the Parsis or Zoroastrians) worship fire in the temple. They use to offer daily prayers (Navjati) particularly hymns uttered by the prophet Zoroaster either in home or in temple before burning the fire. They burn two types of fire on the basis of gradation—the Royal Bahram or Victorians fire and the 'Dar-i-mihr' or the ordinary fire.

They consider God as Ahura Mazde meaning wise lord or wise God. Zoroastrianism prescribed a religions code in the form of scriptures in *Zend Avesta*, their holy book. God is pure and faultless. He is One, the only One, nothing resembles Him. He is immortal. He has no origin or end. He is without body and form. He has no parentage and he has not encumbrance. Human eyes cannot see him. No human being can conceive him. He is above our imagination. He is the creator of the universe, the mighty and the beneficent. He is the savior of mankind. He can distinguish between good deeds and misdeeds. Zoroastrianism also reveals that soul is immortal and when death occurs, good soul goes to heaven and evil soul falls into the hell. This religion gives adequate stress on purity and pollution.

1.20 Judaism and Its Philosophy

Judaism is the religion of Jews. It is the smallest religious community in India. The Jews are a very homogeneous group, conservative in attitude and orthodox in temperament. They strictly adhere to their religions beliefs. This community is mostly found in Israel. History reveals the fact that some Jews came to India before the beginning of the Christian era. There are three main communities of Jews found in India. They are the Bene—Israel, Kerala Jews was Baghadadi Jews. The Jews are strict disciplinarians. This religion is the sum tonal of a set of ideas about the world where were born and grown.

Judaism lays adequate stress on good moral life. It does not advocate asceticism celibacy and self peace. Their sacred religious book *Torah* contains some ideas about God, the universe and the linkage between divinity and human being. They consider masses as their God and Synagogue is their place of worship. The Jews believe that God exist. He is one unique, in corporeal and external. Prayer shmid be directed to God alone. God can look after the welfare of human beings. The actives and inactive will be duly evaluated by God. God will reward in good punish the evil. Ultimately the messiah will come. The dead will be resurrected. Good soul case reach heaven and bad soul will suffer at hell.

Thus, Judaism is a strict religion.

Social Change

2

2.1 Concept of Social Change

Social change is the change in the society and society is a web of social relationship. Hence, social change is nothing but change in social relationships which include social processes, social patterns, social interactions, mutual activities and relations of various parts of the society. It is very difficult to define social change precisely. The term 'social change' is used to describe variations of any aspect of social processes, social patterns, social interactions or social organization. It includes alternations in the structure and functions of society and can be observed in any society. Whenever one finds that large number of persons are engaged in activities that different from those which their immediate forefathers were engaged in small time before, one finds a social change. Whenever human behaviour is in the process of modification one finds that social change is occurring. Human society is constituted of human beings. Hence, whatever apparent alteration in the mutual behaviour between individuals takes place is a sign of social change.

2.1.1 Causal Factors of Social Change

Sociologists are of the view that social relationships undergo constant alterations due to diffusion and invention. A closer scrutiny reveals that the factors causing social change are cultural, technological, biological, demographic, environmental, psychological and others.

(a) Cultural Factors

The main cause of social change is the cultural factor. Changes in the culture are accompanied by social changes. This hypothesis has been proved by Max Weber by a comparative study of religions and economic institutions. It is an incontrovertible fact that changes and variations in culture influence social relationships. Culture gives speed and direction to social change and determines the limits beyond which social changes cannot occur.

(b) Technological Factors

The technological factor has immense influence in social change. As W.F. Ogbum states, "Technology changes society by changing our environment to which we in turn adopt. This change is usually in the material environment and the adjustment we make to the changes often modifies customs and social institutions. Hence, the incessant increase in new machines and methods due to new discoveries has had a very great influence upon social relationships. The form of society is undergoing change due to development of science and technology leading to inventions and discoveries.

(c) Biological Factors

Biological factors have some indirect influence upon social change. Among the biological factors is the qualitative aspect of the population related to heredity. The qualitative aspect of population is based upon powerful great men and their birth is dependent upon the heredity and mutation. Hence, biological factors play a part in social change to that extent.

(d) Demographic Factors

Changes in the quality and size of population have an effect upon the social organizations as well as customs, and traditions, institutions and associations, etc. Rise and fall in the birth rate, change in the ratio of men and women have an effect upon social relationships, economic institutions and associations, etc.

(e) Environmental Factors

The geographists have emphasized the impact of geographical environment upon human society. Huntington has asserted that an alteration in the climate is the sole cause of evolutions and devolution of civilization and cultures. Even if these claims of the geographists are to be discarded, it cannot be divided that floods, earthquakes, excessive rain, drought, change of season, etc., have significant effect as social relationships and these are modified by such natural occurrences.

(f) Psychological Factors

Many sociologists viewed that psychological factors are important elements of social change. The cause of social changes is the psychology of man himself. By nature, man is a lover of change. He tries to discover new things in every sphere of his life and is always anxious for novel experiences. As a result of this tendency, the mores, traditions, customs, etc., of every human society are perpetually undergoing change.

(g) Other Factors

Another factor of social changes is the appearance of new opinions and thoughts. For example, changes in the attitudes towards dowry, caste system, female education, etc., have resulted in widespread social variations and modifications. In fact a majority of the social revolutions take place as a result of the evolution of the new ways of thinking. Similarly, war is also a cause of social change because it influences the population, the economic situations, and ratio of males to females, etc. In the same way, social changes are introduced by the advent of great thinkers as Gandhi and Karl Marx, etc.

2.1.2 Social Change and Urbanization

No society can exist without changes. Social change may be partial or total, though mostly it is partial. We find that changes have been coming rapidly in modern times. One of the main reasons for social change is dynamic nature of the people. As Maclver states "Social change is change in social relationship." Social changes is a process responsive to many types of change to changes in the man-made conditions of living, to changes in the attitudes and beliefs of men" some of the major factors which are responsible for social changes are urbanization, industrialization cultural lag westernization and secularization. In India urbanization has changed the whole economic and social life. We can see comprehensive and wide ranging changes in the Indian socio life in consequence of urbanization. The urbanization have had maximum impact on the family and marriage institutions. In the urban society there is decline in the community and fellowship feeling and relations have become impersonal and revolve around cash nexus. The sense and value of time has increased and the institutional controls have become tax. In areas, where male female relationship has been adversely affected there is increase in alcoholism, gambling and prostitution.

2.1.3 Social Change and Industrialization

The phenomena of industrialization and urbanization are interlinked and interconnected. Thus, there impact on society is more or less than some. The industrialization has resulted in mass exodus of rural labour to industrial areas where they come to live huddled in slums. Usually they cannot bring their families along with them. Therefore in slums, female population is far outnumbered by the male. Therefore the villages folk take to use of alcohol indulge in gambling and begin visiting wayside cheap prostitutes. The incidence of venereal diseases and other acute and chronic diseases is very high in slums. The industrialization has also made people materialistic and individualistic in their outlook. Competitions have come to replace cooperation. There is increase in callousness and indifference to others miseries. These days in residential flats in big cities, people know nothing of their neighbours. Industrialization has made the gap between rich and poor wider.

2.1.4 Social Change and Cultural Lag

In India, one of the basic causes of unwieldy and bewildering social change is the cultural lag. In the past, century, India has borrowed heavily from western science, technology and culture. Big industrial towns have sprung up which easily match their western counterparts in grandeur and lavishness. But whereas there has been tremendous change in the technical and material culture, the spiritual cultural and moral values have changed little, e.g. India women enjoy all freedoms. They vote fight elections, seek all sorts of jobs like men. Indian women are emancipated and are mens equal in all respects but in matter of feelings and sentiments Indian women are close to orthodox tradition. It will be difficult to visualize Indian women preaching lesbianism, as some women are doing in past.

2.1.5 Social Change and Westernization

The biggest impact on society causing tremendous changes in society is to be attributed to the phenomenon of westernization. Due to westernization, the caste system and the joint family system, the most important Indian social institutions have undergone important change. The western culture is a culture of humanitarianism, equality and democratic rights. This has helped to stem the root of epidemics, famines and helped to spread the education. As a consequence of western impact, the Hindu religion has undergone re-evaluation. The traditions like sati, child marriage and untouchability have been mere or less eliminated. But it has also encouraged widow remarriage, feeling of nationalism and interest in scientific investigation. On the negative side, the westernization has been instrumental for the promotion of communism, casteism, regionalism, linguistic fanaticism and other parochial tendencies. As a result of westernization, there has been complete transformation in the status of women. Women education has spread; women have been given economic and political rights. All these have enabled women to play decisive role in social life. Women have discarded the veil and are in the forefront in very walk of life. Under the impact of westernization India has adopted foreign technology resulting in the growth of industrialization and shifting of the newer center of social power from villages to cities. This has affected the personal outlook of people and encouraged the independence of thinking and action.

The traditional styles and manners of marriage and family have given way to love and inter-caste marriage and growth of nuclear families. Under the impact of western culture, the young generation is becoming materialistic and sensualist in outlook. The sources of entertainment have changed.

2.1.6 Social Change and Secularization

Secularization implies rationalism. The process of secularization is anti religious. It does not mean atheism. It lays stress on universality of spiritual values. It is one of the most important and unique feature of Indian democracy. We have deliberately adopted the secular democratic, political and social structure. The implication inherent in this are obvious. The distinction of society on communal religions and caste bases is not officially encouraged. Intermixture of religious groups and different castes is encouraged in as much as government recruits its services with persons who possess requisite qualifications without consideration to their caste and religion. All this is leading to collapse of orthodox distinction in society in low and high born, etc. The religion has ceased to enjoy the paramountcy it once did. Now, it is the merit and ability which counts and not the religions or caste affiliations.

2.1.7 Little Tradition and Great Tradition

Robert Redifield was the first anthropologist who coined the two concepts: little tradition and great tradition, in his book *Peasant Society and Culture*. He held the view every society had two traditions, the tradition of the folk or unlettered peasant and the traditions elite or the learned people. The former is known as little tradition and the latter is designated as the great tradition. The social structure of civilization of any country had operated at these two levels and there is a continuous interaction between these two traditions.

As in other countries, traditional India also exhibited continual instances of social change. These changes were initiated through orthogenetic and heterogenetic sources. Orthogenetic sources included indigenous customs and rituals whereas heterogenetic sources referred to the cultural contact with other civilization. Thus, all civilization from an orthogenetic or primary level of cultural organization. As time passes, they are diversified through internal growth and through the contact with other civilizations. This is the heterogenetic process of social change.

2.1.8 Milton Singer's View on the Process of Social Change in India

India exhibits a cultural synthesis of several civilizations because of the fact that in the passage of time India has passed through many rulers. The study made by Milton Singer on the process of social change in India reveals the following facts:

(a) Little tradition and great tradition not only interact but they are interdependent. It has been proved in India. India has not only accepted modernizing forces, but has also absorbed the same by making in a way of life.

(b) Originally India had a primary on Indigenous civilization which was redesigned by the influence of folk and regime culture as well as foreign culture. Its great tradition and little tradition are continue. This continuity could traced in diverse places like villages, castes and tribes.

(c) The cultural continuity in India was the cause result of a common cultural consciousness and this consciousness was shared by most Indians in the form of outlook and ethics.

(d) The formation of cultural consciousness had been possible by certain processes and factors such as sacred books, sacred objects, Brahmans are other agents of cultural transmission.

(e) The modernization aspect had supplemented Indian culture. It had not affected the primary element inherent in Indian cultural tradition. The structure of the village culture substantiated this fact.

2.1.9 Mikim Marriot's View on Social Change in India

M. Marriot has nicely presented the interaction of little tradition and great tradition in India. He had found out that there is a constant and continuous interaction between the elements of little tradition and great tradition in the structure of the village culture and its social organizations. He coined two terms universalisations and "Parochialization" by the establishing interaction between little tradition and great tradition. When the elements of little tradition like indigenous customs and rites circulate upward to the level of great tradition, this is known as universalization. On the other hand, when the elements of great traditional circulate downward to be a pat of the little traditions, this is called parochialization. He was of the view that Sanskritization proceeded in the village not as an independent process, superposed as cultural forms which are non Sanskritic in nature. Sanskritic rites are very often mixed up with non-

Sanskritic rites instead of replacing them. Universalization is something like Sanskritization and parachialization is an invested process of Sanskritization commit mist be termed as de-sanskritization.

2.1.10 Multiple Traditions

Indian culture is hybrid in nature comprising various schools of thought. It is a curious mixture of Sanskritization and westernization. Various religions had their impact in Indian culture. Considering the diversity of Indian culture, S.C. Dube offers a six-fold classifications of Indian tradition such as classical tradition, emergent national tradition, regional tradition, local tradition, western tradition and subcultural tradition. But none of them provide a comprehensive perspective on social change in India because of the fact that Indian society is having a multiple tradition.

2.1.11 Little Tradition

Robert Redifield defines a little tradition as "a tradition of non-lettered unreflective few. It is the product of men's participation with local condition. It is unsystematic and may have variability to belief and devoid of documentation of codification."

Little tradition is the product of local conditions. It operates at the grass-root level. It reflects local set of needs and problems. It is the tradition of the community as a whole. It is that tradition which is not critically examined by the people. This tradition is orally transmitted. India had a primary or indigenous civilization characterized by homogeneity, isolated, common interest, independent, simple technology and small in size, etc. The social structure of this little tradition consisted of folk artists, medicine men, poets and dancers, etc.

There is no historical evidence to have a clear cut line of demarcation between little tradition and great tradition as primary and secondary stage of growth of civilization. Even the primary or orthogenetic tradition of India was probably the synthesis of many indigenous folk traditions in the early periods of history. The relationship between Indus valley civilization and Vedic culture is still controversial. There is also controversy regarding the relationship between Aryan Vedic culture and non Vedic tribal culture. Thus, it is very difficult to determine the orthogenetic tradition.

The Vedic culture and the epic culture present two stages of growth, but it is found that Vedic tradition of the pre-epic period proved the beginning of the religious ethical values, aesthetic perceptions and lifestyle of the Aryan society at its formative stage. The epics also represent the next stage of development of a period of standardization of the social cultural pattern. The Vedic Hinduism of the epic period shows the consolidation of the bullies, ritual patterns and cultural practices. The Vedas represent the formation period of Hinduism and its cultural pattern.

It is an admitted fact that Hinduism constituted the basic orthogenetic culture tradition in India. It is an example of little tradition. All other religious culture patterns prevailing in India are examples of heterogeneous cultural tradition.

2.1.12 Great Traditions

According to Robert Redifield great tradition is a tradition of large community. It is a product of systematic, well planned and meticulous activities having a philosophical contention. Great tradition is a product of urban area. It is a tradition of reflective few. It operates at formal institutions such as schools and temples. It is a tradition of specialists. It is transmitted through systematic literature, not through oral tradition. Milton Singer has said that the growth of great tradition was continuous with the little tradition.

The continuous process of assimilations and change from Vedic times to the 19th century are being observed in Great tradition of Hinduism. These changes are orthogenetic in nature. Buddhism and Jainism brought some transformation in Hinduism but did not affect the basic philosophy of Hinduism. Thus, the two religions initiated the process of cultural changes in the great tradition. The great tradition of Hinduism has some unique features. It devises a social order after meticulous judgement and wisdom. There is extreme liberalism and varieties in ritual practices. Hindu logic and metaphysic have provided for a social under which is unique in the world. There is no confusion any where. Hindu social structure is based on two things—order and change. The social order is passed on the principle of hierarchy which govern the cultural structure of India. Hierarchy though includes the process of cyclic transition is most dynamic. The theory of karma, the basic of Hinduism which keeps life going in a continuous process of transition through rebirth or transmigration of soul is to counterbalance the Hindu social hierarchy. It has an important role to play in the Hindu great tradition by creating a notion of continuity. The theory of Karma justifies the hierarchical social order of Hinduism.

Similarly the process of social change in great tradition of Hinduism continued uselessly for the classical age to the contemporary times. In the post Gupta period, through interpretation by Shankaracharya and Ramanuja, the basis philosophy of Hinduism were brought nearer to the life of the people. It established a bright to communication between the little and great traditions of Hinduism. Up to the end of the medieval period, changes in the great tradition of Hinduism have been marked by a growth of liberal traditions. Nanak, Kabir, Chaitanya, etc., emerged as the leading saints of Hinduism. They not only liberalized the orthodox conception of religions beliefs but also contributed to reduce the gap between the little traditions and great traditions of Hindu culture. During the British rule, Hinduism underwent a substantial transformation. In the beginning, the western culture made its impact on the local aspect of Indian culture. It created subcultural pattern limited to a specific group of people. In course of time westernizations become an integral part of the Indian social structure. Thus, change in little traditions only with industrialization, urbanization, expansion of modern education and growth of nationalism brought a sea change in the great traditions of Indian culture.

2.2 Threats to Indian Unity

Indian unity on national integration is an emotional, sentiment, a socio-psychological process through which a feeling of unity develops in the heart of the people. Irrespective of caste, creed, colour, language, pattern and style of living and religion, "we the people of India ..." is the feeling which constitutes the very basis of national integration.

'Unity in diversity' is the epitome of Indian culture. In spite of its rich philosophy and cultural heritage today that unity of India has been seriously challenged. The history of India presents a poor record of national integration. The causes of disintegration are diverse and pervasive which broadly assumes two forms—external threats and internal threats.

(a) External Threat

With the creation of India and Pakistan as independent republics, grew a permanent hostile of India, i.e. Pakistan. There might be so many reasons behind this. The most important cause responsible for bitter enmity between India and Pakistan was that at the time of independence, several issues remained unresolved between the two for which bitterness grew over the years. Jammu and Kashmir was the apple of discord between the two newly independent republics. Though Jammu and Kashmir constitute an integral part of Indian union. Pakistan claims it as her territory. She has forcibly occupied a large portions named Paksistan occupied Kashmir (Pok). Hence, there is always a mounting tension in the border keeping the rival armed forces in war readiness.

(b) Internal Threats

Internal threats are too numerous and assume many forms. These may be discussed under the following heads:

(i) Growing Activities of the Terrorists

Terrorism refers to the criminal and violent acts committed by a section of the people against the society and government to get their demands fulfilled. It is a weapon of blackmail and coercion which attempts to force the majority to surrender before the minority. Terrorists are religious fanatics associated with drug trafficking extortions, kind napping and blackmailing. There are many groups of terrorists operating to disrupt in unity of India. In Jammu and Kashmir, the militants are terrorists. In the North East part in Assam and the tribal states, the Naga, the Bodo and Ulfa groups are well armed and demanding for independent states. Assam Gana Parishad in Assam is a militant most which wants demographic changes to stop forthwith the prevention of the entry of Muslims from Bangladesh. In Bihar, Odisha and Andhra Pradesh also the peoples war groups and Naxalites are terrorist outfits creating for political destabilization. Much of the national resources are being wasted by these people.

(ii) Communalism

It is an ideology which emphasizes on the separate identity of a religious group. India is a storehouse of peoples belonging to different religions and there is always of fear of the spurt of communalism elsewhere. Communalism is determental to national unity. It is very powerful and widespread. Its matrix is religious sentiments of a community through lies and misinformation. They spread rumour against the rival communities which may be totally baseless. The irresponsible and pernicious game played by the commend forces ends in riots causing massacre, rape, loot, etc., it weakens the safety and security of the country and destabilizes the administration. The Ayodhya violence, Godhra incident are examples of communal riots.

(iii) Casteism

It is an offshoot of communalism which is dangerous to National integration. It is an abnormal feature of the caste system which is an integral part of Indian society. Though constitutional provision forbids discrimination against any citizen in the basis of caste still of persists. When the consideration of superiority between the castes and the tendency to consider the interest of ones own caste as opposed to other castes are added to the caste, it turns into casteism. It creates particular one side loyalty to the fellow caste men. It generates inter-caste tensions.

(iv) Linguism

There are multiplicities of languages in the plural society of India. It is aptly described as the 'linguistic madhouse', 'a museum of languages', 'a social linguistic giant' and as a 'tower of veritable languages', it lacks a single languages for inter-regional communication. Plurality of language has become a threat to the task of nation building. It has become a source of political articulation, e.g. in south, language sentiments have been aroused among the people for getting power within the state politics. The language issue has become highly politicized in India and it has resulted in linguistic and cultural regionalism.

(v) Multiparty System

India is the largest democracy in the world. It has allowed multiple political parties and associations to be formed on national and regional basis. The emergence of multiparty system has become the cause of disruption in Indian unity. Parties formed in religious issues are promoting parochialism and threatening India's unity.

(vi) Regionalism

Regionalism stands for the love of regions or an area in preference to the county. It is a highly parochial sentiment which finds the people of the region to the broader requirements of the nations as a whole. Like communalism, regionalism is a very dangerous factor in India. Leaders of regionalism lack the love and loyalty for the nation. They demand secession for the Indian union, demand for separate statehood, demand for more powers for the state and they quarrel among each other on different issues such as river water and revenue of border villages, etc.

2.3 Approaches to National Integration

National integration is an informative need for a developing country like India. It involves reconciliation of all diversities to build up national solidarity and cohesion. It symbolizes a process of unifying culturally and socially discrete groups into a single nation state. Unity in diversity from the very foundation of national integration. Social integration is the *sine qua non* for national integration. The unity of a nation depends upon the extent to which its various members look upon themselves as members of the same group.

The proponents of the Indian constitution were very much care of the national integrations of India because of the fact that India is a pluralistic state with multiple culture and languages. They created a federal constitution to absorb the political shock of this multiplicity so that each regional aspiration and dream can be taken care of by the provincial government. The administrative set-up of a province is the replica of the centre so far as legislative, executive and judiciary is concerned. All derived their power from the constitution which also provided for one citizenship. The Central Government was entrusted with additional responsibilities such as the power of finance, defense and foreign affairs so as to superimpose its authority on the provinces, when the national interests will be at stakes. This with the making of the constitution we had the political integration. But this is no enough to have full-fledged national integration. As Jawarharlal Nehru, the first Prime Minister of free India states, "political integrations has already taken place to some extent, but what I am after is something more deeper than that, an emotional integration of the Indian people so that we might be welded into one and make into one strong national unity, maintaining at the same time all our wonderful diversity".

The following pre-requisites are quite inevitable for national integration:

1. An all India language should be evolved for increasing a sense of unity among the people.
2. Social institutions should be given adequate emphases for strengthening cultural unity among people through the promotion of art and literature.
3. Efforts should be directed for the change of attitude of the people in favour of communal harmony. Feelings of social solidarity should be cleared in the mind of the people to secure social integration.
4. There should be a strong urge to combat casteism. Hence inter-caste affiliations like marriages, social gathering and cultural functions should be encouraged. Steps should be taken to promote cultural and economic equality in the lives of the people.
5. Efforts should be made to remove linguistic hostility, social tension and regionalism.
6. Educated people contribute more to the social integration. A country's unity largely depends upon the social unity and this can be achieved by the spread of education.

Education institutions should be used as the agents of socialization to incalculate the value of social integration.

7. Leaders of the political parties should make committed and sincere efforts to promote social solidarity among people through ideologies of democracy, secularism, socialism and social justice.
8. A balanced oceanic development approach should be adopted for satisfying the needs of all localities and regions. Equal opportunity for the oceanic development of all regions will lessen enmity among the people and establish and intimate social relationship among them.
9. Voluntary organization should be formed and the existing organizations should be organized to develop a climate for social change and reform to secure social integration. They should promote social awareness and supplement the activities of the Government.
10. Cultural programmes through cultural organizations should be made at regular intervals both in rural and urban areas to strengthen the band of unity. Cultural organizations should be established for creating awareness among people regarding the cultural heritage of the country and its preservation.
11. Mass media can play a very effective role in integrating the society. Adequate freedom should be given to mass media like Radio, T.V. and Newspaper for popularizing patriotism through songs and films on patriotism.
12. Efforts should be made to create an egalitarian society with complete disregards to any type of discrimination relating to caste, creed, etc.
13. There is a constitutional provision of reservation of seats and jobs for SC, ST and other backward castes on the principle of protective discrimination. But it is alleged that actual benefit is available to the people for which the policy was made. Hence every effort should be made to review the existing reservation policy and evolve a reservation policy so that the actually weaker sections of

the society will get the benefit. It will promote social integration.

14. India is a democratic country and its aim is to establish a socialistic pattern of society without caste, class and gender base. But we have not got reached the goal to achieve this noble objective. Hence, adequate efforts should be made in this direction.

2.4 Communalism

India is a vast country where people belonging to different regions live. The origin and growth of communalism can be traced to the pre-independence day. Different writers have defined the term differently. Asghar Ali Engineer defines it as "the art of skillfully manipulating the religions sentiments and cultural ethos of people by its elite to its political, economic and cultural aspirations by identifying these aspirations as these of the entire community". Humayun Kabir describes it as "a phenomenon by virtue of which persons belonging to a certain community are either discriminated against or shown favour to, regardless of their merits and demerits just on the basis of their community".

Thus, communalism is a multidimensional social phenomenon.

2.4.1 Factors Responsible for the Growth of Communalism in India

Not a single cause is responsible for the growth of communalism in India. A proper analysis of the causes behind communalism reveals that they are historical, economical, political, social, psychological, religious, constitutional and incidental.

(a) Historical Factor

Many scholars opine that communalism is the by-product of historical accidents. The Britishers while ruling over India adopted the divide and rule policy. To disintegrate the people they proclaimed the communal award and made provision which they showed long back germinated with vigour and vitality which was instrumental for the partition of India into Pakistan and Hindustan.

Further, Indian naturalism gave birth to militant nationalists like Bal Gangadhar Tilak and Lala Lajpat Rai. Tilak started Ganapati festival and Shivaji festival to unite Hindus against the colonial rule. Though these leaders were above communalism and suspicion, their activities created resentment among non-Hindus and these was widespread communalism.

(b) Political Factor

Communalism is essentially political in origin. The people of higher class manipulate religions sentiments of their community for their immediate political gain. It happened in most of the places in India. Some politicians maintained clandestine relationship with some antisocial who used to create communal violence. As a result communal blocks were used as vote banks for politicians.

(c) Economic Factors

So far economic factors are concerned, a distorted capitalist development is responsible for the growth of communalism in India, as the capitalist economy failed to solve the basic problem of poverty, unemployment and inequality. As a result, there arose unhealthy competitions to grab the existing inadequate economic and social opportunities. Further the growth of capitalist development created a new social class which was in favour of appropriation rather than creation.

(d) Social

The growth of social inequality brought in its trail communalism. The rich got richer and the poor suffered like anything. The gap between rich and poor started widening day by day and created a congenial atmosphere for the rise of communalism. Marked difference between the social practices, customs, traditions, laws, way of thinking, acting and behaving of two major communities Hindus and Muslims created a gap between them.

(e) Psychological

Communalism is more psychological than human. Communalism is born in the minds of the people when communal violence breaks due to mutual distrust and hatred between communities.

(f) Religious

Religious factors are most patent for giving rise to communalism. Demonstrative religiosity arouses a spirit of competitions for celebrations of religious festivals among the members of different religious groups.

(g) Constitutional

A. Kashyap in his book *Communalism and Constitution* states that our constitution is no way less responsible for the growth of communalism. The absence and presence of certain provisions in our constitution contributes to the growth of communalism.

(h) Incidental

Incidental factors are for numerous giving rises to communalism. The press and other mass media sometimes contribute to the communal tension in their own way. Sometimes they misrepresent facts which cause communal feeling and tension. Further, communalism gets encouragement from neighbouring countries. Foreign powers sometimes play foul in the internal politics which disrupts the administration and breeds communalism.

2.4.2 Suggestions to Counter Communalism

The committee on National Integration has given the following suggestions to counter communalism.

(a) Community festivals should be celebrated jointly. It will bring peace and harmony between and among communities.

(b) There should be fellow feeling, and self-respect among the peoples of different communities. People of one community should have adequate respect for the other community, their beliefs and practices.

(c) There should be a code of conduct for each community. They should refrain from any actions derogatory to each other's religion.

(d) Peace committee should be formed in each community to tackle any unpleasant situation occurred between communities. The committee should take initiative to check the growth of anti-social elements and to maintain a healthy atmosphere.

2.5 Casteism

Casteism is an offshoot of communalism which is dangerous to national integration. It is a grave menace to national integration. It is an abnormal feature of caste system. It is a partial or one-sided loyalty in favour of particular caste. When any made of thinking assumes the form of an ism, it becomes rigid and partial. The sense of caste when it implies a specific status in society does not pertain to casteism. The sense of caste is converted to casteism only when consideration of superiority between caste and the tendency to consider the interest of one's own caste as opposed to the other castes are attached to it. The members of one caste do not hesitate in dealing fatal blooms to the interests of the other castes, if the interest of their own caste is furthered in so doing. Thus casteism may be defined as an undesirable a phenomenon by virtue of which persons belonging to a certain caste group are either discriminated against or shown favour to regardless of their merits and demerits just on the basis of their caste. There is a plethora of definitions of casteism depending on its form and nature. K.M. Panikkar defines it on the basis of loyalty to the sub-caste. He says, "In this way it is only because of casteism that the Smiths want to benefit only the Smiths while the Joneses want to come to the aid of other joneses. It matters little if the members of the other castes are irreparably harmed, it does not cause any concern to the smiths and joneses." D.N. Prasad defines it on the basis of loyalty to the caste. He says, "In this way caste has been dragged into political arena in the form of casteism such as 'Brahmanvada' and 'Kayasthavada'. Kaka Kalelkar defines it on the basis of blind group loyalty. He says, "Casteism is an oversiding blind and supreme group loyalty that ignore the healthy social standards of justice, fair play, equity and universal brotherhood.

2.5.1 Characteristics of Casteism

Casteism has the following characteristics:

(a) Casteism implies blind caste or subcaste loyalty.

(b) Casteism is based on the principle "my caste and my caste men" only with complete disregard to other caste and caste men.

(c) It submits one's sense of justice, fair play and humanity to the interests of his own caste.

(d) It is anti-democratic.

(e) It defies the constitution by discriminating on the basis of caste.

(f) It is a grave barrier to national unity.

2.5.2 Causes of Casteism

Nowadays casteism is at its height in India, the culmination of many causes. Some of the important causes are as follows:

(a) Sense of Caste Prestige

The most prominent cause of casteism in the desire of the people belonging to a particular caste to enhance the prestige of their caste and in so doing see no wrong in adopting even the most downgraded and deleterious methods. But the prestige of the caste can be maintained only on the ground that every opportunity availed of is utilized in order to improve the social status of members. In order to achieve this objective, every caste provides its members with all possible privileges in order to raise their social status. This tends to increase in casteism.

(b) Restrictions Regarding Marriage

Hindu society prescribes certain code of conduct for marriage. Under the caste system the restrictions that apply to marriage turn every caste into a monogamous group in which each individual looks upon himself as related in some way to all the others and for this reason every one pays proper attention to the interests of others. Such action encourages casteism.

(c) Urbanization

Urbanization promotes casteism. Due to urbanization, people moving from rural areas to urban areas encounter an impersonal world to live in the lives of members of various castes become beset with problems of diverse nature for which they need security. They are compelled to seek assistance from their own caste people. Casteism spreads because of the necessity to fulfil the need of security.

(d) Increase in the Means of Transport and Propaganda

The most pertinent factor contributing to the growth of casteism is the increase in the means of both transport and propaganda because this improvement has been instrumental in establishing relations between members of a caste who were previously separated because of distance. Further, the feeling of casteism is being rapidly propagated through the medium of newspapers and communal magazines.

2.5.3 Consequences of Casteism

Casteism is a double edged weapon. On the one hand, it serves to further the interests of a small number of individuals which is socially undesirable and on the other, it proves harmful to the nation as a whole. Some of the major consequences of casteism are the following:

(a) Hinders the Process of Development of Nationalism

Casteism hinders the process of development of nationalism by fragmenting the society into different parts. It causes tension and conflict between their various parts which ultimately shatters national solidarity.

(b) Hindrance to Democracy

Political leaders at the time of election take advantage of casteism to win elections. They ask people to vote for them on communal considerations and they also succeed in their evil practices. This also results in the elections of unscrupulous individuals who do not hesitate in crushing common interests in the consideration and promotion of caste interests. In this way, casteism is fatal to democracy.

(c) Corruption

Casteism breeds politics in the segmented form. People are inspired by the sense of casteism to provide all kinds of facilities to people who belong to their own castes and in doing so they resort to all kinds of immoral and improper activities. Thus casteism promotes corruption in the society.

(d) Hindrance in Technological Efficiency

There is a provision in our constitution that, some seats will be reserved for the people belonging to SC, ST and Backward communities so far job opportunities are consumed. As a result some inefficient people are entering into government offices. Skilled and efficient persons belonging to higher strata of the society are not getting opportunities for employment. Thus, a great obstacle is placed in the path of nation's industrial and technological advance.

2.5.4 Remedial Measures

Casteism has become widespread. It is a deep-rooted problem. It is the foundation of Hindu society. It cannot be uprooted over night. A strong and tremendous revolution is needed to get rid of it. But the artificial simulations of a revolution prove harmful in the long run of time. Hence, as long as the society is not prepared to change the system and to adopt some other social order in its place, it cannot be eliminated.

The following are some of the suggestions for the solution of the problem:

(a) Change in the Existing System of Education

The greatest need for a solution of the problem of casteism is changed in the existing system of education. The educational institutions should be able to provide an atmosphere in which caste distinctions are not encouraged while children are allowed to develop distaste for this kind of discrimination. A healthy point of view in the public for casteism can be generated. Casteism can be eliminated to same extent by the development of new psychological tendencies and behavioural pattern.

(b) Exogamy

In a caste ridden society marriages are confined to one caste. If marriages are held outside the caste, automatically the caste feeling will be wiped out. Exogamy thus, provides an opportunity for two familes belonging to different castes to come together not only for two individuals one male and the other female to do so. Thus, the seed of casteism shall be unable to strike root and even if it does the resulting sapling will be so weak that it will be subsequently wiped out.

(c) Cultural and Economic Equality

Inequality in the sphere of cultural and economic welfare between two communities belonging to different castes promotes jealousy and competitions among them which later assumes the form casteism. Hence, there is an urgent need for the restoration of cultural and economic equality of various castes.

(d) Lesser Emphasis on the Term 'Caste'

People should create a congenial atmosphere of love, affection and team spirit for the promotion of community welfare. They should make less frequent use of the word "Caste" so that there may be no traces of it left in the mind of the impressionable children and they should not be imbued with the idea of caste distinction.

Of late, castes have taken the form of classes through politics and casteism is on increase. It seems impractical to harbour any hopes for the complete removal of casteism from the society. However concerted efforts made in this direction can lessen the problem to some extent. It this connection opinions expressed by different scholars are worth citing. M.N. Srinivas is of the view that most of the shortcomings of casteism can be removed and the door opened to democratic equality through adult franchise, economic planning, provision of education development programmes for the backward classes and the influence of the culture of higher castes on the standard of living of the people belonging to backward lower castes. According to Dr. Ghurye, the conflicts originating in casteism can be removed by encouraging exogamy. Coeducation should be introduced at the primary level so that boys and girls belonging to different castes will be given an opportunity to come closer. This will lead to improvement of the behaviour between different sexes simultaneously with which casteism will be actively refutes. Mrs. Iravati Karve suggests provision for economic and cultural equality between castes as a means to do away with casteism.

According to Probhu, the conflicts created by casteism can be solved only when the internal aspects of conduct are influenced. Hence, it is quite essential and desirable to develop new attitudes in the people. Dr. Rad is of the opinion that in order to wipe out casteism and to deprive it of its very basis, the creation of some optional groups should be encouraged in which the communal tendencies of the individual can be manifested and organized. Casteism will decrease as the number of these groups increases because the individuals will have the opportunity to express their instincts and motives outside the caste.

The caste notion is quite prominent in Indian society from time immemorial. Today it has become an impediment for the progress of the country. Hence attention from all spheres should be focused to change its form to ensure the development of national sentiment and the progress and successful functioning of democracy in the country.

2.6 Linguism

Linguism is a complex problem in a plural society like India. During the recent years, it has been gathering momentum and force and has become a definite threat to the unity and integrity of the nation. India is a multilingual country in which people speak many languages. It is a fact that every state has its own language and sometimes more than one language are spoken in the same region. Though there are so many spoken languages in India such as English, Hindi, Punjabi, Marathi, Tamil, Telugu, Malayalam, Kannada, Urdu, Bengali and others the great number of people speak Hindi. Hindi is the national language and its number is on the increase. But the literatures of various other languages have been appropriately developed. The presence of multi language in a country is no defect in itself. An increase in the literature of the various languages is an increase in the literary wealth of the nation. But when people try to develop the language that they speak and do not attend to other languages and when people consider their language superior to any other language, this tendency is called linguism.

India is a land of many languages. The Census of India 1961 revealed that there are 1018 different languages spokes in different parts of the country. The Census of 1971 recorded 1052 languages spoken all over the country as mother tongues. India is popularly described as 'a tower of variable languages'. Our constitution recognizes only 18 principal languages such as Assamese, Bengali, Gujarati, Hindi, Kannada, Kashmiri, Malayalam, Marathi, Oriya, Punjabi, Sanskrit, Sindhi, Tamil, Telugu, Urdu, Nepali and Konkani.

Language problem in India has two dimensions, i.e. (a) medium of instruction of the educational institutions and medium of expression in public service examinations and (b) Issues relating to the official language. So far the medium of instruction in educational institutions is concerned our national Government have implemented a three language formula such as, (i) teaching the regional language or mother language when the latter is different from the regional language, (ii) Hindi or another Indian language in the Hindi speaking area, and (iii) English or another medium support languages. The second dimension of language problem in India is relating to the official language. Article 343 of our constitution envisages that the official language of the Union shall be Hindi in Devanagari script. The people of south went on agitation with the slogans "Hindi never English for ever". Tamils say that they are Indians not Hindians. The Government of India passed the official language (amendment) Act 1967 which declared that English shall continue to be the official language of India for all the non Hindi speaking states until these states would opt for Hindi. As a result Hindi is continuing as one of the official languages of the Indian union. During the past decades or so, linguism has been gathering momentum and force. Till now it has become a definite threat to the unity and integrity of the nation. In Punjab, the problem of choice between Punjabi and Hindi has created lots of conflict and tension while in Assam the language question has resulted in bloodshed. In Bengal, Bengali has taken shape. It is also revealed that politician with a view to achieve their goal are causing lingual movements.

2.6.1 Factors Causing Linguism

Linguism is a complex problem and it is quite difficult to make a complete analysis of its various causes. However some of the pertinent and immediate causes may be stated as follows:

(a) Geographical Causes

Language is the medium through which people express their thoughts and feelings and come to known each other. There is a bond of intimacy with one who speaks someone's own language while one feels lost among people who speak some other language than one's own. Every language has its own literature which is influenced by its geographical conditions, rivers, plains and mountains, vegetation, animals and local culture. It reflects the life of people who speak that language. Hence it is built natural for a person to which the development of his language and literature. When this mentality develops within individuals living in a particular geographical area, they develop hatred and distaste for other language as a result the sense of linguism prevails and reigns supreme.

(b) Historical Causes

History plays a very significant role in the creation and spread of linguism in India. Indian soil has been experimented with different languages with the advent of foreigners to India. They have made their languages Indianized which have been instrumental for the growth of linguism in India.

(c) Psychological Causes

The most important and primary cause of linguism are of a psychological in nature. People have developed a psychology for love and admiration for their own language and hatred and disrespect for other language.

(d) Political Causes

The politicians and emerging political groups are the potent factor for linguism. Many regional communal political parties raise the language, instigate their people and want to win elections. The problem of linguism has become complex due to its affiliation with politics.

(e) Economic Causes

Government is responsible for linguism in the sense that huge amount of money is being spent for the promotion of Hindi and Urdu in non Hindi and non-Urdu speaking area. It has created resentment among the people having other languages.

(f) Social Causes

Some social factors such as myths, legends, customs and traditions encourage linguism. That language is respected in society which provides a place for these and the society accepts the language. On the other hand the languages which cater to contradictory presumptions are vehemently opposed. Thus, linguism spreads.

2.6.2 Solutions for the Abolition of Linguism

The following suggestions can be made for the abolition of linguism in India:

(a) Enunciation of a National Language

If one national language were to be enunciated, people expressing their views in different languages would have an opportunity to communicate with each other through the medium of national language and the problem arising out of difference in languages of expression will be sensibly lessened.

(b) Encouragement to all Regional Languages

In addition to the enunciation of one common national language and literature, adequate guidelines should be framed and carried into for promoting regional languages. The people will automatically develop the language of expression. Once this is clearly understood, much of the tension caused by linguism would come to an end.

(c) Opposition of Communalism

With a view to free the language issue from the clutches of politicians it is quite necessary to vigorously oppose communalism in the country. The political intrigues that instigate the problem of linguism should be kept in strict vigilance and the Government should see that a national language is developed to communicate among different lingual groups as a result linguism will be decreased considerably.

2.7 Regionalism

Regionalism is one of the most important current micro problems prevailing in our country. Though regionalism has always been present in this country in one form or the other it has never attained such magnitude as it possesses today and neither was it ever as detrimental to any national interest as it is in the present context. It has become a major challenge to nation building.

Regionalism is the sense of affection and attachment for people belonging to one's own region and hatred for those who belong to some other region. As a result of this people of one region in India start looking at people from some other part of the country in the same light in which they are prone to regard foreigners. They want that only people of their own area should run the government in their region while they do not want to make any place for people who have migrated from some other region irrespective of the period for which they may have been living there. Thus, love for a particular region in preference to the country and in certain cases in preference to the state of which the region is a part is called regionalism. According to A.T. Philip and K.H. Shivaji Rao, "Regionalism refers to sub nationalism demanding preference to the regions against the country as a whole." Iqbal Narain states that "Regionalism has both a positive and negative dimension. Speaking in positive terms it embodies a quest for self-fulfilment on the part of the people of an area. Negatively speaking regionalism reflects a psyche of relative deprivation resulting from specific grievance." Seligman and Johnson define it as "A counter movement to any exaggerated or oppressive form of centralization."

In India regionalism assumes several forms in order to achieve some political gain by certain political parties. They demand for a separate state on the basis of language. They claim themselves some of the soil and demand to enjoy opportunities for educational and employment as priority basic. They demand more state autonomy; they produce some organizations in a miniature form to destabilize the government when their demands are not considered. Further regionalism is also formed out of boundary disputes between states, and interstate river disputes and disputes relating to the revenue from the border forest area, etc.

2.7.1 Characteristics

Religionalism is a serious problem which affects the solidarity and integrity of a nation adversely. Regionalism has the following characteristics:

(a) It is psychological state of mind.

(b) It exhibits love and loyalty to the region in preference to the state or nation.

(c) It is the reflection of a narrow outlook aiming at regional development only at the cost of the welfare of other regions.

(d) It doubts the integrity of the people of other regions.

2.7.2 Causes Responsible for the Growth of Regionalism

Regionalism is a complex social process. There are many causes responsible for the growth of regionalism. Some of the major causes giving rise to regionalism are the following:

(a) Geographical

Difference in language, pattern and style of living only with food habits and attitude gives rise to regionalism because. They love their own style and pattern of living and consider it superior to that of other regions. Due to these differences they come to regard each other as foreigners and they acquire an attitudes of fear and hatred for each other.

(b) Historical

There are some historical causes at the root of regionalism. Many of the regions have their local history, and local historical tradition for which they are proved of. If they see their regional tradition is hurt, they form regionalism. History reveals the fact that there has been some difference between the people of the North and South ever since the time of the Aryans and it is continuing as such. For this many South Indians look upon North India as separate and distinct.

(c) Political Causes

A closer scrutiny reveals that fact that the main cause at the root of regionalism present in the country is of a political nature. In different regions some people have demanded the formation of regional governments and in this they have been inspired by regional interests and by aims of gaining power, i.e. a major part has been played by the revolutionary Naga party guided by Phizo, the Akali party in Punjab and the DMK party in the South.

(d) Psychological

The psychological causes have contributed a lot to the development and stability of regionalism. It is the desire of most of the persons that their area in which they live should be progressive with complete disregard to the national interest. This type of feeling promotes regionalism.

(e) Cultural

Each culture has its indigenous custom, tradition and culture. The people of a particular region develop and inalienable identity with the culture of other region. They love their own culture and develop hatred towards other culture. This breeds regionalism.

(f) Economic

Economic factor is the root cause of regionalism. Unbalanced economic development comprising agriculture, industry, trade, commerce, education, transport and communication give rise to regionalism. It has been evident since the colonial rule in India, because some of the states are found to be economically progressive and some others are quite backward. In progressive areas people enjoy all the facilities of modern and sophisticated living whereas in the backward areas people lack the opportunities to live. This type of difference promotes regionalism.

2.7.3 Remedial Measures

The following measures are suggested for diluting if not ending regionalism to some extent:

(a) If regionalism is to be eliminated, the people should be encouraged to indulge in travel and to increase contact with the people belonging to different regions of the country. In traveling to different parts of the country the people will gather sufficient knowledge, mix with different types of people, exchange ideas and views with each other which will help remove regional sentiments.

(b) The history of the nations should be propagated all over the country so that the people may clearly realize that the history of the individual regions of the country is only a part of the history of the nations to which all the regions have to make an important contribution. It will help in eradicating the sense of regionalism.

(c) It is essential for national unity and integration that the political parties propagating regionalism and regional interests should be prevented from doing so.

(d) Efforts should be made to propagate sentiments of nationalism in the country so that the psychological causes underlying at the root of regionalism can be removed.

Regionalism is just like a hydra headed monster. It must be fought with all weapons. It requires whole-hearted support and cooperation both from the government and from the people.

Process of Sociocultural Change in India

3

M.N. Srinivas the first sociologist spoke out the significant social changes taking place in India in the passage of time. These changes can be visualized from various angles of studies like economic, social culture, political, legal, demographic and sociological. All these changes have taken place through specific processes which may be categorized as Sanskritization, westernization, secularization, modernization and democratization.

3.1 Sanskritization

Sanskritization is an ongoing process of social change in India. It is a cut urological concept which explains the process of endogenous change in Indian society and culture. M.N. Srinivas, the sociologist evolved the concept of Sanskritization while preparing his doctoral dissertation at Oxford University and later on used the term in his book *Religion and Society Among the Corgs of South India* to describe the process of cultural mobility in the traditional social structure of Indian society. He defined it as "a process by which the low castes take over the beliefs, rituals, style of life and other cultural traits from those of the upper classes, specially the Brahmins".

Authorities on social stratification and social change give diverse views on Sanskritization. Andre Beteille states, "Sanskritization was an important feature of traditional Hindu society, where it appears to have been the principle of social mobility." Yogendra Singh is of the opinion that "Sanskritization has been a process of social mobility throughout the history of Indian society." Harper treats the concept of Sanskritization as a functional concept distinct from a historical concept of change. According to M.N. Srinivas, "Sanskritization means not only the adoption of new customs and habits but also exposure of new ideas values which have found frequent expression in the vast body of Sanskrit literature, sacred as well as secular." Thus, Srinivas described Sanskritization as the process of mobility of lower castes by adopting vegetarianism to move in the caste hierarchy in a generation or two. Later on, he redefined it as a process by which a low caste or tribe or other groups changes its customs, rituals, ideology and way of life in the direction of a high twice born (*Dvija*) caste.

The very foundation of Indian society is based on caste system. In Indian society two castes prevail, i.e. upper and lower. According to the varna system Brahmins were on the top rang of the society as society regarded them as preservers of culture. The varna system was based on the cultural values. The higher castes were regarded culturally sound. The social hierarchy of varnas is static. In the varna system the social status and position of each varna is predetermined but it is dynamic in case of caste. During the British rule in India, the ideal of the varna system collapsed and each caste tried to improve and reform itself by Sanskritization. Thus, Sanskritization is a cultural process leading to positional change in the society. Sanskritization results only positional changes, not structural. It involves mobility by the upward movement of a caste through the spread of culture. It does not occur in Hindu caste only. It takes place among the tribals and semi tribals. It is a process of cultural transformation.

3.1.1 Forms of Sanskritization

Sanskritization assumes several forms. It refers to an effort on the part of the low caste to adopt the name of the higher caste to have higher sociocultural status. It is an indication of imitation of certain customs and lifestyle of the upper caste. It may be expressed in the form of de-Sanskritization or inverted Sanskritization when a caste is pulled to increased Puritanism and traditionalism higher than the higher caste. It may assume the form of de-Sanskritization. This refers to the process where a formerly progressive group discards many of the cultural symbols of modernization and accepts the original traditional cultural elements relating to dress, food habit, language of expression, style and pattern of living and political ideologies, etc.

Thus, Sanskritization is not universal. As D.N. Majumdar states, "the shrinkage of distances between castes is not due to Sanskritization but its reverse. The lower castes are not moving towards the higher, but the higher castes are abandoning their lifestyle." The effect of westernization has greatly facilitated the process of de Sanskritization. At present several castes are abandoning their social traditions and resorting to that of other. The social mobility among castes is horizontal rather than vertical. As a result the process of de Sanskritization is more evident than that of Sanskritization in Indian society. Like four varnas, Sanskritization has four models such as Brahmanical, Kshatriya, Vaishya and Sudra. It is because of the fact that the process of Sanskritization is very much influenced by the dominant caste factor. The local dominate caste or leader mediates in the process of cultural transformation. If the dominant caste is Brahman, we will have the Brahmanical model of Sanskritization. The model of Sanskritization will be shaped on the basis of dominant caste factor such as Kshatriya, Vaishya and Sudra. The process of change will be determined by the dominant caste. Sometimes it happened that the transmission of culture of the dominant caste had caused disruption in the social organization and eroded social values and had given rise to cultural lag.

3.1.2 Pre-requisites of Sanskritization

The pre-requisites of Sanskritization are as follows:

(a) A change in the self-image of castes or groups followed by higher status aspiration.

(b) Improvement in socio-economic status of these castes.

(c) Upward social mobility.

(d) The aspirant caste do not consider the dominant caste a negative reference group either due to their commitment to the ideology of the traditional society or to the force of habits.

(e) The absence of organized apposition from the dominant caste to such imitating behaviour of the lower caste.

3.1.3 Distinctive Characteristics of Sanskritization

Sanskritization is a broader concept. It possesses the following distinctive characteristics:

(a) Sanskritization involves the imitation of the custom conduct, and rituals of higher caste by the lower caste.

(b) Sanskritization enables peoples of a lower caste for acquisition of higher status in the society.

(c) It denotes a process of upward mobility.

(d) It is not universal. In this process Brahmins are not the object of imitation. Other castes can be taken as models.

(e) By Sanskritization a caste or a group adopts customs and rituals which would qualify it for being treated as twice born.

(f) In this process the unit of mobility is group and not individual or family.

(g) It refers to the cultural change but not to structural change in the society.

(h) Sanskritization encompasses social virtues such as economic welfare, political authority, acquisition of knowledge through spread of education, leadership and a consistent desire to move up in the social hierarchy.

(i) In a particular society when a caste enjoy higher economic power or political authority, but rated low in the society it adopts the process of Sanskritization to gain higher position.

(j) Sanskritization is not a static concept. It is dynamic. The process of Sanskritization is continuous.

(k) It is virtual protest against caste tradition.

(l) The motive force behind this process is not culture imitation, but an expression of challenge and revolt against socio-economic deprivations.

(m) It is a cultural camouflage for latent interclass and inter-caste competition for a acquisition of economic and social power in the social hierarchy.

(n) The process of Sanskritization has been speeded up by acceleration effect such as rapid change in material culture, i.e. industrialization, technological progress, spread of education and scientific knowledge, and cultural revolution, etc.

3.1.4 Factors Leading to Sanskritization

The following factors are responsible for Sanskritization:

(a) The Colonial Rule

The establishment of British rule and impact of colonial culture provided impetus to the lower castes to have the opportunities to Sanskritize themselves and subsequently raised their status. The Britishers encouraged the process of cultural change in India.

(b) Development of Transport and Communication

Development of the means of transport and communication during the British rule enabled people to move from place to place and mix with people of different religions and cultures. It helped in imbibing a spirit of Sanskritization among themselves.

(c) Development of Mass Media

Mass Media particularly the radio, the cinema, the newspaper and various journals contributed a lot for the popularization of Sanskritic values and ideologies. It helped in spreading modern ideas.

(d) Political Factors

The introduction of parliamentary democracy and universal suffrage have helped the growth of Sanskritization.

(e) Education

The impact of western education accompanied by socio-religions movements like the Arya Samaj, the Brahmo Samaj and the Prarthana Samaj contributed a lot to the process of Sanskritization.

(f) Cultural Institutions

People of different areas found the opportunity to meet each other at piligrim centres, temples and holy places and exchanged ideas. They got the opportunity for the spread of Sanskritic ideas and beliefs.

(g) Sectarian Movement

Sectarian movements were also instrumental for the growth of Sanskritization. They attracted members of the low castes and help them raise their status by joining the movement.

3.1.5 Limitations of Sanskritization

Though Sanskritization is a broader concept and the gateway of radical social change it is subject to scathing criticism on the following grounds:

(a) Sanskritization is a westernized concept. The seeds it Sanskritization should not have been transplanted in the Indian soil. The seeds have been germinated and plants have been grown, but these have borne poisonous fruits.

(b) Theoretically Sanskritization is a loose term.

(c) Sanskritization in legal sense is a truth asserting concept which oscillates between the logic of ideal typical and nominal definitions of phenomenon.

(d) Sanskritization as a process of cultural change has failed to account for many aspects of the cultural change in the post and contemporary India as it has neglected many non Sanskritic traditions.

(e) D.N. Majumdar in one of his studies has revealed that there is no tendency among the low castes to adopt the customs and rituals of the higher castes nor do these help in elevating the status of any caste.

(f) Lynch alleges that Sanskritization is culture bound and is not so much useful to explaining all movements for social mobility in the post-Independence India.

(g) Prasad vehemently criticizes the concept of Sanskritization on linguistic ground and suggests kulinization in place of Sanskritization. Kulinization is the process by which the lower status Brahmins acquire higher status by marrying Kulin (high status) Brahmins.

(h) There are evidences that people of lower caste being sanskritized have not been accrued higher social status by the upper caste.

3.2 Secularization

Secularization implies the belief that the state, morals and education should be independent of religion. The word secular has been derived from the Latin word 'seculum' which means age or generation. The word secular stands for things not spiritual civil and not ecclesiastical and for things not concerned with religion. The term secularization was first used in Europe in 1648 to refer to the process of transfer to church properties to the control of the princes. George Jacob Holyoake was the first man to coin the term in the middle part of the 191th century. It symbolized a revolt against the stringent hold and influence of religion on the individual's life. Subsequently, the term was derivatively used to indicate a striking social process. Thus, secularization meant one thing different from the earlier secular. Secularization as a socio political ethos is only an instrumentality to achieve a system of ordering and arranging the human affairs.

Byron Wilson defines secularization as, "the process where by religious thinking, practice and institution lose social significance". Petter Berger considers secularization as, "the process by which sectors of society and culture are removed from the domination of religious institutions and symbols". Bryan Wilson defined the term as, "the process by which religion loses influence within groups and societies". M.N. Srinivas writes, "the term secularization implies that what was previously regarded is religious is now ceasing to be such and it also implies the process of differentiation which results in the various aspects of socio-economic, political, legal and moral becoming increasingly discrete to each other".

Thus, secularization implies rationalism and its process is anti- religious. As Y. Singh puts it, "the spread of the process of secularism implies that various issues and events in personal and social life are evaluated not from a religious point of view but utilitarian".

Broadly speaking secularization refers to a process of change, i.e. from traditional to modern. In this context, Singer says, "The tendency of jobs, products, social relations in the industrial plant and the office become increasingly free from ritual and restriction is commonly referred to as secularization."

3.2.1 Basic Features of Secularization

Secularization becomes increasingly evident from the following basic features:

(a) Erosion of Religiosity

Secularization has been characterized as a process involving the erosion of religiosity. When society tends to upward movements from sacred to secular, the influence of religious on social life starts reducing to the minimum. People lose faith on religious beliefs and practices.

(b) Rationalism

Increase in secularism leads to an increase in the differentiation of various aspects of society. In the process of secularization, the element of rationalism holds supreme. Rationalism means independent thoughts free from traditional beliefs and ideas. It may be understood as a comprehensive expression applied to various theoretical and practical tendencies which regulate the individual and social life in accordance with the principles of reason and try to eliminate every thing irrational. Thus, an outstanding feature of secularism is the rule of reason and discarding of superstition.

(c) Progressive Outlook

Secularism is an embodiment of broad scientific outlook. It makes the individual free from superstition, conservation and narrow-mindedness people experiment with their latent potentials rather this on the fate of inevitability. Secularism has a scientific base. As science develops, secularism develops.

(d) Anti Religious

Secularism stands for religious neutrality. It may require the status to be above religion. Traditionally religion was considered as one of the most important element which influenced various aspects of social life, but the spread of secularization has reduced its importance, as a result, the religions bond over other aspects of social life is breaking day-to-day.

Thus, it is revealed from the analysis of the basic features that secularization is the subway in the process of modernization.

It is a process which helps removing certain sectors of society and culture from the clutches of religion dominance. Secularization has two aspects such as structural institutional and cultural symbolic. Appropriation of church or temple land by the state or removal of educational institutions from ecclesiastical control is an example of the structural institutional aspect of secularization. The cultural symbolic aspect of secularization can be visualized from the ground decline of religions content in Art, Philosophy and Literature.

3.2.2 Causes of Secularization

The following causes are responsible for the evolution and growth of secularization in India:

(a) During the British rule various socio-religious reform movements launched by the Arya Samaj, the Brahmo Samaj, the Prarthana Samaj, the Ramakrishna Mission, the Theosphical Society of India and the Sarvodaya, etc., were instrumental in encouraging rational thinking among people.

(b) The expansion of modern education based on western culture, literature and thoughts reinforced the values of secularism. The educated people started abandoning all the superstition enveloping the society and put all the tradition to critical analysis. A secular man was no more directed by faith or sentiment but by logical thinking.

(c) The development of the means of transport and communication widened the horizon of wisdom of the people, as a result their circle of social contact expanded to a considerable extent. It accelerated the process of secularization.

(d) Increased urbanization and enactment of social laws for social reform influenced religions beliefs and traditions and encouraged the process of secularization.

(e) In the post-independence era, Hindu Code Bill greatly contributed to the secularization of Hindu society. Indian constitution provided that there shall be no discrimination on grounds of religion, race, caste, sex, etc. The Hindu marriage act, the Divorced act, the Removal of

Untouchability Act, the Prohibition of Dowry Act and the prohibition of sati system, etc., encouraged secularization.

(f) The impact of western culture fascinated and enchanted people. There was a radical transformation in the pattern and style of living of the people. Increasing influence of the foreign culture encouraged materialism, individualism and liberalism which promoted secularism.

(g) Lack of strong religious organization is one of the causative factor for speeding the tempo of secularization.

(h) Political organization acted as a stimulant in the process of secularization as they professed secular outlook reducing the influence of religion.

(i) The cultural revolution that took place in the post-independence era detached religion from culture. As a result several cultural activities were organized on democratic, scientific and worldly bases encouraging secularization.

(j) In the past, religion was patronized by kings and emperors. Religion had a political backing. Nowadays there is a lack of patronage and there is complete absence of political support. As a result the influence and activities of religious organizations are waning day by day leading to secularization.

3.2.3 Impact of Secularization

As a matter of fact, the process of secularization in India had its beginning with the advent of the British rule. It was further accelerated with industrialization and urbanization. The impact of secularization may be discussed in the following heads:

(a) Impact on the Ideas of Purity and Pollution

It is a fact that the Hindu social life is governed by the ideas of purity and pollution purity means sacredness or cleanliness and pollution means impurity. In the traditional society the people belonging to the upper caste were considered pure and free from pollution and the people who belonged to the lower caste were considered as untouchable, impure and polluted. On the basis of purity and impurity occupation was determined. The secularism developed in the social life of people has wiped out caste and occupational distinctions.

(b) Impact on Life Cycle Rituals

Secularization has created the move of de-sanskritization in Hindu society. It is evident from the change in the social behaviour of people. Traditionally Hindus used to observe a number of life cycle rituals such as name giving ceremony, the first tonsure, sacred thread ceremony and puberty ritual of girls. Nowadays, these rituals have been made cut short. Even many conservative Brahmins have given up the practice of daily rituals such as praying, fasting and performing sacrifice, etc. It is the result of secularization.

(c) Impact on Monasteries

The land reform measures initiated by the Government have been a death blow to the abbots and monasteries as the landed property of several monasteries have been taken among by the administration and the powers of the abbots have been reduced to the minimum. The process of secularization has adversely affected the religious autonomy of monasteries all over the country.

(d) Impact on Pilgrimage

It was a practice among Hindu devout to go at least once on pilgrimage in their lifetime to satisfy their religious aspiration. Secularization has converted the pilgrimage into pleasure trips. People have forgotten their basic objective of earning 'punya' rather they are interested for luxurious lifestyle.

(e) Impact on Casteism

The age-old caste system which contributed to the personal degradation of millions of individuals and constituted a hurdle in the path of developing the democratic society in India has undergone radical transformation in the process of secularization. Caste is no more considered a determinant of one's position and status in the society, rather in its place education, wealth, efficiency, etc., have emerged as the determinations. Secularization has brought an attitudinal change in the society and there is no caste distinction at all except in some conservative communities.

(f) Impact on Village Life

Of the three major elements in the social structure of Indian society, the village is the most important in the programmes of rural development. Each ancient Indian village was as self-sufficient a local society as ever existed any place in the world. Sir Charles Metcalfe writing in 1832 said, "The village communities are little republics, having nearly everything they want within themselves, and almost independent of any foreign relations. They seem to lost where nothing else lasts. Dynasty after dynasty tumbles down revolution succeeds revolution... but the village community remains the same. The union of village communities, each one forming a separate little state in itself, has, I conceive, contributed more than any other cause to the preservation of the people of India, through all the revolutions and changes which they have suffered, and is in a high degree conducive to their happiness, and to the enjoyment of a great portion of freedom and independence. Now things have been changed. The effect of secularization has transformed the village community. The caste panchayats have lost three powers. They are being used for political ends rather than social objectives. The importance of religion has been replaced by accumulation of wealth. In villages rapid changes are occurring in every aspect of social life.

(g) Impact on Family and Marriage

In India, the powerful combination of social, economic and religions or philosophical functions within the family has made this ancient and respected institution continue to survive in the face of strong forces playing on it to weaken its hold. As a social structure especially adopted to conservative village life, in a folk society, a peasant agricultural economy, it stands in a vulnerable position at this stage of India's development as this nations has moved towards a secular society through vast programmes of change. Changes in the direction of industrialization have moved people from their customary places of habitation and from their usual roles in society. Many village people are seeking jobs in towns and cities. As employment opportunities in various guises are multiplying and becoming more diversified, both men and women of whatever stations in life are enabled to equip themselves through education and training, to rise in social and economic status to better positions. With the framework of horizontal and vertical mobility as an integral part of India's programme of development now under way, the role of the family as an important conditioning factor has undergone a drastic change. People have forgotten their social rituals. There are no elderly persons to guide the people. Spread of education among women has created situations in which young girls do not have time to learn rituals from their mothers and grandmothers. Educated women have cultivated an altogether different attitude towards ideas and practices of pollutions and purity. The impact of secularization on the custom of marriage is becoming prominent. The provision of divorce and civil contract has turned marriage from a religion to a personal affair. Dowry has increased in alarming proportions and has become a precondition to marriage and thereby turning marriage into an economic affair. Further, the Hindu Marriage Act regulated the conditions of marriage including legal age, degree of kin relationship permitted and consent required. It provided for marriages to be registered by the state and specified the grounds for judicial separation by petition and grounds of divorce by either party. Lows provided greater freedom and protection concerning marriage divorce, inheritance and succession and control of property. The social sanctity was deteriorated to a considerable extent.

Thus, the spread of secularization in India has been spectacular and so also its impact.

3.2.4 Secularism in India

The concept of secularism is a product of the west. The rise of secularism in India is due to her contact with the west. Secularism was felt in India in various splendors. The grant of Diwani in 1765 gave rise to complex problems in Indian society. Prudence and commercial interest dictated non interventions giving preference to commercial interests. The reform movement of the utilitarian, Evangelicals, liberals and Humanitarians influenced Indian policy to a great extent before 1830. The reform measures undertaken by Bentik sowed the seeds of liberalism and secularism in India. Brahmo Samaj movement initiated by Raja Ram Mohan Roy created a liberal wave of secular Ideals. By 1885, growth of nationalism and liberalism were felt everywhere in India. The end of the century witnessed the revival of Hinduism of Arya Samaj and vedantism of Vivekananda. Indian National Congress was founded on the basis of secular ideals. Secularism in India was put to an acid test with the evolution of Muslim League demanding a separate state. The Muslims demanded their immediate partition. It gave a death blow to secularism. The British policy of separate electorates for the Muslim given in the Indian Councils Act of 1909 introduced anti secular forces in Indian politics. This separate communal representation laid the foundation of final partition. Though Mahatma Gandhi, Jawaharlal Nehru and Subhas Chandra Bose were great secularists they failed to place permanent imprint of secularism on the Indian masses. As democracy in India is an alien institution grafted on a traditional society, so is secularism western impact still to become an integral part of Indian culture, secularism can survive in India not only by attempting to get support from India's past which will not come but by looking forward to a move hopeful future.

India's historical traditions and its immediate political exigencies following Independence supported India's commitment to secularism. The Indian constitution contains some articles supporting the principle of secularism. In India secularism implies unity among people irrespective of caste creed, colour, language, etc. Secularism means above all religion, i.e. neutrality. The word secularism can better be substituted for nationalism in India. The term 'Secularism' has its own limitations as it is understood, i.e. separation of state from religion, equal and impartial treatment of all communities by the state, approaching religious beliefs in a spirit of objective rationality and ensuring a just standard of living for all people irrespective of community.

3.2.5 Barriers to Secularism in India

India is a vast country having geographical, cultural, ethic, religions and linguistic diversity with a bewildering variety of customs, ideas, values and aspirations. In spite of multitude of diversities, there is also a tremendous impression of unity which proves its uniqueness in the world. The concept of secularism was brought to India by the British utilitarian during the viceroyship of Lord Willim Bentick. The base of secularism in India was strengthened with the spread of education and growth of transport and communications facilities. It received further impetus during the Second World War and the civil disobedience movement led by Mahatma Gandhi. With the independence of India in 1947, there was growing urgency to widen the base of secularism to suit the needs of new India. This was given official recognition when our constitution declared India as a secular state. Secularism was a buzz word in the early post-independence era.

Though India professes secularism, a number of obstacles are observed in the path of secularism. They are as follows:

(a) Lack of a uniform civil code acts as a stumbling block to the country's secularism.

(b) Politics in India is entertained with religions and it is very difficult to separate them.

(c) Hindus in India constitute a majority community. The cultural system adopted by Hindus is not at all accepted by the minority community and it causes misunderstanding among communities.

(d) Secularism in India is not universal in character. Due to limited interpretation of secularism, the religious identities and other subcultural differences of Indian citizens have continued to remain strong.

(e) Emergence of communalism makes the scope of secularism limited.

In spite of the obstacles secularism has been accepted and practiced as a national policy in India.

3.3 Westernization

The biggest impact on society causing tremendous changes in society is to be attributed to the phenomenon of westernization. Westernization is a culturological concept devoting the process of sociocultural change in modern India. It is an inclusive, complex and many layered concept covering a wide range right from western technology at one end to the experimental method of modern science and modern historiography at the other. Its incredible complexity is seen in the fact that different aspects of westernization sometimes combine to strengthen a particular process, sometimes work at cross purposes and are occasionally mutually discrete.

The term 'Westernization' can be interpreted in two senses—one is global and the other is Indian. From a global perspective, westernization refers to the process of social change brought about in non-western countries as a result of prolonged contact with western culture. In the Indian context, it refers to changes brought about in Indian social life as a result of its contact with the British. In India, westernization did not take place as a totality, rather it was selective. It was the result of the traditional, tolerant and receptive attitude of the Indians. Raja Ram Mohan Roy, Ishwar Chandra Vidyasagar, Ramanuj, Vivekananda, Gokhale, and Gandhi who come under the influence of westernization tried to redefine the ancient Indian values in terms of modern enlightenment. Western ideology affected all the sphere of our life. Westernization is the main force behind modernization. Compared to sanskritization, westernization is a simpler concept. Srinivas defines it as "The changes brought about in Indian society and culture as a result of over 150 years of British rule, the term subsuming changes occurring at different level...technology institutions, ideology and values". By westernization, Srinivas primarily meant the British impact. Earlier he had maintained that sanskritization is a prelude to westernizations. Later on he changed his view and maintained that it is not necessary for Sanskritizations occurring prior to westernizations. But the two processes are linked with each other. Emphasis on humanitarianism and rationalism is a part of westernization, which led to a series of institutional and social reform in India. Establishment of scientific, technological and educational institutions, rise of nationalism, new political culture and leadership in the country are all by products of westernization. Srinivas prefers the terms westernization to modernization.

3.3.1 Sanskritization and Westernization

Though Sanskritization and western had some common programme and objectives their approach was different, e.g. both wanted social changes. If the exponents of sanskritization were against meat eating and consumption of liquor, the proponents of westernization were supporters of meat eating and wine drinking. Sanskritization gave a religions touch to their agenda, but westernization gave more emphasis on secular approach. Among lower class people, marriage of widow, divorce and remarriage were no problem. Their wives did not treat the husbands as deities. So this approach was compatible to westernization programme. For the Brahmins, the outlook was conservative and different. But those of them who availed western education did not find it difficult to change the outlook. The lower caste were willing to accept sanskritization with the hope of upgradation. But when that was not possible they turned in favour of westernization. Thus sanskritization is a process of endogamous change and westernization implies exogamous change.

3.3.2 Basic Features of Westernization

Following are the basic features of Westernization:

(a) The process of westernization subsumes changes at different levels of technology, institutions, ideology and values.

(b) Westernization emphasizes on value judgement. It is based on the nation of humanitarianism which implies active concern for the welfare of all human beings irrespective of social inequalities based on caste, economic positions, religion, age or sex.

(c) Westernization is an all inclusive term. It covers a wide range of changes from western technology at one end to the experimental method of modern science and modern historiography at the other.

(d) Westernization process is associated in our food, dietary pattern, cooking, and style of eating, utensils used for the purpose and various other things connected with our eating pattern.

(e) Westernization has no universal impact. It affects certain areas leaving some untouched. It has limited impact in selected areas where educated community is numerically large. But in less educated and less affluent family these changes may not be seen. So westernization has discrete impact.

(f) The form and pace of westernization of India varied from region to region and from one section of populations to another.

(g) Westernizations has created many inter-contradictory forces which instead of consolidating contradict each other. In the political and cultural fields, westernization has given birth not only to nationalism but also to revivalism, communalism, casteism, linguism and regionalism, etc.

3.3.3 Types of Westernization

Taking into consideration the social organization of tradition in general and orthogenetic and heterogenic process of cultural organization, westernization can be categorized into two parts—primary westernization and secondary westernization. Primary westernization means changes induced by the western impact on orthogenetic process of cultural change or Indian little tradition.

Primary Westernization Assumes Two Forms

(a) Subcultural change and (b) supercultural change. Sub-cultural change is associated with minority sections of Indians coming in contact with western culture. This includes the sub culture represented by those Indian intellectuals and scholars who not only adopted money western cognitive patterns and styles of life but also supported its rapid expansion. The second type of primary westernization refers to supercultural change associated with the process of general diffusion of western cultural traits such as the new technology, dress, food and change in the habits and styles of life of people in general resulting from the cultural contact with the British.

On the other hand, secondary westernization was associated with the great tradition of India and refers to changes which contributed to the growth of several forms of cultural structures covering a wide spectrum of education, law, science, technology, new forms of politicization, urbanization and industrialization.

3.3.4 Impact of Westernization on Indian Society

The process of westernization had a deep impact upon the social, cultural and political systems of India. The impact of westernization brought a sea change in the Indians cultural tradition. Many social institutions of India were changed under the process of westernization. History reveals that Indian culture has been influenced by so many western traditions such as the tradition of Portuguese, Dutch, French and British. But the British culture with its substantive qualities like rationality, experimentation, codification, verification and rational utilitarian orientation in behaviour and thought exerted overwhelming influence on the little and great tradition of Indian culture. Thus, the western impact on Indian society has been primarily of British.

The impact of westernization on Indian society can be discussed under the following heads:

(a) Impact on Education

The prevailing system of education in India owes its origin to British. In the traditional Indian society the content of education was metaphysical. It was open for the people of upper classes or the twice born classes and the people of other castes were deprived of getting the education in spite of their best endeavour. Further its structure was hereditary and classed. But modern education under the impact of westernization is open for all. Its content is liberal and approach is secular. Any body irrespective of class and caste can avail it. It is due to the impact of westernization.

(b) Impact on the Communication Network

British people introduced the modern printing press, telegraph, railways and modern postal system in India. Which enabled people to know about world affairs through newspapers and to have interactions with people of distance places. People had a broad outlook which changed their attitude to life.

(c) Growth of Nationalism

Both Democracy and Nationalism are the gifts of westernization. Nationalism means consciousness of one nationhood. Its sociological manifestation is the idea of nation state. Democracy is a special form of political organization and system of values on which nation state can be founded. The feeling of nationality and respect for democratic norms is a consequence of westernization.

(d) Impact on Food Habits and Mode of Eating

Westernization has reached the level of food habits and ways of eating. Traditionally Indians ate their meals sitting on the floor. Food was served either on the leaves or on brass, bronze or silver plates. Among the upper castes and specially among Brahmins, eating was a religious act. Food has to be cooled while the women in charge of cooking and serving it must be in a ritually poor state. Food was being served to children and adults in order of seniority. At the end of the meal, the dining leaves became impure and were thrown out and the places where the leaves rested were purified with a solution of cow dung. Now the westernized groups prefer to eat at tables with stainless steel utensils and spoons, etc. The new mode of eating has contributed to an increase in secularization as the table is not likely to be purified with cow dung after meals and the ritual acts traditionally performed before and after meals are almost dropped. Change in the food habits have brought people never to modern food technologies.

(e) Impact on Dress Factor

Westernization has completely changed the dress factor. Home spun clothes have been replaced by factory made clothes. The mode of dress has undergone a drastic change.

(f) Impact on Language

Nowadays, there is an increasing use of English language. Regional languages have been enfeebled as English language has entered the dialects of rural folk.

(g) Impact on Marriage

The traditional has undergone a perceptible change due to the impact of westernization, marriage today is no longer seen as a relationship between two families, and rather it has been transformed into the relationship of two individuals, i.e. husband and wife. Husband and wife are treating themselves as friends. The superiority and inferiority complex between husband and wife have been minimized.

(h) Impact on Family

Westernization has changed the structural aspects of joint family. The virtues of a joint family such as it is three generational in depth, that its members live under the same roof, that the property of whatever kind is shared by all, that it is a self-sufficient unit socially and economically, that the centre of the universe for the whole family, that it is the reservoir of deep loyalties and bonds of affection that it is a kinship group that serves a place of abode and centre for social, recreational and religious activities have been wiped out. Western culture has preached the individualistic ideology of family which is diametrically opposite to the collective ethos on which the joint family system is founded.

(i) Impact on the Status of Women

Westernization has changed the status of women. They are no more confined within the four walls of a room. Spread of education has prepared them to strive for natural status of equality. In every sphere of socio-economic activity they are competing against their male counterparts. The economic opportunity has made them independent. They are more interested for acquisition of wealth, power and prestige with complete disregard to their duties and responsibilities.

(j) Impact on the System of Social Stratification

Westernization has been instrumental in the complete transformation in the system of social stratification. The roots of ancient system of stratification have been shaken by the process of westernization. The basic values of pollution and purity underlying the Indian caste system have lost their vigour and vitality and in their place some new criteria for socio-economic ranking of the population have emerged. These criteria are based as achievement and not on ascription. Status is allocated on the basis of individual performance and not an charismatic qualities.

The traditional styles and manners of marriage and family have given way to love and inter-caste marriages and growth of nuclear families. Again, under the impact of western culture, the young generation is becoming materialistic and sensualistic in outlook. The sources of entertainment have completely changed which has transformed the humans into beasts.

(k) Impact on Religion

The socio ethical value of religion has undergone significant changes under the influence of westernization. Uncritical acceptance of religious ideas is being replaced by logical interpretation and acceptance. People have become more materialistic than devoted. It is due to the impact of science and modern western education.

3.3.5 Criticisms

Though westernization is favourable process of social change aiming at binding the developing nations to an established goal and a historically determined course it is not free from criticisms. The following criticisms are leveled against westernization:

(a) It is a value loaded term as it denotes the western model. When adopted in the eastern economics it leads to harmful consequences.

(b) Lerner believes that westernization is a more limited concept than modernization. All countries have not become modern due to the influence of the west. The term westernization is ethically neutral.

(c) It is alleged that the term is inadequate and parochial.

(d) Yogendra argues that westernization is a pejorative term, because of its associations with former colonial domination of these countries by the west.

(e) Some are of the view that westernization is not suitable for many reasons. Some like westernization of USA model, but some reject it in favour of USSR model. The middle eastern countries prefer the latter for ethnocentrism. They express their dislikeness for USA model for political reasons and express the hostility with extreme nationalism and passionate xenophobia.

3.4 Modernization

Modernization is a process of social change which involves the transformation of social, political and economic setup of a country. It aims at building an open society. It involves the control of administration by an organized bureaucracy or civil services. The process of modernizations has many aspects. It finds expression in social organization culture, political activities, economy, and education in various ways. The process of modernization involves an increase in social unrest. It institutes appropriate change in the social system to meet the rising expectations of the people. The term modernization is derived from the Latin root mode, which implies just new. In chronological sense, it means, the latest. The term was evolved by American scholars during the 1950 and 1960 and since this it gained currency throughout the world.

The idea of modernization can be comprehended in three senses. The first one is the most general and is associated with all kinds of progressive social change occurring in any society. The second one is more historically specific. It connotes the idea of a complex of social, economic, political, cultural and psychological transformation occurring in the west from the 16th century onwards and reaching its apogee in the 19th and 20th centuries. It involves the process of industrialization, urbanization, rationalization, bureaucratization and democratization, etc., the rise of capitalism, the spread of individualism and achievement, motivation, the affirmation of reason and science and many other processes. Thus modernization means attaining modernity. It refers to the process through which a traditional or pre technological society passes. It is transformed into a society characterized by machine technology rational and secular attitudes, and highly differentiated social structure. Finally, there is the most specific meaning of the term modernization referring only to the backward and underdeveloped societies and describing their attempts to catch up with the most developed countries, co-existing with them in the same historical period within the world society.

'Modernization' is defined by different writers in different manners.

David Lerner defines it as "modernization includes a distinguishing positivist spirit. It touches both public institutions as well as private aspirations."

Robert Bellah say, "where modernization means only an increased effectiveness in goal attainment with no increase in rationalization of the goal setting process, very serious pathologies can result. Empirically such pathologies of modernization have occurred, but they are the product of partial or disturbed modernization, not the inevitable result of modernization itself."

Smelser defines it as "a complex set of changes that take place in every part of society as it attempts to be industrialized. It involves ongoing change in society's economy politics, education, tradition and religions."

Schumel Fisenstadt defines it as "the process of change towards those types of social, economic and political systems that have developed in Western Europe and North America from the 17th century to the 19th and 20th centuries to the South America, Asian and African continents."

Edward Tiryakian defines it as, "From a world of historical perspective, modernization pertains to the state of the art or leading edge innovations or break through in cognitive, moral, ethical, technological and social arrangements that contribute to the enhancement of human condition."

Szymon Chodak defines it as, "a special important instance of the development of societies, an instance where conscientious efforts are made to achieve higher standards".

Wilbert Moore says, "Modernization is a total transformation of a traditional or pre-modern society in to the type of technology and associated social organization that characterize the advanced economically prosperous and relatively politically stable nations of the western world."

All these definitions convey the idea that modernization is a process whereby less developed societies acquire characteristic common to more developed societies. It is a process involving the rationalization of ends aiming at building an open society. It provides for educational service. It implies economic development. It involves the control of administration by an organized bureaucracy.

3.4.1 Characteristics of Modernization Process

Modernization has many facts. It finds expression in social organization, culture, political activities, economy and education in various ways. The result reveals the formation of an open society in which individual talent, enterprise and training can find places.

Modernization possesses the following characteristics:

(a) It is a Revolutionary Process

In the process of modernization, a radical change takes place in human life. Black has compared the transition from tradition to modernity with that of the change from pre human to human existence and from primitive to civilized societies.

(b) It is a Complex Process

Modernization has a complex process. In its wake, it changes the whole of the social system. Change in one factor tends to produce a complimentary change in another factor.

(c) It is a Global Process

Modernization is a universal process. It was originated during 15th and 16th century. Presently it has become a world-wide phenomenon.

(d) It is an Irreversible Process

Modernization is irreversible in the sense that, there is no point of going back. Once society reaches certain levels of urbanization literary and industrialization in one decade, it will not decline to the lower levels in the next decade. There may be casual setbacks but the process as a whole is irreversible.

(e) It is a Dynamic Process

It is an ongoing process of change. With the advancement of scientific knowledge and technical skills, the conditions of life undergo a radical change.

(f) It is an Adaptive Process

This process puts before individuals and groups the need to adopt themselves to the new changes taking place in society. In the process of rapid changes taking place in society, individuals are likely to adopt themselves to the changing environment.

(g) It is a Progressive Change

It is a progressive process. It is quite inevitable and desirable. In the beginning modernization causes pain but ultimately it contributes to human welfare.

(h) It is a Painful Process

Sociological analysts are of the view that modernization is a painful process. It brings changes which produces not only benefits but also conflict, pain and relative disadvantage.

(i) It is an Unending Process

Modernization is a continuous process. Every minute, every second, some changes are visualized and modernization is the end result.

(j) It is a Multilinear Process

Modernization is a multilinker and multipath process. All societies do not necessarily have to take the same road to modernization. Each society can follow an attractive path.

3.4.2 Pre-requisites for Modernization

Yogendra Singh, one of the famous exponent of modernization is of the view that, a unique feature of modernization in India is that it being carried forward through adaptive changes in the traditional structures rather than structural break down. Regarding the pre-requisites of modernization diverse opinions emerge from different scholars. S.N. Eisenstadt has stated that modernization requires three structural characteristics of a society such as a high level of structural differentiation a high degree of social mobilization and a relatively centralized and autonomous institutional framework. In similar view, Narmadeswar Prasad points out that for modernization certain pre-requisites are to be present in the society. They include the awareness of purpose and an eye on future, awareness of existence beyond one's own world, of many other societies, a sense of urgency, availability of a variety of opportunities and roles, emotional preparedness for self-imposed tasks and sacrifices and emergence of a devoted dynamic and committed leadership, etc.

David Apter is of the opinion that three conditions are required for modernization to take place. They are: (i) an innovative social system, (ii) a flexible structure, and (iii) a social framework backed by advanced technology. Christopher Bates Doob has identified certain conditions for promoting modernization which include economic, social politico administrative, psychological and demographic, etc. Economic pre-requisites for modernization includes modern tools, transportation, communication media and technological up-gradations. Social pre-requisites include the evaluation of individuals on the basis of their worth and potential. Politico administrative pre-requisite requires acceptance of legitimacy of the established authority. Hence, political and administrative institutions with differentiated and specific functions should be well developed. Prevalence of efficient and trained bureaucracy is an added advantage. At that psychological sphere, modernization requires certain significant changes in the dimensions of human personality and in patterns of motivation. Empathy, mobility and high participation are the basic attributes of personality and that should be consciously fostered in the interest of modernization. Finally, demographic feature particularly the control of pyrulation growth is a significant pre-requisite to country's modernization.

3.4.3 Factors Facilitating Modernization

The factors which facilitate modernization may be discussed as follows:

(a) Education

Explosion of knowledge and skill are very much essential for human development. It is possible only when people go beyond the traditional education. Specialized education in the areas of science, technology, medicine and management, etc., as a booster to modernization.

(b) Mass Communication

Mass communication comprising newspaper, radio, TV, telephone and movies accelerate the tempo of modernization. Modern ideas can spread at a faster rate through mass communication.

(c) Ideology Based on Nationalism

Spirit of nationalism is the character of people. In a democratic set up of administration, people are organized into political parties and each party is based on some ideological principle. Nationalism and democracy are generally whole-hearted supporters of modernization.

(d) National Leadership

Leadership is an art. It requires for sighted vision which is quite indispensable for modernization. A leader with a missionary zeal and spirit can help promote modernization.

(e) Initiative of the Government

A government bent upon adopting progressive policies can motivate the people to accept reforms essential for all round economic development. Government should be dynamic and result oriented.

(f) Urbanization and Industrialization

Both urbanization and industrialization are complementary. They promote economic growth. They are to be supported by modern transport and communication, better education, employment opportunities and facilities for expansion and growth. These are stimulants to modernization.

3.4.4 Modernization in India

Yogendra Singh, the eminent sociologist in his famous book *Modernization of Indian Tradition* has attempted to analyse the process of modernizations in India from a systematic sociological perspective. In course of his analysis, he has concentrated on two key concepts such as social structure and tradition because they constitute the core of social realities. He has classified the social structure in to two parts—macro and micro. Macro social structure includes the changing nature of the political industrial and urban structures and categories such as industrial workers, middle classes and the elite. The micro structure consists of relations limited to religion, territory, language and kinship communities.

On the other hand tradition refers to value themes characterized by four attributes such as hierarchy, holism, continuity and transcendence. He has divided the tradition into two categories such as great tradition and little tradition. Great tradition refers to the cultural beliefs and practices and little traditions comprise the cultural beliefs and practices held by the folk through oral tradition and coalessed adaptations of cultural roles and values of the great tradition. Modernization of tradition in both the traditions means a change from hierarchy to equality, from holism to individualism, from continuity to historicity and from transcendence to the worldly rationalism and secularism.

He says, the "unique feature of India's modernization is that it is being instituted through the adoptive changes in the traditional structure rather than structural breakdown". He has attributed the sources of breakdown of Indian process of modernization to the structural inconsistencies such as democratization without the spread of civic culture, bureaucratization without commitment to universalistic norms, rise in media participation and aspiration without proportionate increase in resource and distributive justice, verbalization of a welfare ideology without its diffusion in social structure and its implementation as a social policy, over urbanizations without industrialization and finally modernization without meaningful changes in the stratification system. He holds the view that modernization in Indian society has taken recourse a conciliatory to pattern. It has shown a wonderful capacity to absorb the shocks of tensions and contradictions. Thus, it has minimized the chance of structural breakdown.

3.4.5 Impact of Modernization in India

The impact of modernization on Indian economy is manifold in nature. It has contributed a lot to the Indian society in the form of the emergence of entrepreneurial class or business elite, increase of industrial workers in factories and trade unions, urban ward migration of population and expansion of cities in the Indian society. There has been the growth of various political parties and democratic political framework. It has been instrumental for the common mass of people participating in politics. It has brought forth eye catching structural changes in the society. The impact of modernization on Indian society and culture may be discussed in the following manner:

(a) Modernization has changed the structure of social institutions such as marriage, family and caste, etc.

(b) The introduction of modern means of communications has affected man's life in various aspects.

(c) The emergence of the middle class has changed the dominant values of the society.

(d) It has brought radical changes both in the primary sector and secondary sector of the economy.

(e) It has led to the breakdown of the caste system.

(f) As a result of modernization, the outlook of general masses in respect of religions has become broad-based. It has broadened the outlook of the people in respect of their rights and freedom.

(g) Due to modernization, the transition from the extended or joint families to conjugal forms or nuclear families has become much more accelerated and the socialization of children in the family has taken on a new direction.

(h) Modernization has initiated a profound change in the Indian cultural tradition. Further, it has brought about a radical change in the orientation and organization of education. People have been initiated into political modernization.

(i) It has brought changes in the customs and laws of the Indian society. It has led to the emergence of universalistic legal system based on the principle of universalism, rationalism and individualism.

(j) Modernization has enlightened Indian elite for introducing political institutions based on the values of democracy, equality, liberty, freedom and justice.

(k) With the process of modernization, the Indian society has experienced tremendous changes in the technological sphere which comprise development of new techniques, new inventions new modes of production and new standards of living. It has led to the decay of old traditional craftsmanship and diversification of occupations and has also brought men and women to factory and office. New industrialism has brought in modern value patterns. Technological advancement has resulted in greater functional inter-dependence and differentiation between parts and greater mobility of the members with respect to location and occupation.

3.4.6 Impediments to Modernization

The impediments to modernization can be classified into five categories such as ideological, motivational, institutional, organizational and other.

(a) Ideological Impediments

Lack of proper articulation of ideology obstructs the process of modernization and strong and progressive ideological motivation quickness the process of modernization.

(b) Motivational Impediments

The success of any programme for development largely depends upon motivation, unless people are motivated, there is little chance for its success. The elite, planners and the political leaders can formulate different plans and programmes for modernization, but their implementation can be a distant dream if people are not motivated to take part in them.

(c) Institutional Impediments

The institutional framework is quite indispensable for modernization of a society. It is observed that the institutional network of the third world societies is tradition bound. They are characterized by such attributes as ascription, particularism, affectivity and diffused expectations in parsonian language which are detrimental to the growth of modern values.

(d) Organizational Impediments

Modernization requires a proper integration among local, national and political process. But this has not happened to an expected degree in the third world countries. On the other hand, there are many inconsistencies and contradictions due to lack of sincere effort to bring a proper harmony between micro and macro political processes. Hence, there is an informative need to strengthen organizational base.

(e) Other Impediments

Quantitative expansion with complete disregard to quality is a serious obstacle to the process of modernization. Adequate stress should be given an qualitative expansion.

Modernization is not only necessary but also essential for all round development of the country. People all over the world aspire after and strive for it. Although modernization process is occurring at a rapid stride, it is facing a lot of obstacles in the third world economics including India due to structural rigidities. Hence, adequate steps should be taken to overcome these impediments.

3.4.7 Modernization and Social Change

Social change is the change in society and society is a web of social relationship. Hence, social change is a change in social relationship. Social relationships are social processes, social patterns and social interactions. These include the mutual activities and relations of the various parts of society. Whenever one finds that a large number of persons are engaged in activities that differ from those which their immediate forefathers were engaged in sometimes before, one finds a social change. Human society is constituted of human beings. Whatever apparent alteration in the mutual behaviour between individuals takes place is a sign of social change. This fact of social change can be verified by introspection at the history of any society. Man is a dynamic being. Hence, society can never remain static, it undergoes constant variation.

The factors responsible for social change are manifold. Some writers regard diffusion to be the main factor of social change while some others consider invention in a similar capacity. As a matter of fact, both diffusion and invention have a hand in the change which besets social relationship. The causal factors of social change are cultural, technological, biological, population, environmental psychological and others.

Cultural Factors

The main cause of social change is the cultural factor. Changes in the culture are accompanied by social changes.

According to Max Weber, changes and variations in culture inevitably influence social relationships. Culture gives speed and direction to social change and determines the limits beyond which social changes cannot occur.

Technological Factors

The technological factor has immense influence in social change. As Ogburn states, "Technology changes society by changing our environments to which we in turn adopt. This change is usually in the material environment and the adjustment we make to the changes often modifies customs and social institutions. The form of society is undergoing change as a result of the technological advancement. The explicit effects of technological advance are labour organization, division of labour, specialization high speed of life and increase in production, etc. In the modern age, technological factors are among the predominant causes of social change."

Biological Factors

Biological factors have some indirect influence upon social change. Among the biological factors is the qualitative aspect of the populations related to heredity. The qualitative aspect of population is based upon powerful and great men and their birth is dependent to a large extent upon heredity and mutation. Hence, biological factors play a part in social change to that extent. In addition to this the biological principles of natural selections and struggle for survival are constantly producing alterations in society.

Population Factors

Changes in the quality and size of the population have an effect upon the social organization as well as customs and traditions, institutions and associations, etc. Expansion and contraction of populations, a change in the ratio of men and women, young and old have an effect upon social relationships. Contraction and expansion in the population has an immediate effect upon economic institutions and associations.

Environmental Factors

The geographists have emphasized the impact of geographical environment upon human society. According to Huntington, an alteration in the climate is the sole cause of the evolution and devolution of civilizations and cultures.

Psychological Factors

Sociologists are of the view that psychological factors as important elements in social change. The cause of social changes is the psychology of man himself. By nature, man is a lover of change. He is always trying to discover new things in every sphere of his life and is always anxious for novel experiences. As a result of this tendency, the more traditions, customs, etc., of every human society are perpetually undergoing change.

Other Factors

Other factors of social change include appearance of new opinions and thoughts. Changes in the attitudes towards dowry, caste system, female education, etc., have resulted in widespread social variations and modifications.

The form of each aspect of social life is being continually transformed due to the effect of all these factors which cause social change. New institutions and associations are being formed and destroyed in the social, economic, political, cultural and verily in all spheres. The form of family, marriage, state, religion, culture, educational system, economic and social structures is continually changing and transforming as a result of which, a change occurs in the life of the individual and subsequently in the relations with others.

The process of modernization has brought forth some significant changes in the structural and cultural spheres of Indian society which may be categorized as structural change and cultural change.

Structural change means the growth of new roles and group structures. It involves role differentiations and role accretion. Structural changes can be visualized at two levels—the micro structures and the macro structures. Micro structures are autonomous in nature. They provide a social space for primary relationships. Their organization is less formal and the relationships are more affective and particularistic. The new work relationship is limited family, community, clan, tribe, caste and sub-caste are examples of micro structures of the Indian society. On the other hand, macro structures refer to these organized roles and relationships which are more extensive, more formal and which are organized on universalistic principles and which have to do with the integration or regulation of the larger system of society and involve secondary and higher order of relationships. Political and other types of elite, administration and bureaucracy, industrial workers and entrepreneurs and other urban and industrial groups and other classes are examples of macro structures.

3.5 Cultural Change

So far cultural change is concerned, it is revealed that modernization has initiated a profound change in the Indian cultural tradition. The cultural traditions in India can be classified into (a) the great tradition and (b) the little tradition. The great traditions refers to those traditions which grow because of outside contact and are found at national level whereas the little traditions are local in origin and are found at the folk or at the peasant level. Great traditions include industrialization, urbanization, expansion of modern education, growth of universalistic legal system, transportation, mass communication, mass politicization, social and technology, etc.

Thus, modernization and social change are complementary to each other.

3.6 Democratization

Democracy is the buzz word of the developing nations today and the process of democratizations has always been interest to political sociologists and social scientists. It is a process of change which turns the system of the government of a country according to the wishes of the public, speaking precisely, it is a process that helps the democracy to develop.

The term 'democracy' has been defined by different experts differently. So also the term democratization. Democratization may be defined as the process of becoming democracy. It involves adoption of not only a form of government, but also internalizations of liberty, equality and fraternity in everyday life. Therefore it is a move on than mere regular participation of elections.

The concept of democratizations is related to democracy. The term democracy is derived from two Greek words—'demos' which means people and 'kratia' which means rule. Thus, democracy means the rule of the people. Theoretically speaking, the term democracy conveys different meanings such as a form of government, a type of state, a pattern of social system, a design of economic order and a way of life. Precisely speaking, it is a form of government in which people are the supreme or sovereign ruler. It is a form of government in which the rulers are responsible to the ruled. As a form of state, it implies governmental machinery which should run on democratic basis. As a pattern of social system, it implies liberty, equality, fraternity, free discussion, tolerance, adjustment and compromise and respect for the views of the minorities. As a design of economic order, it presupposes absence of grass economic in equalities.

The preamble of Indian constitutions declares it is a soverign Democratic Republic. The system of government is parliamentary democracy which runs a government of Republican character headed by the President as the chief executive. He is not a hereditary monarch. He is elected for five years. The democratic set up is based on the basic principle "Government of the people, by the people and for the people". The various institutions set up under the constitution seeks to give effect to democracy which is sustained by adult franchise, fundamental rights and independence of judiciary.

Indian constitution provides for parliamentary form of government at the centre as well as at the states. India has adopted the British model. Parliamentary democracy contains their features:

(a) The executive is responsible to the Lok Sabha or the Lower House.

(b) The Lower House is elected on democratic basis by universal adult suffrage voting.

(c) Legislative and financial control is vested in the Lower House.

The President of Indian union and the Governors of States act as constitutional heads and are guided by the council of ministers under the leadership of the Prime Minister at the centre and under the Chief Minister in the States.

Democracy presupposes people's government. The citizens enjoy some fundamental rights. These rights can neither be curtailed nor cancelled. Like fundamental rights, the citizens also have some fundamental duties. Rights and duties go hand in hand. These duties cannot be enforced in a court of law if they are violated. These duties are for the guidance of the citizens.

In a democratic country like India, the parliament is vested with supreme powers. The members of the parliament enjoy freedom of speech in the parliament, freedom from arrest for anything said in the parliament. They are elected by the people who can elect members to the federal and state legislature by universal adult franchise. Every Indian citizen above the age of 18 has the right to vote. It is this spirit of equality and national participation which pervades behind all national constitutions and their working in India.

3.6.1 Need for Democratization

The need for democratization arises because of the following reasons:

(a) Democracy helps peaceful resolution of conflicts. It helps social change without disorder.

(b) Orderly political succession is facilitated in democracy. A government is changed through elections rather than through force or violence.

(c) It accommodates and respects diversity. It allows difference of opinion as it respects people's liberty to ventilate their own views.

(d) Justice is likely to be attained through promoting equality and equal share which everybody gets in a government of this type.

(e) People can truly enjoy freedom in a democracy.

(f) It provides training ground for people while participating in the elections; they come to know about the working of the government.

3.6.2 Base of Democratization

The bases of democratization include the Indian constitutions and decentralization of power.

Indian Constitution

Chapter III (Articles 12-35) of the constitution guarantees fundamental rights to Indian people. The freedom guaranteed by the constitution provides a sound basis for decentralization of Indian society. The constitution is not an alliance between democracies and dynasties but a real union of Indian people, built on the basic concepts of sovereignty of the people. The intent of the rights enshrined in the constitution is to respect human personality. By article 32 of the constitution, a citizen has the right to approach the Supreme Court for the enforcement of the fundamental rights. Personal freedom is the cornerstone of a true democracy. Besides equality and fraternity, freedom is the most essential constituent of democracy. This freedom is guaranteed by the rule of the law and Judiciary is its protector. Articles 14, 19, 21, 22 and 32 guarantee freedom to Indian citizen. According to these articles it is guaranteed that the citizens, men and women equally, have the right to an adequate means of livelihood, that the ownership and control of material resources of the community are so distributed as best to subserve the common good and that the operation of the economic system does not result in the concentration of wealth and means of production to the common detriment.

Decentralization of Power

It is another basis of democratization in India. Power is distributed at various levels. So that a large number of people participate in decision-making process. Democratic decentralization in the context of India assumes the form of Panchayat Raj system. Panchayat Raj is directed towards decentralization of administration at the villages, block and district levels. Thus, Panchayat Raj has a three-tier structure consisting of three self-governing institutions namely Village Panchayat at the village level, Panchayat Samittee at Block level and Zilla Parishad at the district level. These institutions are vested with vast power and authority. As a decentralized form of administration, Panchayat Raj encourages people's participations not only in the management of local affairs but also in the implementation of development programmes. Thus, Panchayat Raj has been a basis of democratic decentralization.

The growth of Panchayat Raj institutions has been instrumental in transmitting power to the lower section of the society. Now they enjoy political power as well as economic and social power. On the other hand, the higher castes are found losing power.

Thus, it may be concluded that democratization has come to stay in every social, cultural and educational institutions. Provisions are made for deciding every issue in a democratic way. Similarly, provisions are also made for holding elections at regular intervals. Today, it is very difficult to find an institution which is not democratized.

3.6.3 Impact of Democratization in India

The process of democratization has a deep impact on Indian economy. It is discernible from the following factors:

(a) Politicalization

The process of democratizations has developed politicalization in the country. A number of political parties have come into existence. They are of regional and national in character. The Socialist Party and the Janata Party are national in character whereas small political parties such as Akali Dal, Lok Dal, DMK, etc., are regional in character.

(b) Federal System

Indian Constitution has given rise to a federal form of government. Our country is a union of several states with autonomous powers. Central government keeps control over the state governments but they enjoy independence in certain matters. The states have been recognized after Independence on the basis of language, culture and political equality. In Indian democracy the government holds joint responsibility. The entire cabinet of ministers is responsible for anything done by one ministry. If the Prime Minister or the Chief Minister of a State resigns, the whole ministry is deemed to have resigned. There are two houses at the centre—the Lok Sabha and the Rajya Sabha. Both houses are empowered to enact laws. Similarly in the states there are Legislative Assemblies and Legislative Councils. The Indian democracy mainly rests upon the centre.

(c) Constitution

The Constitution of India adopted in 1949 towards after independence was granted like all written constitutions, was a character for the kind of government, indeed the kind of society, the leaders of India desired and determined to build. It stated some things to be done immediately; other things as long-term and ultimate objectives. Its preamble stated:

> We, the people of India, having solemnly resolved to constitute India into a sovereign Democratic Republic and to secure to all its citizens: Justice, social, economic and political, liberty of thought, expression, belief, faith and worship. Equality of status and opportunity and to promote among them all fraternity assuring the dignity of the individual and the unity of the nation, in our constituent assembly this 26th of November 1949 do hereby adopt, enact and give ourselves this constitution.

The Indian constitution deals with political freedom and the rights and duties of the government at specific times the government has been vested with powers to regulate and curb the political freedom of the people. Every day, new effort at making the state a welfare state is being made. Every citizen has freedom to form a political party to be its member and express and propagate his thoughts.

(d) Decentralizations of Power

It is a special characteristic of Indian politics. Several political units from the village panchayat to the central parliament have been organized. The common village man should have a feeling to freedom to this object. Village panchayats have been set up on the basis of adult franchise. The Gram Sabha acts like a legislature. Gram Panchayat is an important political unit.

(e) Political Parties

Political parties assumed much prominence in Indian politics. Evolution and growth of a number of political parties is a peculiarity of Indian politics. There are large numbers of political parties in India.

(f) Elections

Election is an integral process of democracy. Election takes place in every five years. In spite of crises and obstacles, elections have generally been held in time. Many facts have surfaced during elections. The ruling party uses the government machinery to its advantage. Casteism is given prominence. Voters vote for the candidates of their own caste. Regionalism and linguism are also given importance during elections.

(g) Floor Crossing

Change of party has developed to large extent. There is no rigid principle for defectors. It rests purely on selfish motive. People also get elected as independents on a party tickets and join the ruling party to get some advantage such as a ministry. Similarly these who do not get a portfolio thereafter to go out.

(h) Social Institutions

Democracy has also influenced the social institutions as well. Democratic outlook and constitutional changes have demonstrated religion fields also. The social effects of differences in religion have disappears. No institution can afford to be prejudiced by religion. Caste system had a very important place in Indian social structure. Democratization has declared casteism illegal. Democracy lays emphasis on justice and equality.

(i) Community Life

Democratization has influenced village life to a great extent. The outlook of rural folk has been transformed radically. Their political consciousness has arisen. Now they are awakened to their rights. Cartels have been formed among farmers to fight for a common goal. Several economic and social organizations have been formed in villages. Panchayats and Cooperatives have become a part of democracy. The democratic experience in the rural setting has given birth to democratic leadership in villages.

3.6.4 Barriers to Democratization in India

Democratization in India suffers from a lot of impediments. They are as follows:

(a) Ignorance and illiteracy poses a serious constraint in the way of successful working of democracy in a traditional society.

(b) There is no strict party discipline. Defection is very much common in every party.

(c) Low living and power economic standard makes Indian democracy ineffective.

(d) Corruption has become rampant. The evils of corruption is posing serious threat to our socio-economic and political system.

(e) Fragmented electoral verdicts have caused political instability in India.

(f) Mafia groups have infiltrated in all the major political parties and subverted their functioning.

(g) Militant separatists are getting arms and funds from neighbouring countries smoulding insurgency in different parts of the country is a threat to Indian democracy.

(h) It is observed that most of the Indian elites are least interested in politics. They do not have interest in public affairs and do not even vote in the election.

(i) The hypocrisy of the Indian politicians has destroyed the sanctity of democracy. It is evident from the history of past elections.

The process of democratization will definitely yield desired results of social equality and economic growth provided the bureaucracy shows dedication and the politicians eshew corruption. Without national integrity and honesty of character, the democratic experiment in India is likely to be founded on the bedrock of corruption and violence.

3.7 Westernization

The term westernization is a culturological concept, which was used by Srinivas to explain the process of socio-cultural change in modern India. It is an inclusive, complex and multilayered concept. It covers a wide range from western technology to the experimental method of modern science and modern historiography. The term westernization implies two meanings—one is global and the other is indigeneous. Globally, westernization refers to the process of social change brought about in non-western countries as a result of their prolonged contact with western culture. On the other hand, from Indian perspective, it refers to a change brought about in Indian social life as a result of its contact with the British. In this context, Srinivas observes that, Indian society and culture experienced changes as a result of over 150 years of British rule in India which was instrumental in bringing changes in several spheres comprising art, science, literature, technology, institution, ideology and values.

3.7.1 Features of Westernization

Westernization combines the following features:

(a) The process of westernization subsumes changes at different levels of technology, institutions, ideology and values.

(b) The most important change was the value preference of the non-western societies. The most important value which in turn subsumes several other values is what may be broadly characterized as humanitarianism. It implies active concern for the welfare of all human beings irrespective of social in equalities.

(c) Introduction of reforms and new laws by the British led to several changes in the Indian customs which were earlier enforced as part of one's religious duty. As the British rule gained roots in India, the value of rationality and humanitarianism also become firmly entrenched in the caste ridden society.

(d) Westernization is an ill inclusive term which covers a wide range of changes from western technology of one end to the experimental method of modern science and modern historiography at the other.

(e) The process of westernization in India was uneven, only a minority section of Indian population came into direct face to face conflict with the British officers did not always become a force of change.

(f) The process of westernization was intensified in multiple ways. The first and most critical step in westernization as the establishment of Pax Britannica and the communication revolution that took place in the country which opened up avenues for new contacts.

(g) The form and pace of westernization of India varied from region to region and from one section of population to another.

(h) The process of westernization created many inter-contradictory forces which instead of consolidating contradicted each other.

3.7.2 Types of Westernization

Westernization can be classified into two types on the basis of influence on little tradition and great tradition, such as primary and secondary.

Primary Westernization

It means changes induced by the western impact on Indian little traditions. It assumes two forms:

(i) The emergence of a westernized sub-cultural pattern through a minority sections of Indians who first come into contact with the western culture. This includes the sub-culture represented by those Indian intellectuals and scholars who not only adopted many western cognitive patterns and styles of life but also supported their rapid expansion. Thus, westernization is its first stage was sub-cultural in nature.

(ii) The second category of primary westernization refers to the process of general diffusion of western cultural traits such as the use of new technology, dress, food and changes in the habits and styles of people in general resulting from the cultural contact with the British.

Secondary Westernization

This category of westernization was linked with the great tradition of India and it refers to the changes which have contributed to the growth of various forms of cultural structures extending over the whole of the country. This form of westernization has all Indian character and has contributed to the emergence of a new great tradition of modernization in India.

3.7.3 Impact of Westernization on Indian Society

The impact of westernization on Indian society may be discussed under the following heads:

(a) Impact on Education

The prevailing education system is of western origin. Initially the content of education was metaphysical and was confined to upper class only. Its structure was hereditary and closed. The roles of both the teachers and the taught were qualitative inscriptive. The modern system of education is very liberal having scientific worldview.

(b) Impact on Communication Network

The British rule in India was instrumental in spreading the communication network throughout the nook and corner of the country. Through the western contact printed newspapers came into being. The Britishers introduced the telegraph, railways and modern postal system in India. Expansion in transport by the railways, road ways, and water ways contributed a lot to the intensification in the volume of interaction and contact between one region with other.

(c) Growth of Nationalism

Both nationalism and democracy in the contemporary form are said to be the gifts of westernization. Nationalism means consciousness of one nationhood and democracy is a special form of political organization and system of values on which nation states can be found.

(d) Impact on Style of Living

Style of living implies food habits, mode of eating and dress pattern. Westernization has changed the style of living of Indians. Before British came to India, people used leaves, plates made of brass, bronze and silver to serve food. Among the upper castes especially among Brahmins, eating was a religious act. Food was being cooled while the women in charge of cooking and serving it were in a ritually poor state. Food was being served to children and adults in order of seniority. At the end of the meal, the dining leaves were thrown out and the place where these used dining leaves were dumped was purified with a solution of cow dung. But westernization has made people sophisticated and they are sitting at tables with stainless steel utensils and spoons etc. The new made of eating has contributed to an increase in secularization as people belonging to different castes and creeds are using the same table and there is no need of purification. Traditionally people were using homespun clothes but now-a-days they have opted for mill made clothes like nylon, terrylene and terrycot, etc. The mode of dress has undergone a drastic change.

(e) Impact on Language

Before Indians come into British contact people used very selective terms. But westernization has popularized so many terms of English language and even rural folks are using such terms in their day-to-day life.

(f) Impact on Marriage

Westernization has brought about perceptible changes in matrimonial relationship. Today marriage is not contained only to two families, it is confined to two individuals. Husband and wife do not consider them either superior or inferior rather they treat them as friends. The impact of westernization has developed individualistic ideology which is not at all beneficial to the Indian society. It has adversely affected the sanctity of the family.

(g) Impact on the Status of Women

Westernization has a deep impact on the status of women in India. Before the British rule in India women were denied their legitimate rights. They were not allowed to move to places. But things have been radically changed during British rule. Spread of education has prepared women to strive for natural status of equality.

(h) Impact on Religion

Impact of science and western education has brought about a significant change in our perception of religion. Uncritical acceptance of religious ideals is being replaced by logical interpretation and acceptance. The social values of religion have gone down.

(i) Impact on Art and Literature

The English literary tradition has greatly influenced Indian literature. Romanticism and psychiatrist of the west can be found in every kind of literary expression of today. Experimentalism, hedonism and romanticism have found place in Indian poetry. Equality, environment, freedom and other related topic have also got place in Indian art and literature. Modern art is a by-product of westernization.

(j) Impact on the Worldview

Western values have inculcated a worldly attitude in the Indians. Prior to westernizations Indians were very much god fearing and their lives were based upon the doctrine of karma. Now they are leading a luxurious life. Materialism has dominated them and they have become materialistic.

3.7.4 Criticisms

The concept of westernization is criticized on the following grounds:

(a) The term westernization has limited applicability because it primarily analyses social change in Indian society in cultural but not in structural term.

(b) Though the concept is considered as ethically neutral it is not really so. It contains certain value preferences.

(c) Yogendra Singh argues that westernization is a pejorative term, because of its association with former colonial domination of these countries by the west.

(d) Daviel Learner has commented that the term is in adequate and parochial. Hence he preferred modernization.

3.8 Modernization: The Concept

The word modernization is derived from the Latin root 'modo' means just now. Chronologically it means the latest. The idea of modernization can be comprehended in three senses. The first one is most general and synonymous with all kinds of progressive social change. The second one is more historically specific which connotes the idea of a complex of social, political, economic, cultural and psychological transformations occurring in the west from the 16th century onwards and reaching its apogee in 19th and 20th centuries. It involves the process of industrialization, urbanization, rationalization, bureaucratization and democratization, etc. Thirdly, there is the most specific meaning of the term modernization referring only to the backward and underdeveloped societies and describing their attempts to catch up with the most developed countries, coexisting with them in the same historical period within the world society.

Modernization can be defined in three ways such as historical, relativistic and analytical. Historically, modernization refers to a particular time and place, it is dated and localized. In this sense modernization is synonymously used as westernization. Schemel Eisenstadt defines it as "the process of change towards those types of social, economic and political systems that have developed in western Europe and North America from the 17th century to the 19th and 20th centuries to the South America, Asian and African continents". In this context Wilbert Moore says, "Modernization is a total transformation of traditional or pre-modern society into the types of technology and associated social organization that characterize the advanced economically prosperous and relatively politically stable nations of the western world."

In the relativistic sense, modernization implies purposeful emulation of standards which are considered modern either by the population at large or by its enlightened sections or by the ruling elite. In this context Edward Tiryakian defines it as "from a world of historical perspective, modernizations pertains to the state of the art or leading edge innovations on break through in cognitive, moral, ethical, technological and social arrangements that contribute to the enhancement of human conditions."

So far the analytical definition of modernizations is concerned, Neil J. Smelser describes it as "a complex, multidimensional transition embracing six areas—economic, political, education, religion, family life and domain of stratification. In the economic area it means rooting technologies in scientific knowledge, moving from subsistence farming to commercial agriculture, replacing human and animal power with inanimate energy and machine production and spreading urban forms of settlement and spatial concentration of labour force. In political sphere, modernization signifies the transition from tribal authority to system of suffrage, representations, political parties and democratic rules, etc. in the field of education, it involves elimination of illiteracy and growing emphasis on knowledge, trained skills and competence. In religious sphere, it indicates secularization. In family life, it is marked by a diminishing role of kinship ties and greater functional specializations of the family. In the domain of stratification it means emphasis on mobility and individual achievement rather than on ascription.

Thus, modernization is not a philosophy but it is a process of change. It is one of the few terms that have come to be the key words in contemporary discusses on the dynamics of social change.

3.8.1 Features of Modernization

Modernization possesses the following characteristics:

(a) A Revolutionary Process

In the process of modernization, a radical change takes place in human life. Black has compared the transition from tradition to modernity with that of the change from pre-human to human existence and from primitive to civilized societies.

(b) A Complex Process

Modernization is a complex process which cannot be reduced to a single factor or single dimension. It involves changes in all areas of human thought and behaviour.

(c) A Systematic Process

Modernization is a systematic process which helps changing the total social system. Change in one factor tends to produce a complimentary change in another factor.

(d) A Global Process

Modernization is a universal process. It originated in the 15th and 16th century Europe. Now it has assumed a worldwide phenomenon.

(e) A Phased Process

The process of modernization proceeds in phases and subphases. All the societies have to move through some stages. The pattern of modernization varies from one society to that of the other.

(f) A Lengthy Process

Modernization takes a long time to occur. It is evolutionally in nature. Sometimes it takes generations to move from tradition to modernity.

(g) A Homogenizing Process

Modernization is a homogenizing process. It produces tendencies towards convergence among societies. It involves movements towards integration of societies in the long run so that the formation of a world state can be contemplated.

(h) An Irreversible Process

Modernization is an irreversible process. In it, there is no point of going back. Once a society reaches certain level of urbanization, literacy and industrialization in one decade it will not decline to lower levels in the next decades. The rate of change may vary but the direction of change remains static.

(i) A Progressive Process

It is a progressive process. It is inevitable and desirable. In the very beginning of its occurrence, it may cause pain, but in the long run it contributes to social welfare.

(j) An Adoptive Process

Modernization is an adoptive process. It puts before individuals and groups the need to adopt themselves to the new changes taking place in the society. In the process of rapid socio-economic changes, individuals are likely to aspire after various positions and are supposed to perform different roles.

(k) A Dynamic Process

Modernization implies an ongoing process of change. With the advancement of scientific knowledge and technical skills, the conditions of life undergo a radical change.

(l) A Multilinear Process

Modernization is a multilinker and multi path process. All societies do not necessarily have to take the same road to modernization. Each society can follow an alternative path.

3.8.2 Pre-Conditions for Modernization

Modernization cannot occur overnight. It takes a considerable period of time. S.N.E. Senstadt states that modernization requires three structural characteristics of a society such as a high level of structural differentiation, a high degree of social mobilization and a relatively centralized and autonomous institutional framework. Narmadeswar Prasad points out that for modernization certain pre-requisites need to be present in the society. These include awareness of purpose, awareness of existence, a sense of urgency, availability of a variety of opportunities and rules, emotional preparedness for self-imposed tasks and sacrifices and emergence of a dynamic and committed leadership. David Apter says that there are three conditions of modernization such as an innovative social system, a flexible social structure and a technologically advanced social framework for healthy living, etc. Christopher Bates Doob has identified certain basic conditions for promoting modernization which include economic condition, social condition, politico administrative condition, psychological condition and demographic condition, etc.

Economic condition includes modern tools, transportation, communication media and technological advances in agriculture sufficient enough to allow increased proportion of population to take up industrial jobs.

The social condition for modernization requires that individuals should be evaluated on the basis of personal worth and potential. Norms should apply uniformly to all cases of citizens.

The political administrative condition requires acceptance or legitimacy of the established authority.

At the psychological level, modernization requires certain significant changes in the dimensions of human personality and in patterns of motivation. Empathy, mobility and high participation are the basic attributes of personality that should be consciously fostered in the interest of modernization.

Further, growth of population (demographic factor) is considered as a significant precondition for modernization.

3.8.3 Impact of Modernization

Modernization has a deep impact on the society, culture, and environment and above all on the economic development of the country. This may be discussed in the following manner:

(a) Modernization brings structural transformation in social institutions like marriage, family and caste and it has been realized through the process.

(b) The introduction of modern means of transport and communication have affected human life in various forms.

(c) The emergence of middle class and new rich class have changed the dominant values of the society.

(d) Modernization has promoted both agriculture and industry leading to the economic development of the country.

(e) Modernization has minimized the obstacle of the caste system existing in the society.

(f) Modernization has broadened the outlook of the people.

(g) Modernization has removed the boredom of the people. Life has been smooth, rapid and mechanized.

(h) Modernization has changed the traditional cultural values.

Thus, modernization has affected every sphere of human activity.

3.8.4 Obstacles to Modernization

Modernization, in fact is desirable for all round development of every economy whether developed, developing or under developed or undeveloped. Although modernization process is occurring at a rapid pace a lot of obstacles are found in the path of modernization. Sociologist have made an humble attempt to locate and understand the obstacles of modernization and have found out certain obstacles which they have subdivided into four categories such as ideological, motivational, institutional and organizational.

(a) Ideological Obstacles

Strong ideological motivations quickens the process of modernization whereas the process is obstructed ideology is not properly articulated.

(b) Motivational Obstacles

Motivation is a nostrum for development of any kind. Unless people for whom development is intended and motivated, there is little chance for its success. The elite, planners and the political leaders can formulate different plans and programme but these can be implemented successfully when people are motivated effectively.

(c) Institutional Obstacles

Institutional framework provides infrastructure for building plans for modernization of a society. But in the third world economics the institutional infrastructure is very weak to cope with modernization. Hence, there is an urgent need for the change in the mindset of the people along with the development of institutional infrastructure.

(d) Organizational Obstacles

Modernization needs a proper integration among local and national political processes. The third world economies lack an integration. Further, there are many inconveniences, in consistencies and contradictions due to lack of sincere effort to bring a proper harmony between micro and macro political processes.

Some sociologists have made these individual studies to locate the obstacles of modernization.

Rama Ahuja has located six obstacles to modernization. They are: (i) rise of unrest due to lack of coordinated pattern of growth, (ii) conflict between modern and traditional institutions, (iii) uneven structural change, (iv) outer modernity in the absence of inner modernity, (v) lack of cooperation among the modernizing agencies and (vi) failure of social system to meet the rising expectations, etc.

Gunar Myrdal has pointed out five obstacles to modernization such as:

(i) The growth of nationalism and democracy in an uneven form.

(ii) Adoption of India's soft policy.

(iii) A gap between verbalization and implementations of policies.

(iv) Centralization of power in the hands of a few.

(v) Unenthusiastic leadership.

Further Yogendra Singh has visualized certain structural in consistencies associated with modernization. They include democratization without spread of civil culture, bureaucratization without commitment to universalistic norms, rise in media participation and aspiration without proportionate increase in resources and distributive justice, verbalization of a welfare ideology without its diffusion, social structure and its implementation as a social policy, over urbanization without industrialization and finally modernization without meaningful changes in the stratification system, etc.

3.8.5 Modernization and Social Change

The process of modernization has brought forth some significant changes in the structural and cultural spheres of Indian society. These may be categorized as structural change and cultural change.

(a) Structural Change

This type of change relates to the growth of new roles and group structures. It involves role differentiation and role accretion.

Structural changes can be discussed at two levels—the micro structure and the macro structure. Micro structures are autonomous in nature. They provide a social space for primary relationships. Their organization is less formal and the relationships are more affective and particularistic. The new work relationship is limited. Family, community, clan, tribe, caste and subcaste are examples of micro structures of Indian society.

On the other hand, macro structures refer to those organized roles and relationships which are more extensive, more formal and which are organized on universalistic principles and which have to do with the integration or regulation of the larger system of society and involve secondary and higher orders of relationships.

(b) Cultural Change

Modernization has initiated a profound change in the Indian cultural tradition. The Indian cultural tradition can broadly be classified into two—the greater tradition and the little tradition. The great traditions refer to those traditions which grow because of outside contact and are found at national level whereas the little traditions are local in origin and are found at the folk or the present level. Great traditions include industrialization, urbanization, expansion of modern education, growth of universalistic legal system, transportation and mass communication, mass politicization and science and technology, etc.

The cultural traditions may be discussed under the following heads:

(a) Industrialization

Industrialization in India has been the cause and consequence of modernization. The process of industrialization has changed in the whole social system based on the principle of ascription and a subsistence agricultural economy.

(b) Urbanization

Urbanization has brought about transformation in various social institutions such as family, social stratification patterns of social interaction and value preference to people, etc.

(c) Expansion of Modern Education

Modernization in Indian society has brought about a radical change in the orientation and organization of education. The organized structure of education has undergone a significant change. People have been initiated into political modernization through education.

(d) Change in Legal Structure

Modernization has also brought changes in the customs and leaves of the Indian society. It has led to the emergence of a universalistic legal system based on the principle of universalism, rationalism and individualism, etc.

(e) Spread of Transportation and Communication

Modernization has led to the growth and expansion of a nationwide network of transport and communication. As a result, the barriers between regions have broken down. People have become physically and morally mobile. Mass communication has accelerated the process of industrialization and urbanization and at the same time it has strengthened primordial ties like caste, religion and race, etc.

(f) Mass Politicization

Due to the process of modernization in India, the enlightened Indian elite could think of introducing political system based on values of democracy equality, liberty, freedom and justice.

(g) Change in Little Tradition

Modernization has been instrumental in changing the little traditions, i.e. daily life, customs and habits of the people.

(h) Technological Changes

With the process of modernization the Indian society has experienced tremendous changes in the technological sphere comprising development of new techniques, new inventions, new mode of production and new standard of living. The process of modernization has brought insignificant changes in political, social, economic and cultural spheres of the Indian society.

3.9 Globalization

Ordinarily globalization refers extending of economic activities across national boundaries. It means integrating the economy of the country with world economy. It is a complex process by which the world is becoming highly inter-connected world though economic, social, political and cultural contacts. It signifies borderless growth and internationalization of all aspects of human living. It is an ongoing and dynamic phenomenon characterized by transactional movement of capital, labour and cultural practices. Ronald Robertson is said to be the father of globalization because he has employed the term in its technical sense for the first time. Globalizations appeared as a central concept in his celebrated article "mapping the Global condition—Globalization as the central concept" in the year 1990.

D.N. Danagare defines it as "the growing integration at international level based significantly on activities of multinational corporations".

Anthony M.C. Graw defines it as "globalization refers to these processes, operating at a global scale, which cut across national boundaries, integrating or connecting communities and organizations in space time combination making the world in reality and in experience more inter-connected".

Macolm Waters defined it as "a social process in which the constraints of geography on social and cultural arrangements recede and in which people become increasingly aware that they are receding".

Anthony Giddens writes about globalizations as "the intensification of worldwide social relation which link distant localities in such a way that local happenings are shared by events occurring many miles away and *vice versa*".

Friedman and Kaplan have defined it as "a process of integration of markets, finance and technology specially information technology in a way that shrinks the world to a miniature in size and enables people from different parts of the globe to reach around the world faster, deeper and cheaper".

The European Commission defined it as "the process by which markets and production in different countries are becoming increasingly interdependent due to dynamics of trade in goods and services and flows of capital and technology".

Rubens Ricupero Secretary General of UNCTAD says, "Globalization is the integrations of the world economy as a result of three main forces, (i) Increase in trade in goods and services, (ii) Increase in the investment of transactional companies and the consequent change in the nature of production. Production becoming no longer no time but as a process that takes place in different countries, and (iii) International financial and exchange rate transaction."

3.9.1 Implications of Globalizations

Globalization in its totality implies the following:

(a) There is a spread of International trade.

(b) People migrate from one country or region to another temporarily or permanently.

(c) Money or means of payment are exchanged on an increasing scale between countries or regions.

(d) Capital flows from one country to another to help produce goods and services.

(e) Finance not necessarily linked to the production of goods and services—flows between different countries.

(f) Transnational Companies arise which increasingly engage in the activities listed so far.

(g) Technology is traded as between different countries. Increasingly with the spread of patent regimes governed by the WTO, frontier technologies take an increasingly proprietary form.

(h) Spread of print and electronic media.

(i) Growth in trade and production of services of all kinds shipping, insurance, banking, health care and of course finance.

Briefly speaking, globalization implies being able to manufacture in the most cast effective way possible any where in the world, being able to procure raw materials and drawing management resources from the cheapest source any where in the world, having the entire world as a market.

3.9.2 Characteristics of Globalization

(a) Globalization is Historical

It is argued that globalization is not new. It marked its beginning during industrial revolution of 16th century.

(b) It is a Composite Process

It results from the convergence of a series of developments such as contemporary revolution in science and technology of communication high velocity of movements of finance, capital and market, increased social mobility and emergence of cultural diaspora.

(c) It is Multidimensional

It has many forests such as economic, cultural, political, ideological and environmental. Economic dimension means the economic policies of national governments dominated by movements in the matrimonial financial market resulting in the reduction of earning autonomy of nations of the nation states. Cultural dimension refers to an increased cultural interconnectedness across the globe. Because of the spread of mass media, migration, tourism, people all over the world are opportuned to live a similar life pattern, political dimension is marked by erosion of autonomy and sovereignty of the nation states and building world society and world governance. Ideological dimension marks the victory of liberalism and capitalism over socialism. Further, technological dimension is connected with the spread of information technology and telecommunication.

(d) Globalization is Associated with New Technology

The process of globalization is marked by the arrival of new technology which includes electronic media like T.V. computer, internet and satellite, etc.

(e) It is Dialectical

Globalization process is dialectical having both positive and negative consequences. It contains certain dualities such as universalization...particularization, homogenization vs., differentiation, integration vs., fragmentation, centralization vs., decentralization and juxtaposition vs., syncretization, etc.

3.9.3 Factors Leading to Globalization

Michael Porter has identified the following factors leading to globalization:

(a) Growing similarity of countries in terms of available infrastructure, distribution channels and marketing approach.

(b) **Fluid Global Capital Markets:** National capital markets are growing into global capital markets because of the large flow of funds between countries.

(c) **Technological Restructuring:** The reshaping or competitions globally as a result of technological revolutions such as in micro electronics.

(d) The integrating role of technology reduced cost and increased impact of products have made them accessible to more global consumers.

(e) **New Global Competitors:** A shift in competitions from traditional country competitors to emerging global competitors.

(f) **End of the Cold War in 1990:** It set the stage for most developing countries to liberalize their economies and undertake structural reforms aimed at higher growth of their economics and create a climate for attracting foreign investments to supplement domestic resources.

3.9.4 Case for Globalization

The case for globalization can be discussed as follows:

(a) The main argument in support of globalization is that it helps remove X in efficiency. In absence of globalization prolonged protection of domestic industry will have serious distortionary effects on cost structures.

(b) Globalization of UDCs will improve the allocative efficiency of resources, reduce the capital output ratio increase the labour productivity, help to develop that export culture, increase the inflow of capital and updated technology into the country increase the degree of competition in the domestic economy, reduce the relative price of industrial and manufactured goods, improve the terms of trade in agriculture in general and give a boost to the average growth rate of the economy in the years to come.

(c) Globalization will help to restructure the production and trade pattern in a capital scarce labour abundant economy in favour of labour intensive goods and labour intensive techniques. As a result, the overall resource productivity will go up.

(d) Foreign capital will be attracted to exploit the professional export opportunities along the above lines. With the entry of foreign capital, updated technology will also enter into the country.

(e) With the entry of foreign competition and the removal of import tariff barriers, domestic industry will be subject to price reducing and quality improving effects in the domestic economy.

(f) With the entry of foreign capital the aggregate gross and net investment properties to GDP will go up and with a reduce capital input ratio the growth rate will go up.

(g) It is also believed that the main effect of integration will be felt in the industrial and related sectors and cheaper and qualitative consumer goods will be manufactured at home. Employment opportunities will expand; trickle effect will operate the proportion of people below the poverty line will go down.

(h) It is also believed that the efficiency of banking and financial sectors will increase with the opening up of these areas to foreign capital and foreign banks.

3.9.5 Case Against Globalization

Globalization has certain demerits. It has a very disruptive impact on the economic activity and social stability in many countries. The adverse impact of globalization may be discussed under the following heads:

(a) Globalization will multiply the human and social castes in view of the fact that capital moves across borders which increase the pressure for structural and conceptual readjustments.

(b) Globalization process causes tremendous redistributions of economic power at the world level which translates into a distribution of political power.

(c) An analysis of data presented in UNOTAD's Trade and Development Export Zone and the IMR's world economic outlook Sept. 2002 reveals that in the globalization, economics of the world are ironically moving away from one another more than coming together. This change has a profound destabilizing effect.

(d) Globalization process challenges some familiar assumptions. Prior to the adoption of globalization it was believed that technological change and increases in productivity would translate into more jobs and higher wages. After India adopted the policy of globalization it is found that technological changes have eliminated more jobs than they have created.

Globalization can be compared to a bickney bathe suit. What is revealed is interesting and what is not revealed is much more exciting.

3.9.6 India's Response to Globalization

India adopted the new economic policy on 24th Oct. 1991. Globalization being a part of the new economic policy initially offered significant opportunities for India. These may be discussed as follows:

(a) India has a terrific opportunity to become the premier production centre of the world.

(b) In several sectors, particularly in agro-based industries India has the skills and the investments which makes it the lowest cost producer in the world. These investments can easily obtain a share of the world market and all that is required is to develop alliance with partners overseas and support it with national policy for each sector.

(c) From the colonial past it is revealed that India was benefited to develop her capabilities to achieve self-sufficiency. It is, therefore, hoped that globalization will promote economic self-sufficiency in India.

(d) It is also important for Indian corporations to go into world markets and to become India's multinationals abroad with markets and later production centres spread across the globe. Globalization will bring certain national advantage in certain sectors such as knowledge led services sector and wide range of agricultural, industrial and fashion products.

(e) An out word looking approach to investment will help spread the risks of entrepreneurship.

(f) Barriers could be built to protect domestic industries from foreign competition. Policies could be changed of times of adversity and if need be, the government could even subsidies economic activity.

(g) Recent economic reforms have ended the scarcity of capital that placed Indian business men since independence and this has transformed their finances and competitiveness. Indian companies are no longer limited by the modest size of domestic capital market and can tap the huge global market through Euro issues and sales to fills in India. Since India has better growth prospects than mature Indian markets, it merits a higher price earnings ration and lower dividend yield. The result is that Indian corporate sector can actually raise equity move cheaply than others.

(h) The policy of globalization will help in attracting foreign investors to make India there home base for their world markets.

In spite of the growing resistance to the ongoing process of globalization it can be said that globalization cannot be an unmixed blessing, just as it is not an unmixed curse. On the whole we have an optimistic and positive picture of the implications of globalization in India. The experience may not have been extremely rosy, but it has been fairly encouraging.

Hence, each country is required to choose its own path of globalization in a way most favourable to it.

3.9.7 India and Globalization

By globalization, Indian economy was opened for world market through international competitiveness. It indicates interaction of the country in matters relating to production, trading and finance with the developed industrialized countries of the world. Globalization offers opportunities and challenges to a developing country like India.

(a) In 1991, New Economic Policy (NEP) of India was prepared. It prepared a list of high technology and high investment priority industries. In these foreign direct investments up to 51 per cent of foreign equity would be automatically permitted.

(b) In respect of foreign technology agreements of automatic permission is provided in high priority industry worth ₹ 1 crore.

(c) Indian rupee currency was developed by 20 per cent to promote export. It raised the inflow of foreign capital.

(d) To facilitate the integration of Indian economy Indian rupee was made partially convertible in the budget of 1992-93. In 1993-94, it was made fully convertible the Government introduced an exchange rate system and transactions on trade account were made free of exchange control.

(e) A new five-year export import policy was announced on 31st March 1992. Its aim was to establish globalization framework of India's foreign trade. Besides its aim was to promote productivity, modernization and competitiveness of Indian industry in order to enhance its export capability.

(f) The Government modified the custom duties further reducing the customs rate from 25 per cent to 40 per cent in the budget of 1999-2000.

(g) The Government took several steps to increase the flow of foreign investment.

(h) The Government took steps to correct its balance of payment deficit and also to increase the share of India in international trade.

3.9.8 Globalization—A Review

(a) Globalization represents the most modern trend in the creation of one world. It deals with processes that cross national boundaries to link states all over the world. It ensures worldwide flow of capital, communication and manufactured goods from region to region. It creates a social world with fluid boundaries. It represents a world that has accepted great uniformity in its modes of internal articulation and construction of social meanings.

(b) The process of globalization has economic overtones that involve movement of factors like production technology. This has created new imbalances in the developing societies by destabilizing local markets, labour and industry. It has also corrected their social organization, culture and polity.

(c) Globalization has promoted the culture of consumerism. This culture has inflamed violence against women.

(d) It has brought an end to protectionism provides justification for free market economy. The entry of multinationals is a welcome sign for making production quality conscious and price conscious. State intervention was considered a negative value of development.

(e) Globalization may be equated with modernization.

(f) Globalization and postmodernization affected men and women differentially.

(g) The devaluation of rupee and the resultant inflation reduced the purchasing power of people.

(h) Globalization has failed to promote human development in the developing economics. The decline in the facilities of essential services and increasing emphasis on consumerism has led to violence and crime.

(i) Globalization in its trail has given rise to modernization and mechanization which have brought many paradoxical situations for the poor.

(j) Agricultural mechanization and inflation have caused pauperization of agricultural labour.

(k) The grim picture of Globalization is reflected in its socio-cultural impact. The values of communicationism, spiritualism and accommodation have been replaced by colonialism.

3.10 Liberalization

Liberalization as a component of New economic policy was launched in the middle of the year 1991 by the Government of India. The main thrust of the policy is that greater freedom is to be give to the entrepreneur of any industry, trade or business and the governmental control in the same to be reduced to the minimum. It implies less control of the government in matters of trade and investment. It is the knell of state control. In the Indian context liberalizations come as a response to crises in Indian economy. The Government at the helm of affairs in 1991 in the octopus of a grave fiscal crisis, P.V. Narasimah Rao, the then prime minister with Dr. Manmohan Singh the then finance minister of the central government accepted liberalization as the economic policy of the government of India.

The basic philosophy behind the policy of liberalization is that the government instead of keeping with itself all the power and authority to take decisions on economic matters must share the same with the private entrepreneurs so that better control will be established in the market.

The basic purpose of the process of economic liberalization is to set business free and to enable it to run on commercial lines. Liberalization requires that government restriction over economic and commercial activities and the flow of goods and services to be lifted. It intends to liberalize commerce and business and trade from that clutches of government's control.

3.10.1 Features of Liberalization

(a) Minimizing Government Control

The main feature of liberalization is that government control over industries, trade and business goes on diminishing and in these fields the participation of the non-governmental agencies and individual entrepreneurs goes on increasing.

(b) Simplification of Licensing Policy

Liberalization has led to a total review of the simplification of licensing policy. There is no need of license to start a business only the entrepreneurs opting for starting a new business have to follow certain guidelines prescribed by the Government. License and permit system which rested with the government has been liberalized in favour of private sector.

(c) Capital Markets Opened for Private Entrepreneur

As a result of liberalization policy the capital markets have been opened to private enterprises seeking capital. Any new company can now be floated with new issue of shares and debentures, etc. without obtaining prior permission from the government.

(d) Opportunity to Purchase Foreign Exchange at Market Prices

Liberalization policy has become so liberal that if an imported equipment is needed for an industry there is no need to approach the government for foreign exchange or to obtain the import license. They can buy foreign exchange in the market at market rate.

(e) No Governmental Intervention in Taking Decision

The new economic policy does not put any restraint on the new entrepreneurs to make their decisions themselves. Without any interference of the government, the entrepreneurs can take their decisions regarding price and profit.

(f) Opportunity for the Competitors

The present day economy is virtually market oriented and the economic environment provides better opportunities for competition. Due to this competition between entrepreneurs will continue and the quality of the product will be improved to capture the market. The competitors will utilize their productive potential by improving their talents.

(g) Widened Liberty to Business and Trade

The process of liberalization provides sufficient liberty to the private entrepreneurs in the realm of business and trade. Liberalizations remove import restrictions by taking out licenses and by reducing custom duty on imports and allows buying or selling of goods, technologies and services from or to any country in the world. As per the provision the labour laws are liberalized permitting free flow of labour. This policy also helps allowing conversion of currency.

3.10.2 Assessment of the Liberalization Policy

The policy of liberalization adopted by the Government of India under New Economic policy has brought some mixed consequences comprising both gain and loss.

The liberalization process has been instrumental for the free flow of goods and services leading to better industrial performance. The interim assessment of the process reveals the fact that industrial organizations have become more efficient and market responsive. It has helped in the increase of exports. There is considerable progress in the field of computer software and information technology. Banks have been more responsive to the financial needs of the industries. Competitive spirit has been developed among entrepreneurs. Apart from all these success has been achieved in different fields.

On the other hand the policy of liberalization suffers from certain deficiencies. Liberalization as a part of the new economic policy was introduced all on a sudden for which adequate infrastructure was not developed to take the full advantages of the policy. It is observed that the policy of liberalization was found suitable for richer section of the society and big business companies. But it was proved to be a castly experience for small scale industries and poor labourers. The policy of liberalizations is a western concept which did not bear fruit. Wherever it bore fruit it was bitter. The policy in course of time fractured and damaged the power of nation state. The agriculturists in India were the worst suffers.

3.11 Civil Society—Its Origin

The word 'civil' owes its origin to the Greek word 'civicus' implies a diversity of people living together peacefully (city). The city represents a qualitative evolution from what initially was a small, primary homogenous community, where every body did basically the same thing and where solidarity was based on similarity. A city has both diversity and organic solidarity based on mutual interdependence. This is the beginning of civil society. Generally civil society is connected to urban community and implies the coexistence of individuals who were able to find ways of resolving differences and disputes. Thus, civil society can be traced back to the beginning of a city, the metro polish and its diversity.

Though the concept of civil society is a modern concept it is a product of 17th century. The concept was derived from the contractualists—Hobbes, Locke and Rousseau. Hobbes is credited to have offered a theory of absolute sovereignty. He was the first individualist to emphasise that the state is merely a means for the promotion of the interests of the individual. Locke was the pioneer of individualism and liberalism. He believed in the supremacy of the community. He asserted that Government exists only for the welfare of the individuals. Further, Rousseau was of the opinion that state was retained as an instrument of the general welfare of individuals. The theory of general will advocated by Rousseau has been considered as most evolutionary doctrine.

There are no coherent and consistent definitions of civil society. Hence, it is very difficult to define it precisely. The term has been conceptualized in a number of ways. First, the term refers to a site for contestation. Hence, people stand against the state and work towards the replacement or reformation of state power. Second, it is interpreted as civic association performing the role of watch dogs in a democracy. The third stream of conceptualization completely divorces civil society from the state. It refers to uncoerced realm of society where social affairs are conducted without any interference by the state. Fourthly the term is conceptualized as a separate sector different from the state and the market.

There is a plethora of definitions of civil society. USAID defines it as "civil society is the multi trade of non-state organization around which society organizes itself that may or may not participate in the civil polity process in accordance with their shifting interests and concerns". Anthony Gidden defines it as "the realm of activity which lies between the state and the market including the family, schools, community, associations and non-economic institutions".

Connon states, "Civil society is composed of autonomous associations which develop a dense, diverse and pluralistic net work. As it develops, civil society will consist of a range of local groups, speacialized organizations and linkages between them to amplify the collective voice of civil society as a partner in governance and the market."

Satis Barwal says, "By civil society we mean a social space which has two main qualities, (i) decisions and choices have to be made on the basis of reason and knowledge, (ii) its members have to relate to each other open-endedly, without exclusion of grounds of religions.

3.11.1 Features of Civil Society

Civil society has the following features:

(a) Civil society is quite distinct from the state and the market.

(b) A civil society is formed by people having common needs, interests and values.

(c) It has its own systems and structures with entrenched values, norms and practices.

(d) It develops through a fundamentally endogenous and autonomous process, which cannot easily be controlled from outside.

(e) It allows individuals to discuss, debate, argue and launch peaceful protest.

(f) Liberty and tolerance are the basic ingredients of a civil society.

(g) It is a network of all different organizations that have been created voluntarily of their own free will.

3.11.2 Forms of Civil Society

Civil society assumes several forms. Some major forms of civil society are as follows:

(a) Civil society is space free, open and accessible. It is space for ideas, fraction for debate discussion and contestation.

(b) It can be seen as a movement for advancing causes such as women's rights, human rights, children's rights and tribal rights, etc. It also includes movements for protest—rotest against the policies and actions of national and international institutions.

(c) Civil society is a set of organization, such as self-help, mutual help and mutual support groups.

3.11.3 Significance of Civil Society

Civil society plays a pivotal role for the promotion of good governance and acceleration of the process of economic development. It acts as an instrument of social change and effective democratic governance through:

(a) Advocacy and policy analysis.

(b) Regulation and monitoring of state performance and the actions and behaviour of public officials.

(c) Building social capital and enabling citizens to identify and articulate their values, beliefs civil norms, democratic practices and a collective definition of public good.

(d) Mobilizing the poor and socially disadvantaged people to participate effectively in politics and public affairs.

(e) Reducing the socially isolated and unsettling effects of market forces.

(f) It mediates between state and market and helps to contain state power. It represents a sphere out side state control and one which gives maximum scope for individual freedom and self-determination.

Thus, civil society manifests when people combines themselves to pursue their common objectives. It is free from state authority. State and civil society are mutually interdependent. Both are complementary to each other. Civil society always aims at the realization of human welfare. It supports self-help association. It makes the state responsible. As M. Vilas writes, "Civil society refers to a sphere of collective actions distinet from both the market and political society—parties, legislatures, courts, state agencies. Civil society is not independent of politics, but clearly, when people identify themselves as civil society, they are seeking to carve out a relatively autonomous sphere for organization and action." In this context Prof. A. Ghosh writes "Civil society is just the entire body of the citizens of a country, and here, there are neither any given or well defined institutions nor any unity of interests of purpose, of authority, civil society consists of divorce, frequently conflicting interest groups in every society, and more so in an underdeveloped country. The state has, therefore to necessarily intervene and arbitrate between different interest groups in the larger interests of both peace and orderly development of civil society.... The state would (or should) attempt to reconcile conflicting interests. Different societies have divergent institutions to subserve the innumerable interests of the large members of civil society. The most organized of these institutions is the church (all religious institutions) and of late the so-called NGOs (Non-Government Organization), which in turn represent diverse interests, interest groups, objectives and aspirations of different sections of civil society."

In India, the interest in civil society initiative has been inspired by both the democratizing impulses as well as the new liberal interest in strengthening civil society as a counterbalance to the regulatory state. Civil society and social activists are being encouraged to take up responsibility for the development welfare functions which the state wants to shed. The compulsions of survival in globalize financial and a capital market necessitates such a division of responsibilities between the state and civil society. State can no longer guarantee employment and redistribution of assets. They need to be able to attract capital and maintain investor confidence by developing a pool of skilled manpower, good infrastructural facilities and low cost of production. On the other hand, civil society could offer scope for the exercise of creativity and self-reliance by people. People should consider themselves stakeholders in the society rather than passive recipients of benefits. The individualist values which lie behind neoliberal theories project the notion of a society in which individuals find their due place in terms of the effort and merit they show.

3.11.4 Civil Society and The State

There is an intimate relationship between civil society and the state. Both Hobbes and Locke considered the state to be the creation of civil society for protecting the life and property of citizens. The relationship between the civil society and the state is complementary. Sociologists also emphasis this truth. It is a fact that no civil society exists without the rule of the land. The ultimate guarantor of the land is the constitutional state. The relationship between the state and the society is mutual. Each has to care for the other. But in the modern world we find certain conflict between the state and the civil society. It is because of the intrusion of the state into the sphere of the civil society. The state should be vigilant for the survival and growth of the civil society.

3.11.5 Civil Society and Democracy

Democracy and civil society are inalienable. An active civil society could build support for democratic government by encouraging greater public participation in different schemes. It is believed that a partnership between civil society and state would be able to revitalize the democratic step up a country. Thus civil society is a precondition for democracy.

In the contemporary world, modern democratic states are characterized by contradictory beliefs—religions and non-religions, liberal and non-liberal. In a democratic society, plurality of views concerning good life is a permanent feature of societies. Pluralists hold the view that multiplicity of cultures can coexist within the boundaries of one political order. In a multi-cultural society, social integration is established by shared liberal political values. Civil society provides the arena for finding a common ground and integrative and collaborative mode of action. Thus, civil society stands between government and private sector and helps in conflicting institutions and belief systems coexist.

3.11.6 Civil Society and Globalization

In the globalized era, the structure of the civil society has been transformed. This has posed a challenge to the nation state. The role of nation state in sponsoring autonomous organization and helping them compete with one another in a healthy manner is under threat by international government organization and multi and transnational NGOs. Civil societies have assumed leading roles in meeting the challenges of globalization and fostering sustainable development. In India, there is a great divide on the theme of globalization. Supporters of globalizations consider it as the unique path for accelerating economic development and the opposents consider it as a recipe for economic subjugation. From the interim assessment of the process of globalization, it is revealed that the process has led to a decline in the role of modern nation state in regulating the nature of growth of the political economy at the national level. Economic reforms are imposed as the action states so that national economics can be restructured in accordance with the external changes taking place at the level of the global economy.

Globalization has sown the seed of consumerism culture. The narcotic effect of consumerism has destroyed the social ethics inherent in human beings. The media has captured the hearts and minds of the viewers. Indian views have accepted this culture as their own. Constantly viewing the glamour of dominant western culture, they have tended to imitate sexual behaviour and western lifestyle. The chronic addictions to media programme have withdrawn people from reality. The sanctity of Indian social life has been tarnished. The commodification of art and culture has affected our attitude towards women. Our perceptions to women have changed. The Indian women are being used a purchasing agents of their families by the MNCs. There is an unholy nexus between the state and religion. For the success of the new economic policy, the Indian family values, discipline cohesiveness and education are being given a subsidiary role. The adoption of the process of globalization is based on electoral politics which is not at all a healthy sign for future development. Cultural imperialism is in-built in the long-term strategy of globalization.

India being an agricultural economy cannot be governed by adopting the strategy of globalization neglecting her base culture, i.e. agriculture. We have to generate and multiply wealth from agriculture and agro-based industries through labour intensive technologies of production in order to have sustainable development. The growth what we have achieved through the adoption of globalization strategy is jobless, ruthless, rootless, futureless and voiceless. We have to explore the alternative between traditionalism and westernism which will help preventing the political and cultural hegemonization of the western economics through globalization.

The recent trend exhibits the fact that India is experiencing transition. In the process, the resilience of a modernizing democratic Indian society in the face of ever growing differentiation and polarization based upon hardening categories and social ruptures seems to be lost somewhat. Our economic system continues to be skewed in respect of economic justice. In spite of several developmental programmes initiated by our national government, people are not getting the desired benefits. Poverty is rampant everywhere. About one-third of the populations are deprived of the basic amenities. Health and education sectors are completely distorted. This has prevented civil society organizations from playing the advocacy role. Further, the socio-cultural values have failed to promote healthy democracy and effective civil society. Social behaviour in most of the areas is guided by particularistic values. This has resulted in conflict and confrontations. Many civil society organization are governed by norm ethnic, regional, communal and linguistic considerations. This has stifled democratic process and weakened the capacity of civil society to render help to the state to function.

Hence, there is an urgent need for restructuring the civil society for the promotion of human welfare and all round development of the economy.

Indian Culture

4

4.1 Concept of Bharatvarṣa

Bharatvarṣa is the earliest name of India. It is believed that the name is derived from the Bharat tribes that inhabited the land. Some people also believe that it is named after Bharata, the mighty son of king Dushyanta and queen Shakuntala. There is no historical evidence to this effect. Bharatvarsha (the land of Bharat), the ancient name of India is also mentioned in the preamble of the Constitution of India. There is also different story behind the name. The ancient Greeks called the river Sindhu as Indus. The Persians called it Hindu. So it came to be known as Ind or Hind. The land of Ind or Hind has become known as India or Hindustan. The Britishers called it India.

The history of every economy is very much influenced by its physical features. So also is the case of India. Its history has been shaped by its geography. India is a peninsula. Its geographical area is 32,87,782 sq. kms. Its length from north to south is 3214 kms. and breadth from east to west is 2933 kms. It is a subcontinent in Asia and has a population of over 100 crore.

Geographical unity of India is its unique feature. The geographical location of Bharatvarsha is described in *Vishnu Puran* as follows:

> "Uttarm yat Samudrasya, Himadreschaiva dakshinam
> Varsham tad Bharatam name, Bharatyatra Saritatih"

The meaning of this version is that the country which lies in the north of the sea and in the south of Himalayas is known as Bharat. It is inhabited by the descendants of king Bharat.

4.1.1 Geographical Division of India

India is divided into four distinct geographical divisions such as:

(a) Mountainous region of the North.

(b) Plain region in the Gangetic Valley.

(c) Deccan plateau.

(d) Eastern and Western Ghat regions.

(a) Mountainous Region of the North

This region stretches about 2450 kms. covering Kashmir, Kungra, Tehri, Kemann, Nepal, Sikkim and Bhutan. The distinctive feature of the region includes the Himalayas which series as a protecting wall for India. It also acts as defenisive wall for India and protects her from external aggression. The Himalayan wall has an opening in the North East and North West. These passes act as gateways for foreign traders. The Himalayas is the source of many useful rivers such as the Indus the Ganges and the Brahmaputra, etc. The northern plain of India is very fertile because of the impact of the Himalayas region.

(b) The Indo Gangetic Plain

This region is the most thickly populated region in India. The river system of northern India namely the Indus and its tributaries, the Ganges and its effluents and the Brahmaputra and its feeders irrigated this vast plain. These rivers have contributed a lot to the evolution of Indian culture. The fertility of the soil and the richness of the region have been instrumental for the establishment of big empires. A nature has gifted this region abundantly and have made it populous and prosperous. History reveals that this region was the centre of great intellectual activity. The environment of this region was so congenial that the Aryan preferred to settle here and developed their sublime religious thought and philosophy in these regions.

(c) Deccan Plateau

Geologically, the Deccan plateau is the oldest part of India. Western Ghat and Eastern Ghat mountain ranges act as the two sides of the region and strike southwards into a single subsidiary massive ending in cape comorin. Vindhya and Satpura mountain ranges act as a dividing line between Deccan plateau and the Indo Gangetic Plain. The tableland slopes from west to east and therefore all rivers like Godavari, Mahanadi, Krishna and Kaveri flow from west to east. The Hill tops of the Western Ghat provide an ideal location for strategic forts. The flat mountain tops of the deccan volcanic trap furnish excellent sites for maratha fortification. The coastal plain on the east is broader and drier than on the west. The north of this plain is formed by the alluvium of the Krishna and Godavari. The carnatic plain watered by the Kaveri contains some of the fertile lands in India. The history of the deccan reveals that it has played a creditable role in the past for preserving the Hindu culture.

(d) The Eastern and Western Ghats

The Eastern and Western sea coast, being very close to the sea, support for the growth of ports and port towns like Mumbai, Goa, Cochin, Visakhapatnam, Paradeep and Kolkata, etc. They constitute important trade centres of India. As centres of trade, education and industries, these port towns have served the lifelines of Indian economic and social growth. They have facilitated Indian maritime relationships with Java, Sumatra, Burma and Sri Lanka, etc. The culture which developed in this region has a lasting impact on the life of the people of India.

4.2 Features of Culture

Culture is an integrated system and language is the chief vehicle of culture. It is a continuous process which is transmitted from generation to generation. Culture denotes everything relating to man and his activities. Behaviour which is learnt is called culture. It assumes two forms—material culture and non-material culture. Material culture includes physical objects which can be seen, touched, exchanged and transferable. On the other hand non-material culture includes religion and art, etc. Culture is symbolic, continuous and progressive process. It implies the socially transmitted system of idealized ways of knowledge, practice and beliefs. It is the short-hand version of the rules that guide the way of life of the people. It is the embodiment of customs, traditions, thoughts, etc., of a social group throughout the ages. Though culture and civilizations are used interchangeably and are considered as synonymous it is wrong. Civilization is mechanical, external, utilitarian and concerned only with means, but culture is an end in itself. Unless one becomes cultured, he cannot be called civilized.

The word 'culture' is a 16th century innovation which means cultivated. During the 19th century, the word was used in a wider perspective to refer to all aspects of the social life of a community. It belongs to the whole community of the people. It is social and not individual heritage of man. It is idealistic. It is an acquired quality.

India is an ancient country with great cultural traditions. The culture of India is ancient and persistent. Indian culture is reflected in its religious rites, rituals and social ceremonies. In India, religion is the binding law which accounts for the cohesion in the social system throughout the history of Indian society. Since the dawn of the civilization mankind has been making cultural experiments. Many of them have failed to stand the taste of time and have been disappeared. But Indian culture has been survived even in adverse circumstances. Indian culture is a living force which originated thousand of years ago and continues till today. We find the glimpses of cultural heritage of India in our philosophy and religion. India has stood like a rock of ages, weathering many a fierce storm, because her foundations are the eternal values of philosophy and religion. The culture of India has always been integral in its approach. As A.L. Basham puts it, "In no other part of the ancient world were the relations of man and man and the man and the state, so fair and humane. In no other early civilization were slaves so few in number and in no other ancient law book are their rights so well protected as in the *Arthashastra*. India was a cheerful land, whose people each finding a niche in a complex and slowly evolving social system, reached a higher level of kindliness and gentleness in their mutual relationships than any other nation of antiquity."

4.2.1 Features of Indian Culture

India is a big country protected and nourished by nature. It has the proud privilege of possessing an unbroken tradition and continuous history. For several thousands of years India has maintained her tradition with unbroken continuity. In religion and literature, this continuity is most vibrant. India is an ancient land having deep historical significance. It stands for one vast cultural and political unit. The sense of unity of this land stretches from the Himalayas to the Indian Ocean. Though diversity is very much fundamental to India it has maintained its unity all through.

The distinctive features of Indian culture are as follows:

(a) Regional Identities

Regional identifies are implicit in spite of geographical diversities. We find a variation in the climate, rainfall, temperature, flora and fauna, deserts and forests because of geographical location of mountains and valleys, placing and coastal regions. They foster regional disparities and differences. It is a unique feature of Indian culture. In spite of heterogeneity, India is one. It is a conglomeration of regional diversities.

(b) Predominance of North India

Since culture is associated with civilization and the civilization flourished at Harappa and Mohenjodaro, they constitute the starting point of Indian history. Though history of Deccan came later, geographically it is older than north India. North India has played a dominate role in the evolution of Indian history due to its physical features.

(c) Social and Religious Diversity

Indian society is complex and heterogeneous. It lacks uniformity. Customs and traditions, fairs and festivals, food and dress habits and the general attitude to life vary from place to place and region to region. India has been a fertile ground for the growth of spiritualism. India boasts of her ancient religion, i.e. Vedic religion which stands for universal humanism and fraternity. Later on, Hinduism came to manifest itself in various sects like Vaishnavism, Saivism and Shaktism, etc. Even protestant sects like Buddhism and Jainism are regarded in India as branches of Hinduism. In course of time, cultural contacts with Islam, Christianity and Zoroastrianism, etc. led to harmonious coexistence of these religions with Hinduism in India. India is a polyglot gamble. Nearly 133 communities exist in India, each having its own language. The literature of India has been enriched by the multiplicity of languages.

(d) Political Diversity

Political diversity is one of the most important features of Indian culture. The Vedic system was one of the political accountability of all to the government through institutions such as Sabha and Samiti. Kautilya's *Arthashastra* is considered as the grammar of Indian politics. The glorious reigns of the Maurya's, Gupta's and Moghul's and great rulers like Ashok, Kharavela, Akbar and Shivaji have enriched the diverse political tradition of India. This diversity grows in volume as the people of India become more conscious of their fundamental rights than of their fundamental duties. The former has been imported from the west and the latter is the heritage handed down by our ancestors.

(e) Absence of Historical Unity

India has no systematic, complete and chronological history of its own. It is a collection of local histories. The absence of centre for Indian history has placed a great hurdle in the path towards national unity and solidarity.

4.2.2 Roots of Indian Culture

Indian culture is considered as one of the oldest cultures in the world. Indian culture and civilization are quite distinct from other parts of the world. It has evolved among multiethnic groups of people. It has a fundamental unity. In spite of diversities in the field of language, religion, custom and political system India possesses cultural homogeneity. This unity is reflected in the social ceremonies, religious rites, festivals and life style.

The roots of Indian culture can be studied under the following heads:

(a) Village Committee

Indian culture is village centred. In each Indian village there is a common life pattern. The villagers live like a family and share their pleasure and suffering among themselves. Though they are not economically prosperous, they are self-contended.

There is a sense of interdependence among themselves. Caste factor does not pose any problem before them. Despite caste barriers, there is a strong bond of community feelings based on fraternity, sympathy and cooperation. The villagers very well understand the ethics and philosophy of life. They are loyal, dutiful and law abiding.

(b) Vedic Tradition

Indian culture has been influenced to a great extent by the powerful Vedic tradition. The Vedas represent the oldest literature of the world. The Vedas are of four kinds: Rig, Sam, Yajur and Atharva. The Vedic literature is a magnificent contribution of the Aryans to the Indian culture and civilization. They indicate about social, economic, political and religious conditions of the time. The Vedas are considered as divine and sacred. They are written in Sanskrit. The Vedic language is precise and powerful. Though the authors of Vedas had no script they memorized the words and passages of many generations and centuries without making any change in the basic structure. This served as a powerful force for the growth of other Indian languages.

(c) Religions Tradition

The Vedas laid the foundation of Brahmanical religion. In course of time it was popularized as Hinduism. Hinduism is a catholic religion which encourages worship of nature, universality of one God and many Gods and Goddesses. There is complete freedom to choose religion. The religious tradition in India is based on tolerance and respect and it encourages humanism kindness and service to man. Though Hinduism believes in idol worship it also says that God is formless. Bhakti, Karma, Jnana and Yoga are various means for spiritual attainment. Hinduism believes in Karma and rebirth. It speaks of transmigration of soul and incarnation of God. Karma is a very powerful factor in human life. Reward and punishment are prescribed for good deeds and bad deeds. Karma is the most important and very significant part of Indian culture which serves as the root.

(d) Epics and Puranas

The *Ramayan*, the *Mahabharat* and eighteen Puranas and Upapuranas from the great vehicle of Indian cultural tradition.

Of the Puranas the *Bhagawat Puran* and the *Vishnu Puran* are the most important. They deal with social, political and religious life of ancient India. The Puranas are invaluable records of the ancient days. The Purans and epics are stories about Gods and Goddesses and their incarnations which are replete with didactic values. For centuries, these stories have acted as polestars to guide people on the right path in life. These stories are having deep religious values for our guidance. Due to the religious importance and ethical values these stories have been translated in all languages of the world.

(e) Sanskrit Language

Sanskrit language is the language of India's culture and civilization. It is the language in which all her past greatness, her rich thought and spiritual aspirations are enshrined, e.g. the Vedas, the Upanishads epics and Puranas and scriptures are written in Sanskrit. The language has a powerful legacy. The Gupta kings used Sanskrit as the vehicle of culture in Indian and South East Asiatic countries. Sanskritization is the end result of the spread of Sanskrit language by the Aryans. Further all the non Aryans in South India and Indian Archipelago accepted Sanskrit as the medium of academic and political activities. The Brahmans propagated Sanskrit through large scale migration. They created an efficient network of Indian culture. They received royal patronage and settled down in the new islands. A hermitage established in non Aryan location thrived as a veritable centre of Aryan culture. Further, *Arthashastra* the great masterpiece of Kautilya was written in Sanskrit. *Panchatantra* by Vishnu Sharma which served as the learner's first book for children was written in Sanskrit. Thus, Sanskrit was the lingua franca of the country.

(f) Philosophy

The Vedas and Upanishads constituted the foundation of Indian philosophy based on Brahmanical religion. Philosophy is clear and consistent enquiry into the nature of ultimate reality. God and his creation, man and his salvation were the main subjects of Indian philosophy. According to Indian philosophy, life was to be meaningful. There was no conflict between present and future. Life's purpose was defined as Dharma, Artha and Kama. Life is a harmonious unit.

The Aryans believed in monotheism, polytheism and monism. God exists and he is the creator of the universe. God may have multiple names, but he is essentially one. In Indian philosophy, there was much emphasis on asceticism. All the saints and sages were ascetics. They were great philosophers who dedicated their lives for the reform of the society. They propounded theories of Karma, rebirth and spiritual attainments. The saints possessed great spiritual power. Asceticism had great contributions to philosophical development.

On the other hand, the Upanishads propounded many mystic theories about God and the universe. Upanishad formed the part of Vedas and was the real foundation of Hinduism. They were full of metaphysical speculation. They speak of Brahman and consciousness, the human soul and the self. A realization of all these can free a man from transmigration. The Upanishads with their message of Universal spiritual religion represented the first renaissance of Hinduism. Thus the Upanishads contain the essential features of Indian philosophy and ethics.

(g) Doctrine of Karma

The Hindu culture is predominantly self-restraint. It is based on the ancient Vedic teachings of spiritualism. The teachings of the Gita present recorded evidence of ancient Hindu culture and civilization. The notions of Dharma and Karma are closely interlinked to each other. The doctrine of Karma is the essence of Hinduism. Karma implies work or deed. It determines the nature of next life, man's fortune, his social status, his surround and happiness. Every good deed brings its results in happiness and every evil act in sorrow. One cannot escape from the law of Karma. Belief in Karma does not involve fatalism. Hindu teachers do not support fatalism. Nobody can escape from the law of Karma. Further, Samsara is an important concept which determines human behaviour. It is the wheel of life. Karma identified with life cycle rituals of Hindus. A typical Hindu wants liberations from the cycle of birth, death and rebirth. *Gita* emphasizes on the accomplishment of karma rather than the abandonment of karma. *Gita* teaches the ethics of altruism. If one performs one's duty in a spirit of sacrifice, eliminating one's ego and self-interest. One is liberated from the fruits of action even before death. The direction of life can be determined through the performance of karma. Indian mind thinks of salvation to get rid of illusion and suffering associated with samsara. There are six systems of salvation. These are called saddarshana or six doctrines. These are called six schools such as Nyaya, Vaisesika, Sankhya, Yoga, Mimansa and Vedanta. Nyaya refers to clear thinking and logical argument. It is the system of reasoning. Vaisesika is the school of individual characteristics. It is closely associated with Nyaya. Vaisesika accepts nature as atomic. The atoms are eternal and quite distinct from soul. Vaisesika accepts matter and soul as different. Salvation depends on recognizing the atomic nature of the universe and its difference from soul. Sankhya is explained in *Bhagawat Gita*. It comprises of Sattva, Raja and Tama. Sattva is virtue. Raja is passion and Tama is dullness. Indian life is very much influenced by these three elements. Yoga means spiritual discipline. Mimamsa is more a school of exposition than salvation. Its primary purpose is to explain the Vedas. Further Vedanta is the end of the Vedas. It is founded on the triple authority of the Upanishads, the *Gita* and the *Brhma Sutram* of Badarayana. It brings out the mystical, ethical and metaphysical aspect of philosophy.

(h) Social Tradition, Customs, Rites and Ceremonies

Hindu society is based on the principle of Dharma. Dharma is that holds people together. It means man's innate urge to live together. It also implies law, justice and duty, etc. The Manusmritis divide the society into four castes—Brahman, Kshatriya, Vaishya and Sudra. Brahman and Kshatriya are considered as upper castes. They are most influential castes dominating the religious and political life. The Vaishyas control the economic life as they belong to the trading communities. The Sudras belonging to the lower caste and the people of this caste serve the people of upper classes.

The idea behind the ancient system of classes was that each man had a place in society ordained for him and that it was his sacred functions to perform the duties connected with it.

The Hindu social system is designed to enable each individual to achieve the highest goal of life, i.e. Purusartha (Dharma, Artha, Kama and Moksha). Purusartha means the fullest development of man's personality.

Among social functions, Namkaran, Upnayan, Marriage and funeral are commonly practiced. Apart from these, there are many other social functions like religions ceremonies, ceremonies relating to the laying the foundation of a house, entry into a newly built home, consecrations ceremony, inauguration ceremony and pilgrimage, etc. The Hindus are a liberal minded people. They have not inhibitors in sharing religious merits with others. Catholicism is the dominating spirit of a Hindu. He believes in tolerance. Further, Hinduism encourages national integration. Hindu pilgrimages know no barriers of caste, creed, religions and language. This spirit encourages national unity.

The family bond in India is very strong. Wife is taken as a life long companion. Son is taken as a guarantee of continuity of the family. He conducts the funeral ceremony of the parents and takes care of old parents. In Indian family charity is observed as a virtue. It is believed that service to humanity is service to God.

(i) Saints and Sages

Saints and sages play a very important role in the expansion of Indian culture. India, being an ancient country with a high standard of religious and cultural life gave birth to many saints and sages who added to the glory by their own contributions. Gautam Buddha and Vardhaman Mahavir along with their followers were not only great thinkers but also religious reformers. India has produced large number of sages, saints and philosophers like Sankara, Ramanuja, Madhava, Nimbarka, Ramananda, Vallabhacharya, Sri Chaitanya, Kabir, Nanak, Gandhi and Aurobindo, etc. They have given new life and vigour to Indian culture.

Sankara, an orthodox Brahmin propounded the doctrine of Advaita (monism). To him the world appeared an illusion—a maya, a dream, a mirage, a product of an imagination. He said that the only reality is Brahman the universal soul. Sankara was a great dialectic who investigated truth through reasoning.

Ramanuja, a great philosopher of 11th-12th centuries popularized the doctrine of salvation through knowledge. According to him, devotion was the best meaning of salvations and Bhaktiyoga was the best yoga. Both are essential for the fulfillment of the goals of life.

Madhava was a renowned philosopher of the 13th century who emphasized on the doctrine of the unity of God and human soul. He was the profounder of Dvaita philosophy.

Nimbarka was the profounder of Bhakti doctrine. He held the view that Krishna was the supreme lord of the universe.

Vallabhacharya was a renowned vaishnavite saint. He was an avowed champion of Bhakti and was a scholar and philosopher of high order. He advocated penance renunciation and austerity.

Sri Chaitanya was a saint and reformer. He propagated the cause of Radha Krishna cult. He posed himself as the embodiment of Radha and sang Samkirtana with great emotion. He denounced caste and accepted people of all castes as his disciples.

Kabir, a noted saint and true disciple of Ramananda made sincere efforts to establish communal harmony among the Hindus and the Muslims. He was a religious reformer. He advocated Bhajan and devotional songs along with simple worship for salvation. He disapproved idol worship and caste system.

Nanak was a famous Indian saint and founder of Sikh religion. He believed in the unity of Godhood and toleration. He was against idol worship and caste system. He was a patron of monotheism.

(j) Indian Heritage

India has a very rich and glorious heritage. These constitute the milestones of Indian culture and serve as the roots. Ashokan pillars, Ashokan art, Ashokan edicts, monuments of Gupta period, Ajanta and Ellora Cave, paintings and sculpture, Elephanta Cave, temples of Orissa, Tamil Nadu, Andhra Pradesh, Forts of Doulatabad and Golkunda, monumental architecture of the Mughal period in Delhi and Agra are brightest example of Indian artistic heritage, which speak volumes of her culture. They also represent the visible symbols of Indian creativity and the values they cherished over the centuries. They are the epitomes of Indian culture which represent universal values like art, aesthetics, technology, love and security.

(k) Indian Ethics

Indian culture is deeply rooted in ethics which prescribe there basic objectives of life such as—Dharma, Artha and Kama. These are all mundane things before man enters into efforts for salvation. The Indian Shastras contain certain principles for the king who is the supreme sovereign of the country. The king should abide these rules strictly such as he should avoid untruth and treachery illicit intercourse with women, avoid envy, contact with low and out caste, respect all Gods and Goddesses sanctify cows and Brahmins, revere his ancestors, feed his guests, bath in sacred water, nourish the poor, orphan, widow, semants and relations, protect these who seek shelter, etc. A successful king is he who performs all these things. Further he should possess virtues like hospitality, charity and honest.

Indian ethics also prescribes eight virtues to be observed by the Aryans. These include compassion of all beings, patience, contendedness, purity, sincerity, good thoughts, freedom from greed and freedom from envy, etc. Indian literature has urged at all times for kindliness, tolerance, non-violence, mercy, compassion and friendliness love and forgiveness. These virtues have universal appeal.

(l) Indian Polity

It is very difficult to determine the nature of political system in India. From the description of kingdoms in the *Rig Veda*, we find some hints about the political activity and organization in the early period. Politics in ancient India was not studied as a branch of philosophy. There was no school of political philosophy discussing the orgin of the state and the form of government, etc.

Dandaniti was known as the principle of administrations. It was closely associated with Rajaniti or politics. Though vedic literature refers to the responsibilities of a king, there were some important books dealing with the science of government like Kautilya's *Arthashastra,* Kamandaka's *Nitisara* and *Sukraniti*, etc. *Arthashastra*, a treatise on political economy was written by Kautilya, the Prime Minister of Chandra Gupta Mourya. His work was based on the belief that the success of the ruler depended solely on the material prosperity of his subjects. The *Nitisara* or the essence of politics of Kamandaka, the *Sukraniti*, *Nitibakyamitra* of Samadev Suri all deal with the details of state craft. Apart from these, the Santiparva of *Mahabharat*, *Manusmriti*, passages from Vedas and Upanishads throw light on what was thought to be the ideal human conduct as well as government.

Tradition of monarachy is as old as the Indian history. Gods created the king to lead them in war against demons. The king was endowed with divine power at the time of consecration. He used to perform Rajasuya (Royal consecration), Vajapeya (Drinking of strength) and Asvamedh (Horse sacrifice) for the purpose. In those day the Divine Right of kingship held the field. The duties of kings included protection of life, property, religion and custom of his subjects. Theoretically, the king was absolute, but in practice, his absolute authority did not exist. Hindu kingship was not arbitrary. In course of time, Ashok, Samudragupta and Chandragupta governed the state as per the account for the epithets paramesvara, param Daivata, etc. The ideal of Ashok was to utilize the resources of the state for the benefit of the people. The rulers of ancient India become the models for future generation king. They were inspired by their ancestors develop a sense of unity among the people as well as to project themselves as ideal ruler.

Thus, Indian culture has the capacity to assimilate all the protesting web and it has been happening since the dawn of Indian civilization. Indian culture is an embodiment of certain values which have been nourished by the people over several centuries through innumerable generation. There is a close association between religions belief, moral ethics, expectation of the people and values. The culture of India has grown over centuries though the converted efforts of sages, seers, thinkers, philanthropists, etc. Indian culture is very much flexible. Adoptability to the changes of time is a distinct feature of Indian culture. Indian culture aims at the integral development of man. It transmits spiritual ideals into life with a message for the entire human race. Indian culture has maintained its continuity since the down of civilization without losing its inherent spiritual essence. As stated in the Atharva Veda:

> O, mankind, come together
> Towards one objective—the
> Welfare of all.

These sacred lines from *Atharva Veda* highlights the message of Indian culture.

4.3 Protestant Religious Movements During the 6th Century B.C.

The 6th century B.C. marked the period of spiritual unrest and intellectual ferment. In the Aryan society Brahmanical religions get consolidated with wide public support. The Hindu religion with its caste system and social hierarchy became the order of the day. It heralded the supremacy of the Brahmans over the social and religious order. They formulated religious rules to support the system. The Hindu religion acknowledges the supremacy of the Brahmanas. Sanskrit was their monopoly and they controlled education and mindset of the public. But the Brahmanical supremacy did not last long. The ruling caste Kshatriyas wanted to curb the supremacy of the Brahmans and started revolting against the prevailing social system. They raised their voice against the Brahmans. They also acquired necessary moral strength to challenge the oppressive caste system and injustice of the Brahmans. Such challenge appeared in the form of two religious movements called Jainism and Buddhism. Jainism and Buddhism rose as revolt against the prevailing evils of the society under the supremacy of the Brahmanas. As R.C. Majumdar writes "the 6th century B.C. saw the rise of Buddhism, Jainism and other religious sects heralding that protestant movement which was destined to bring to an end to the questioned supremacy of the Vedic religion and culture".

Both Buddhism and Jainism were a reformed form of Hinduism. They neither taught any new dogmas, nor any new rituals nor a new philosophy. It was an attempt to reform the spiritual life of India. These two religious movements rendered a valuable service to the reformation of the existing religions.

4.3.1 Causes for the Rise of Jainism and Buddhism

Jainism and Buddhism were called protest movements against the vices of existing Hindu religion. These were formed by Mahavir and Gautam Buddha respectively. Both were princes of Madhyadesh. Both flourished in the 6th century B.C. Mahavir belonged to Jnatrika clan and his father was Siddhartha. Gautam Buddha was of Sakya clan and his father's name was Suddhodana. They were intellectuals. They had the leadership to protest against the superior Brahman caste. They rejected the authority of Vedas, denounced animal sacrifice and other unnecessary rituals. They gave new interpretations to the concept of Karma and Samskaras. The teachings of both of them showed the path of salvation to the suffering humanity for a better and nobler life.

Following factors are responsible for the rise of Jainism and Buddhism:

(a) The Brahmanical religion had become complicated due to frivolous ritualism and irrational attitude of the Brahmans which made the common people grown under the heavy burden of the ceremonial rituals.

(b) Brahmanism had lost its original simplicity and purity. Its ceremonies had become costly and meaningless.

(c) All the religious literatures and scriptures were written in Sanskrit language. In the passage of time its simplicity had disappeared. Majority of the people did not understand it. People wanted a religion which could be explained to them in simple intelligible spoken language.

(d) The Brahmanical religion depended more and more on animal sacrifice which caused a lot of violence and blood-shed which created resentment among the common men. The people realized that senseless killing of animals would not be able to please God.

(e) The Brahmans used to misuse their powers and corruption crept in to all corners of the society. By encouraging superstitions and pretending to invoke their desired purpose by chanting the mantras, the Brahmans kept the other castes in constant suspense. The people did not like the supremacy of the Brahamans.

(f) The Hindu religion in course of time became expensive. Performance of Yajna was considered as a sacred duty of every Hindu but it was not alterable for the common man who started murmuring against the existing faith. Further austerity, renunciation, penance, meditation and self-mortifications prescribed by the Brahmans did not appeal to the common man. They wanted to lead a normal life which was not allowed by the Brahmans.

(g) The caste system was very rigid which gave a privileged position to the Brahmans. While the upper caste enjoyed social privilege, the lower caste people felt oppressed. They did not like to be treated as inferior human beings. The existing social system disrupted the smooth functioning of the society. This created a lot of discontentment and resentment among masses.

(h) Contemporary economic and political developments helped the emergence of new social groups which acquired considerable economic power. Various social groups were opposed to the social positions defined for them by the Brahamnas on the basis of their heredity.

(i) The leaders of the religious ferment were the Kshatriyas. They were respected for their scholarship in reforming the existing social structure. They believed in the theory of transmigration of soul and consequences of karma and were of the view that the world was in a perpetual process of creation, dissolution and rebirth filling eternity with an everlasting rhythm. The philosophy of new protestant religion attracted everybody.

(j) It was also thought that the prevailing system of corruption, oppression and suppression of the lower class people, inequality and injustice will harm social life.

Hence the masses very much demanded a change and reformation for the prosperity of the society—moral, ethical, spiritual, socio-economic and political.

4.4 Jainism and Vardhaman Mahavir

Vardhaman Mahavir was the founder of Jainism. He lived during 599 B.C. to 527 B.C. He was the 29th tirthankar (Saint with divine power of granting salvation to his disciples). Rishabhadeva was the 1st tirthankar and Parashvanath was the 23rd tirthankar. It is said that Parashvanath was the real founder of Jainism. He happened to be the son of king Asvasena of Varanasi. From his very childhood he developed a fascination for an ascetic life. He discarded the worldly life and went out as an ascetic in search of spirituality. After 84 days of penance, he received enlightenment. He developed four main principles to be followed by every human being to get salvation. They are Ahmisa (Non-injury/Non-violence), Satya (Truth), Astaya (Non-stealing) and Aparigraha (Non-acquisition). He believed in the eternity of matter.

Jainism as a reformed Hindu religion is the amalgamation of the teachings of 24 tirthankars.

Vardhaman Mahavir was born in a royal family in Kundagram in ancient Vaisali or modern Bihar. His father was Siddhartha and mother was Trishala, a Lichhavi princess. His parents made all efforts to provide him the best education. He was married to Yasodhara and was blessed with a daughter. After the demise of his parents he renounced the world at the age of 30. He become a wandering ascetic in search of truth. He lived the life of severe austerities and deep meditation. At the age of 42 he attained knowledge. He was called Jina, the conqueror. He preached his religion which was popularly known as Jainism. He (Vardhaman Mahavir) the great hero or Jina (the conqueror) or Niggannatha (free from bondage) or Nataputta (scion of the Nata on Jnatrika dan) or Kevalin (omniscient) was more of a religious reformer than the founder of Jainism.

4.4.1 Basic Tenets of Jainism

The basic tenets of Jainism may be discussed in the following manner:

(a) Panchayama Dharma

Mahavir, being the disciple of parsavnath (the 23rd tirthankar and original founder of Jainism) was very much fascinated by the teachings of his guru accepted and developed the later's doctrines. He asked people to give up completely four great vices or Kasayas such as Krodha, Moha, Mada and Lobha. He advocated five important virtues of human life such as Ahmisa (non-violence), Satya (truth), Achourya (non-stealing), Aparigraha (non-attachment) and Brahmacharya (celibacy). He strongly urged to free the atman from all Kasayas. It is the real triumph. The atman can follow the panchayama dharma without any obstacle to attain self-realization or eternal bliss.

(b) Three Jewels (Tri Ratna)

The panchayama dharma is very much essential for leading a pure and noble life. To attain this objective, he prescribed a three-fold path such as proper faith, proper knowledge and proper conduct. In Jain terminology this is known as Three Jewels or Tri Ratna. Practice of triratna helps in purifying the heart and making the practitioner conscious of the irrelevance of worldly attachment on bondage.

(c) Ahimsa (Non-Violence)

Mahavir and his followers laid great emphasis on the theory of Ahimsa. It is the greatest contribution of Jainism to the society. Ahimsa means a love of life in all living beings and a firm belief in the principle of live and let live. "Jewevan Jeevasya Jeevanam"—Life is the basic element of any living being. He emphasized that unnecessary and aggressive violence should be discouraged. Even the smallest creature on the earth should be given adequate protection for his survival. With a view to develop the practice of non-violence one has to give up the thoughts of attachment and aversion. He prescribed that complete renunciation from worldly passions and vanity should be the precondition for perfect practice of non-violence.

(d) Justice and Equality

In order to give justice to everybody, he preached the path of peace, Ahimsa and equality. His philosophy aimed at the welfare of both the individual and the society. Jainism treated everybody equal. Utmost importance was to be given to refine the character and behaviour of each individual. Jainism also stressed to provide equal opportunity for women in social spheres. Women were actively encouraged to get them educated and playing social roles equal to men. Mahavir was an rodent advocate of women's liberation and empowerment.

(e) Doctrine of Anekantavada

Mahavir put forward the doctrine of Anekantavada or many sidedness. He used to advise his disciples to discover the truth after scrutinizing all aspects and giving them due importance. This helps in broadening one's outlook and tains the mind to accommodate the feelings and the way of life of other faiths and communities. Anekant encourages interpersonal and communal harmony through promotion of tolerance in the community. Tolerance is the very basis of Jainism. According to the principle of Anekanta, no element is either different or same as the total. It is both separated and integrated. A person is not entirely different from the universe. Yet he is not the same. So anybody who tries to analyse and comprehend himself also understands the entire universe.

(f) Theory of Syadvada or Maybeism

Jainism is based on one of the most important practical teaching, i.e. Syadvada. It is the theory of conditional prediction which may be called maybeism or perhapism. It is very realistic in the sense that it accepts the manifoldness of reality and postulates a multiverse in contrast to the concept of universe. When we operate on a relative plane, we are open to other possibilities, creativity happens in the space of openness which is a great virtue emanating from the practice of syadvada.

(g) Theory of Living Being

According to Mahavir, the universe was build by two self-governing components such as Jeeva (living) and Ajeeva (non-living). The concept of Jeeva states that whatever remains outside the whole body after death as its shadow is Jeeva. Jeeva is inactive and weightless. It is pure, deathless or eternal without attributes. It is found in countless numbers. Jeeva stays above the earth. It descends on the earth to assume the form of a material body.

(h) Theory of Non-living

The concept of Ajeeva or non-living consists of five elements such as Dharma, Adharma, Kala, Akash and Pudgala. While Dharma remains the yardstick of dynamics, Adharma represents everything that was static. Kala regulates time, Akash symbolizes the void and Pudgala determines the attributes of matter.

(i) The Karmic Body

The karma sharira or material body is constituted by the tenets of pudgala. Mahavir prescribes eight such tenets. They are Jnana baraniya (preventing wisdom), Darshan baraniya (preventing faith and righteousness), Mohaniya (attracting delusion), Vedaniya (Source of happiness and pain), Ayustka (determining life span), Namna (giving human qualities to man), Gotra (indicating lineage, community and caste of man) and Antargua (hindering the path of salvation). A combination of these pudgala attributes and constitutes the material body of each human. These are bound to each other by different shapes and men knowledge. An assimilation of such material forms constitute the world. The endless cycle of life and death is basic to the creation of the world.

(j) Theory of Action

Mahavir espoused the concept of action or karmavada. According to him every human being determines his own destiny. Action brings fulfillment. Bad action brings bad results and good action brings good results and ultimately liberation.

(k) Soul

According to Mahavir, soul is the main component of Jeeva. It gets vitiated by coming in contact with matter which causes suffering. As such, there is a succession of rebirth for life with soul. The sole aim of soul is to free human beings from the bondage of action. Only knowledge or wisdom and meditation can help the humans to achieve this.

(l) Bondage and Elevation of Soul

Mahavir was of the view that one's action determined his destiny. Action surrounds soul and gives it a particular shape. Good action elevates man while bad action relegates him. The soul is bound by the bondage of one's one nature, ignorance and craving. Good action liberates human being from the bondage. As a result the soul of the man goes up.

(m) Liberation of Soul

The liberation of the soul from the bondage of actions is called moksha. In Jainism, every matter consists of two parts—material and spiritual. The form consists of all actions. This part is gloomy, impure and destructive. On the contrary, the spiritual part makes the soul bright, pure and eternal. Predominance of the material part over the spiritual part plunges the latter in darkness. As such, the soul fails to manifest itself properly. The soul's own manifestation is called siddhasila. This happens when the soul liberates itself from the material part and this manifests itself in a pure, luminous, pervasive, endless and divine form. Liberation from all bad actions alone can fetch this stage for oneself. Consequently, there is no rebirth and this can be attained through severe meditation, self-restraint and penance.

(n) God

Mahavir was an atheist. According to him every activity in the world is managed by God. He had identical views as the Buddha in emphasizing the importance and significance of human activity. He exhorted the people to solve their own problems with their own activity to attain liberation instead of depending or delegating their activity to some abstract, metaphysical force.

(o) Denial of Vedas

Mahavir was not in favour of the contents in the Vedas and he denounced the Vedic descriptions as a bundle of lies which misguided the society since long. The Gods and Goddesses as depicted in the Vedas were imaginary and all rituals as meaningless and fanciful. Such ideas led the society astray. Mahavir repudiated outright Brahmanical superiority. According to him, Brahmins were parasites exploiting the society through fake religions and rituals of the Vedas. Jainism is highly reformative in approach which could curb the Brahmianical supremacy.

4.4.2 Spread of Jainism

Jainism as a religion was very much attraction to the people for its simple doctrine. This religion marked an improvement over the existing belief. Teachings of Mahavir became very popular among the masses. The use of common dialect (Prakrit) the simple moral precepts and royal patronage were instrumental for the spread of Jainism.

The causes responsible for the spread of Jainism can be enumerated as follows:

(a) Use of Simple Language

The religious message of Mahavir was in very lucid language which attracted the attention of the people. The common masses were drawn to it as it was the language they could speak and understand. Acceptance of the masses led to spread in the nook and corner of Indian subcontinent.

(b) Simple Doctrine

Before Jainism came into being the masses were fed up with the existing complex Vedic rites and rituals. Jainism was simple religion. It was a reformed form of Hinduism. Since it was based on the theory and philosophy of non-violence and insisted on non-injury in speech, deed and action, it attracted the people who suffered a lot under the existing Brahmanism.

(c) Personality of Mahavir

The strong and impressive personality of Mahavir was an important factor for popularizing Jainism. His simple way of living and impressive manner of conversation and pious admonitions drew the masses to him. A prince by birth, leading a life of spiritual recluse, free from worldly bondage thinking passionately for the common men drew to him wider popularity, sympathy, support and acceptance. The spread of Jainism was thus a resounding success.

(d) Royal Patronage

The popularity of Jainism got instant royal patronage. The Kshatriya kings and prince who were unhappy with the increasing influence of the Brahmans in the society came to accept Jainism and patronize it. Jainism was patronized by Ajatsatru, the mighty king of Magadha, rulers of Nanda dynasty, Chandragupta Maurya and Kharavela. Apart from these rulers, the ruler kings of southern dynasties like the Chalukya, Rashtrakuta and Ganga also patronized it.

(e) Role of Jain Monks

The role of Jain monks and mendicants was unique for the spread of Jainism. The mendicants directly indoctrinated by Mahavir moved to various places of India to spread Jainism. Jain saint Bhadrabahu was instrumental in spreading Jainism in South India during 4th century B.C. He had taken emperor Chandragupta Maurya to Sravan bel gola in south where the later breathed his last. Jainism was very much popular among businessmen and traders. In south India most of the traders belong to Jaina community.

(f) Role of Jain Writers

The Jain writers contributed greatly to endear Jainism to the masses. Principles of Jainism were highlighted by writers such as Hemachandra, Haribhadra, Somadeva, Gunabhadra and Ravi Kirti. Their writing warmed the hearts of people with its religious heat and spiritual radiance.

4.4.3 Contribution of Jainism to Indian Culture

The contributions of Jainism to Indian culture are very great. These may be described under the following heads:

(a) Literature

Jainism had a powerful literature. It had made a tremendous impact on the Indian civilization. It rendered valuable contribution to the growth of vernacular literature. The earliest works of the Jains were written in the form of Pali language called Apabhramsa. In a later stage Jains were reflected in prakrit language, i.e. spoken language of the people which promoted the growth of prakrit literature. Jainism also promoted the growth of Tamil and

Kannada literature. The Jains also took to Sanskrit and wrote legends and fables, etc. and several other books on grammar and poetry which greatly contributed to Sanskrit language.

(b) Jain Architecture

Jainism has utilized art for the popularization of its doctrine. Jain Art and architecture embellished Indian Art. Jain stupas were built of stones and were decorated with gate ways, stone umbrellas, carved pillars and huge statues. The Jain temples at Mount Abu and Chittorgarh in Rajasthan are fine specimens of architecture. The Jains also cut rocks to build caves and rock temples. Exquisite Jain images are found in Mathura, Bundelkhand and Northern Madhya Pradesh. The image of bahubali, in Sravan bel gola, of Karnataka, popularly known as Gometesvara, is a living testimony to the richness of Jain sculpture. Equally unique in their artistic content is the cave art of Udayagiri in Bhubaneswar, Madhya Pradesh, Ellora and Maharashtra. The Parshavnath hill, Rajgir in Bihar, Girnar and Palitan in Kathiawad, Dilwara a top Mount Abu in Rajasthan and Khandagiri and Udayagiri in Odisha are the famous centres of Jaina religion.

(c) Social Life

Mahavir was basically a social reformer. His principal objective was to wipe out the social evils and imbibing a culture among people to attain satisfaction and salvation. In the social sphere Mahavir and his followers did a great job by removing inequality and the evils of the existing caste system. The principle of brotherhood, team spirit, social equality and recognition of basic human rights placed in on a higher pedestal.

(d) Religion

Jainism was a universal religion. It aimed at doing away with the complicated and expensive rituals and free the common man from the clutches of the Brahmans. It helped the people to avoid unnecessary religions ceremonies. Jainism pointed out the deficiencies that had developed into Hinduism. Jainism propagated and prescribed certain principles such as right faith, right knowledge and right conduct for the spiritual growth of an individual.

4.5 Buddhism and Gautam Buddha

Buddhism was founded by Gautam Buddha. This was another protest movement in the religious history of India. Gautam Buddha was a young contemporary of Mahavir who was born in 576 B.C. in a royal family in Nepal. His father Suddhodana was the chief of the Sakya clan of Kapilavastu in Nepal and his mother was Maya, princess of Kaliya clan. His life span was in between 566 B.C. and 486 B.C. The legend about his birth is depicted in art and narrated in literature. Though he was born in a royal family with a silver spoon in his mouth, he was a completely different man. He had a contemplative mood and a compassionate nature and he took little interest in worldly affairs. At the age of 16, he was married to Yusodhara or Gopa and at the age of 29, he was blessed with a son named Rahul. Once, after seeing (four great scenes) i.e. an old man, a sick man, a corpse and an ascetic. He realized the true nature of the world. With a view to find a solutions to the misery of mankind he left home at the age of 29. This event is described as great Renunciation. He becomes a wandering hermit. In the course of his traveling, he become a disciple of two great Brahman scholars Arada Kalam and Udrak Ramputra and acquired knowledge on philosophy, on the art of Meditation. At Urvela near Bodha Gaya on the banks of Niranjana River he sat under a Pipal tree (Bodhitree) and practiced religious penance. Ultimately he attained the truth of Bodhi after such meditation and was known as Buddha or Tathagat (one who attained truth). It was after the attainment of enlightenment, Gautam Buddha went first to the Deer Park of Saranath near Benaras where he preached his first sermon which was known as Dharma Chakra pravartana or turning the wheel of law.

4.5.1 Basic Tenets of Buddhism

Gautam never imagined that one day he would be the founder of a new religion. He only said that materialism creates desire which brings sorrow and sorrow is the end result of desire. One can put an end to sorrow when he puts an end to his desire. End of desire will lead to end of rebirth. The end of rebirth is Nirvana of final deliverance. He did not advocate for a new religion but he sawed the seeds of revolt against the conventional practice of the religion of the day which ultimately germinated and grew as a worldwide religion. He was a realist and Buddhism is a clear and simple religion to lead mankind for the attainment of salvation from the bondage of suffering.

The basic tenets of Buddhism are as follows:

(a) Arya Satya

The concept of Arya satya lays down four noble truths such as:

(i) The world is full of sorrow.

(ii) Desire is the main cause of sorrow.

(iii) One can escape from sorrow by suppressing the desires.

(iv) One must know the right path to conquer the desire.

(b) Eight-fold Path

The very essence of Buddhism is ingrained in the noble eight-fold path or Arya Astanga marg. They are right views, right resolve, right speech, right conduct, right liverlihood, right effort, right recollection and right mediation. On the whole, the eight-fold path regulate the humility and conditions the spirituality in man and they also generate his wisdom. The Arya Astang marg was also known as the middle way as it kept away from the extreme paths of severe penance on the one hand and comfort, luxury and pleasure seeking on the other. The middle way symbolized the Buddhas personal experiences in life. Neither the pleasures of royalty nor the extremities at Urnvilva could lead him to enlightenment. He sustained his life only after accepting milk from Sujata which finally led him to enlightenment. The eight-fold path is called the middle path because it lies between the laxity of Brahmanism and extreme austerity of Jainism.

(c) Nirvana

According to Buddhism the chief aim of man's life is the attainment of Nirvana. Nirvana means blowing out or end of craving of the desire (trishna) for existence in all its forms. As a result, all sufferings should also end. Nirvana does not mean disappearance or extinction. It is a peaceful condition to be realized by a person who is free from all craving or want of desire. It is deliverance or freedom from rebirth. It is beyond disease (abyadhi), beyond decay (akashaya), beyond death (amrita), beyond sorrow (asoka) and beyond bondage (asasmkli). Existence through the physical body brings suffering. So it is quite desirable to free oneself from all types of desire. Freedom from desire is the ultimate path to attain salvation (Nirvana).

(d) Law of Karma

The doctrine of Karma is the essential part of the teachings of Buddha. Buddha said that it was the eternal law that a man reaps the fruits of his deeds. None can escape the consequence of his deeds.

(e) Ahimsa or Non-Violence

Buddha was a strong advocate of non-violence. He preferred non-violent action to any good action. He advocated it not only in words, but in thoughts and deeds. Non-violence of Buddha was not negative but positive in contents. He denounced the bloody sacrificial rites and rituals.

(f) Panch Shila (The Five Commandments)

The Buddha preached a moral code of conduct consisting of five commandments to be followed by all throughout their lives. They do not cause injury to living beings, do not steal, do not tell lies, do not commit adultery and do not use in toxicants.

(g) Brahma Vihar

Good conduct alone enables one to conquer desire. A pure mind is the base of all good conduct. This pure mind comprises four good qualities such as equal disposition to all (*Upekha*) friendship for all (metta), happiness at other's success (mudita) and kindness (karuna). These four attributes or qualities are known as Brahma Vihar in Buddhism. It helps in the purity of mind that can gain salvation through the eight-fold path.

(h) Moral Code

Buddha preached that a man can achieve happiness not only by observing rituals but also by observance of ethical and moral principles in day-to-day life. Truthfulness, charity, purity and control over passion are the salient aspects of the moral code. It taught the code of practical ethics and laid down the democratic principles of social equality.

(i) The Three Jewels of Tri Ratna

The Buddha put a premium on dharma (religion) and Sangha (religious order). At the beginning, he admitted the monks (*bhikshus*) into the Sangha after personally initiating them to Buddhism. Subsequently, it was done by his dependable disciples. An innovation of immense significance was the allowance of women for their attainment into the sangha or order. This was a contrast to Vedic Brahmanism where increasing limitations were being placed on the activities of women in the Dharmasutras. The funding of an order for nuts (*bhikshunis*) was a striking innovation. A monk was required to join the sangha with no attachment whatsoever. He was also required to shave his head and take an oath of allegiance to the head of the sangha. The oath was

Buddham Saranam Gachhami
Dhamam Saranam Gachhami
Sangham Saranam Gachhami.

Which means I consecrate myself to Buddha, I consecrate my self to religions and I consecrate myself to the monastic order? These three are known as the Buddhist three ratna. Right after initiations, the monks were taught the ten-fold principles and asked strictly to follow the eight-fold path.

(j) Disbelief in Vedas and Silence Over the Existence of God

Gautam Buddha rejected the authority of Vedas. He was against priesthood, elaborate rites and rituals, idol worship and animal sacrifice. He denounced caste system. Buddha opened the doors of Buddhism for the person of all castes. Hence, Buddhism can be rightly called a protestant Hinduism. Buddhism was liberal, democratic and acceptable to common men. Further, Buddha was bitterly opposed to the caste system. He emphasized that a person is known by his inherent qualities and not by his birth to a particular caste. To him, all castes were equal and all ·ilty persons must be given equal punishments. Buddha called against caste distinctions. He advocated the establishment of a casteless society.

4.5.2 Causes of the Popularity of Buddhism

Buddhism was popular because of the following reasons:

(a) The personality of Buddha and his method of preaching fascinated people to accept the religion within no time.

(b) People were aggrieved with the supremacy of Brahmanism. They wanted a change and a new religious outlook.

(c) Buddhism was free of the superstitions and orthodox views of Hinduism.

(d) It was a simple and rational religion.

(e) It was free of priestly exploitations.

(f) It was above caste system.

(g) It received royal patronage and state support.

(h) The Buddhist missionaries did very good work in India and outside.

(i) Buddhism used the popular language of the area he lived in. It was known as Prakrit which helped in developing Pali. During the reign of Ashok, Pali became the lingua franca of the state. In Buddhism people found their own language and it become popular.

(j) Buddhism appeared in India at a time of spiritual turmoil and people felt the necessity for religious reforms. People were tired of social hurdles, religious dogmas, useless rituals, animal sacrifices and caste restrictions, etc., in this critical situation Buddha raised his voice for reforms which got popular support.

(k) The role of Buddhist sanghas and monks were no less significant in the spread of Buddhism. The Buddhist monks took the message of Buddha to the common people.

(l) There were beautiful Buddhist monuments at Sarnath, Gaya, Mathura, Ajanta, Ellora and many other places attracting people and pilgrims leaving a undeniable impact on their mind.

(m) Buddhist doctrine of non-violence had great social appeal.

(n) The Buddist approach to life and aversion to materialism had their impact.

(o) With the growing distaste for orthodox and priest ridden Hinduism, an alternative religion was considered essential for the people. Buddhism filled up the void to meet the popular need.

4.5.3 Impact of Buddhism

Buddhism had a tremendous impact on the existing social order and on the future development of politico religions ideas. It asserted a driving force in the life and thought of the people of India. The impact of this liberal religion fascinated every body rich and poor, have and have-not. The Buddha endeared himself to the vast multitude of the suppressed and oppressed section of the society. It created a new socio-religions order which antagonized the Vedic Brahmanical principles. Brahmanical rituals especially the sacrifice of animals became more and more acceptable. One of the most outstanding ideas to be expounded by Buddhist teachings was to dissociate itself from the Gods with the origin of government. Buddhism, on the contrary, described it as a process of gradual social change which could only be brought about and controlled by people by electing a person to govern them and to establish laws for their protection.

The impact of Buddhism on the life and thought of the people of India can be discussed under four heads.

(a) Social impact.

(b) Religious impact.

(c) Political impact.

(d) Cultural impact.

(a) Social Impact

Buddhism refuted the existing caste system and advocated the formation of a casteless society. It believed in and propagated the equality of all men and denounced the supremacy of the Brahmans. Since it was a liberal religion it kept its doors open for the low caste and women. A Sudra would no longer feel segregated or a woman would not be perceived merely as a child producing machine. The conversion to Buddhism freed people from the marks of inferiority. The doctrine of Ahimsa is a great gift of Buddhism to Indian culture and society. Buddhism gave a tremendous fillip to education. Numerous Buddhist monasteries were great centres of learning running schools and colleges which were opened to all. It made education practically universal. The scholarship, simplicity and devotion to duty of the Buddhist monks earned universal acclaim. It laid stress on living a pure life. The preservation of wild life was given utmost attention.

(b) Religious Impact

Buddhism was by and large a sort of reformed Hinduism, when it denounced rituals, sacrifices and priesthood which extended into Hinduism of the later Vedic age. For the first time in the history of the world, Buddha proclaimed a salvation which each man could gain for himself and by himself in this world during this life without the least help from a personal God or Gods. As K.M. Pannikar states, "To the common man, Buddhism was a new gospel. There were no secret mantras, no expensive sacrifices and indeed no difficult as in the Upanishads." Buddhism insisted on virtues like charity, truthfulness, control over passion and non-injury, etc. These virtues were put into actual practice and raised the moral standard of the people. Buddhist thought exercised a profound influence on the Brahmanical religion. Idol worship in India was mainly a fruit of Buddhism. Gandhar Art is solely a Mahayana Buddhist sculpture and heralded a new era in the history of Indian Art. Besides, the monastic order was a creation of Buddhism. As N. Dutta writes "monastic institutions were the most remarkable contribution of Buddhism to Indian culture. It also developed a new awareness in the field of culture. It taught the people not to take things for granted, but to judge them no merits. Now the place of superstition was taken by logic and this promoted rationalism."

(c) Political Impact

Buddhism promoted a feeling of peace as most of the rulers who adopted Buddhism followed the policy of non-violence. The rulers began to take more interest in the welfare of the subjects.

Many rulers tried to carry message of Buddhism to far and wide and thereby developed friendship with other countries. It helped in the promotion of International peace. With its emphasis on non-violence, Buddhism boosted the cattle wealth of the country. The path taken by the Buddhist mission to foreign countries opened new trade contact between India and foreign countries. The non-alignment movement over its origin to the Buddhist doctrine of non-injury and non-violence.

(d) Cultural Impact

The most important contribution of Buddhism to Indian life was made in the realm of architecture and sculpture. Buddhism revolutionized the architecture of India. It remained a powerful social force in India for almost one thousand five hundred years to exercise great influence on the people and their culture. It was not merely an Indian tradition. By transcending the frontier of India it could go to far off countries like Sri Lanka, Myanmar, China, Japan, Indonesia and Cambodia, etc., thereby it could become a world religion.

Buddhism created great movements which served as landmarks of Indian culture. The monuments of Ajanta, Ellora, Bagh, Saranath have immortalized Indian values.

Buddhist literature like the Jataka Stories, scriptures like the Ptakas, Philosophy of Nagarjuna, asvaghosh the logic of Mahayana Buddhism, the tantrik texts of Vajrajyana, the chronicles like Mahavamsa and Deepavamsa are of profound importance. Buddhism produced great philosophers. The Buddhist enters of learning of Nalanda, Takshasila, Ratnagiri, etc., were internationally famous drawing scholars from different parts of the world.

Buddhist Art of Gandhara and Mathura have their everlasting value in culture. Buddhism exercised influence in the culture of South East Asia, China and Japan, etc. For making Buddhism a world religion, credit must go to Ashok, Kaniska and Harshavardhan. Their efforts could spread Indian culture abroad. The isolation of India was broken. For outside countries having Buddhist followers, India become a holy land.

Thus, Buddhism exercised a profound influence on Indian culture. Its unique contributions in the field of religion, art, sculpture, language and literature enriched Indian culture to a considerable extent.

4.6 Cultural Attainment during Gupta Period

The Gupta period heralded a new era in the cultural history of India and constituted the beacon light of ancient Indian culture. After the break down of the Kushan empire, the political solidarity of India was devastated. During this turmoil, the Guptas, a family of uncertain origins, began to build up an empire from the beginning of the 4th century A.D. The so-called imperial Guptas ruled from Pataliputra over the Magadhas empire. With the rise of the Guptas, a new era was dawned which is popularly known as the classical period of Indian civilization. The rule of the Guptas for more than two centuries is considered as one of the most formative era and glorious epochs in the history of India. Four important rulers of the Gupta empire namely Chandragupta-I, Samudragupta, Chandragupta-II and Kumargupta-I changed the fate of India and brought glory and fame through their endeavour. It was during the Gupta era, that the Indian intellect reached its high watermark in several fields and more particularly in the field of art, science and literature. Indian culture and civilization reached a unique stage of development and it left its deep impression upon succeeding ages. Due to the massive cultural development, the Gupta age is known as the Golden age in the history of ancient India. The factors contributing to the growth of culture are political unity, absence of foreign invasion, ideal administrative system, internal peace and prosperity, abundant wealth religious toleration and above all trade and cultural contact with foreign countries. The Gupta were avowed champions of Brahmanical religion and Hindu culture. With their rise to power, the bad days of Hinduism seemed to be over. The imperial Guptas ushered in an era of cultural revival which included revival of Hindu rule and culture and the Sanskrit language. The dedication and work culture of the Gupta rulers paved to way for all development.

The cultural attainment during imperial Guttas may be discussed under the following heads:

(a) Education and Literature

The Gupta rulers tried their level best of imbibe the spirit of creativity. Poetry and prose in Sanskrit were encouraged through royal patronage. The Gupta age witnessed a dominance of Sanskrit. It was recognized as the state language and the language of culture knowledge of Sanskrit become a symbol of culture. During the Gupta age, there was the revival of Sanskrit literature. The beautiful Sanskrit in Kavya style which was in the process of growth prior to the Gupta era reached its maturity during 4th and 5th century A.D. The political unification, peace, stability and prosperity under the Guptas compiled with their rich and liberal patronage to Sanskrit resulted in the flourishing of Sanskrit literature in all its branches.

Respect to scholarship was the unique characteristics of Gupta rulers. The courts of the Gupta kings were adorned by learned scholars. Harisen was the poet laureate of Samudragupta and author of Allahabad prasasthi. Samudragupta himself was a poet of repute for which he was known as Kaviraja or the prince of poets. The court of Chandragupta-II was adorned by a galaxy of nine celebrated scholars known as Navaratna or the nine gems. They were Dhanwantri, Kshyapanaka, Amarsingh, Sanku, Betalbhatt, Ghatkarpar, Kalidas, Barhamhir and Bararuchi. Kalidas was the towering genius of the age. As R.C. Majumdar writes "Kalidas was the most brilliant luminary in the literary firmament of the Gupta age who had shed luster on the whole Sankrit literature. He is by common consent the greatest poet and dramatist that ever lived in India, and popularity through the ages." In his poetry and drama, one finds a unique combination of knowledge and sentiment, artistry and sincerity, morality and idealism. Kalidas was a versatile genius. His works include Raghuvansa, Kumar Sambham, Meghadutta, Ritu Samhar of his plays mention may be made about Malavikagri Mitr, Vikramarvashi and Shakuntala. Vivid portrature compact and elegant expression and an ardent love of nature mark his poem and drama. A part from Kalidas, a few more literary talents adorned the Gupta ages. They are Visakhadatta, Sandrak and Bhairavi. In addition to poetry and drama, the Gupta age had attained perfection in prose writing too. Of these works, *Panchatantra* written by Vishnu Sharma is a collection of fables which assumes a pride of place even today. The *Amarkash* is a famous Sanskrit dictionary of words compiled by Amar Sinha. Vatsayan's *Kamasutra* and Bharatuhari's *Sringar Satak* are two commendable works of the age. The most famous philosophers were the Buddhist philosophers such as Vasubandhu, Asanga, Dignag, and Buddha ghash. Religious books, puranas, smritis, Ramayan and Mahabharat were also given final touches during the reign of Guptas. The famous Buddhist book *Diparasma* and *Mahavamsa* were compiled during the age.

(b) Science, Astrology and Medicine

In the field of science, the highest development was achieved in mathematics, astronomy and chemistry. The decimal fraction and the principle of cipher also originated during this period. Aryabhatta and Varah Mihir were the famous scientist and mathematician respectively. Varah Mihir was a scientist for excellence who propounded the principle relating to Arithmetic, Geometry and Algebra. He was the greatest astrologer of his age. *Brihat Samhita* and *Brihat Jakaka* were his great masterpieces of the time. Brahmagupta was another famous astrologer of the age who composed *Brahma Siddhanta*. Gupta age also witnessed the development in the field of Ayurvedashastra. Sushruta was a prominent physician of ancient India and he belonged to this period.

The science of metallurgy also made good progress during this period. A Buddha image found at Sultanganj near Bhagalpur is an indication of high degree of proficiency in metal work. A gigantic copper image of Buddha placed at Nalanda is a testimony to it. The famous iron pillar at Mehrauli is the best evidence of the striking metallurgical progress of the period.

(c) Art, Architecture, Sculpture and Painting

The Gupta reached a high degree of sophistication in the domain of fine arts. Coins, cave dwellings and their frescoes, remounts of temples and monasteries terracotta plaques and figurines and various images made of stone provide the greatest manifestation of excellence of the artistry and workmanship of Gupta age. Elegance refinement and balance are the outstanding features of Gupta art. The heart and soul of the artists of the Gupta period were purely Indian. The main characteristics of the Gupta art are Indianization, simplicity, spirituality and aesthetic presentation.

The buildings, temples, pillars and stupas, etc., constructed in those days were beautiful, attractive and displayed a mark of excellent workmanship. The two prominent features of the Gupta architecture were, it was free from foreign influence and stone was used in place of bricks. Many temples were constructed during this period. The temples were built on a raised platform with the flight of steps of all sides. There was a Garbhagriha in the temple in which the statue was installed. Round the Garbhagriha, there was the Pradakhina Patha. The early Gupta temples were flat roofed and later on Sikhars were found on the temples, four pillars were constructed on the four corners of the temples, the outer wall was simple, but the door way was well decorated with sculpture. The beautiful Dasavtar temple at Deogarh (Jhansi), the picturesque Vishnu temple at Tigowa (Jabalpur), the exquisite Bhitargaon temple at Kanpur, the Siva temple at Bhumra are the finest specimens of their architectural achievements. The Buddhist caves at Ellora and Ajanta, the Jain caves at Badami and Aihole and the Hindu caves at Udaygiri (near Bhopal) are the indication of architectural greatness.

The Art of sculpture reached its classical height in the Gupta period. The Sarnath statue of Buddha, Buddha statue at Sultanganj, erect Buddha statue at Mathura are the most remarkable. A number of brahmanical images of Vishnu, Shiva and Surya have been finely carved in this age. The Siva Parvati relief at Kasam, the Ramayan panels at Deogarh, Vishnu reclining on Ananta at Deogarh, the image of Ganga from Bisnagar, the Varath image at Udayagiri rank among best specimens of Hindu sculpture of this age.

Painting also reached at its perfectness in this age. The best specimens of the art of painting of this age are preserved in the wall frescoes of Ajanta caves at Hyderabad and the Bagh caves in Gwalior state. The Ajanta paintings have great importance in the history of Indian painting. The paintings of Gupta period left no sphere of human life untouched.

The coins of the Gupta age are the best specimen of numismatic art. The Gupta emperors issued coins of gold and silver to artistic taste. They are excellent in shape, names and pictures engraving of kings, queens and animal are quite artistic. As P. Browon states, "The excellent modelling of the kin's figure the skillful delineation of features, the careful attention to details and the general ornateness of the design in the best specimens constitute this type as the highest expression of Gupta numismatic art." Thus, the Gupta age marked the progress of India in every field of life. The ideal administrative system revival of Brahmanism, adoption of secularism, priceless literature and useful science, growth of trade and commerce were such achievements that have provided the period a distinct place in ancient India. The liberal patronage of the Gupta rulers, a strong feeling for nationalism and love of learning all helped to build up the prosperity of the Guptas. This showed the spirit of the day and that is why the liberal Hindu culture spread to foreign countries without any barriers.

4.6.1 Golden Age Nomenclature

During Gupta age, so many distinctions were achieved in several fields. So historians rightly designated it as the golden age of Indian history. The factors contributing to this status can be discussed under the following heads:

(a) Imperial Unity

The most important achievement of the Gupta period was the establishment of an imperial Government with a powerful capital centre at Pataliputra headed by the Gupta emperor. The emperor was supported by a vast army and a powerful bureaucracy. The imperial Guptas circulated an era of their own. All their feudatories adopted the Gupta era for any reckoning in the records and inscriptions. The circulation of Gupta gold coins in the empire was another manifestation of the imperial authority.

(b) Monarchical Government

The Gupta monarchy was hereditary. It was based upon ancient Indian tradition. His powers, functions, responsibilities, status and ideals were as per Hindu tradition. He could bear high sounding titles like Maharajadhiraj, Paramesvara, and Chakravarti, etc. His led military expeditions for conquests and defense. He could conduct judicial administration as the highest authority. He was the personification of God and had to be obeyed by all. His royal decree had the force of law in the realm which had to be followed by governors and members of the bureaucracy. On the other hand, it was obligatory for the monarch to be benevolent. As reflected in the smritis the kings used to make assiduous efforts to muster politics, protect his subjects, cultivate fortitude and acquire leadership, otherwise he could be a failure. The kings were exponents of music, poet of high caliber and source of infinite strength and courage. The Gupta monarchs had all the qualities for successful monarchs.

The monarchs and emperors possessed supreme severing authority. Their quality of leadership, political excellence had deep impact on the social, economic and religious life of the people.

(i) Social Life

The social life of the people was prosperous and contended. It is evident from literary sources as well as from the accounts of foreign travelers like Fa-Hien, a Chinese pilgrim. According to him, the people were virtuous, rich and prosperous. The material prosperity provided impetus for cultural activities. Most of the people were vegetarians and supporters of non-violence. Criminal activities were minimal. Life was safe and smooth. There was the prevalence of the caste system, but changing of profession was allowed. The untouchables lived outside the village. They were hunters scavengers and chandals. Regarding marriage, it was observed that both Anulama and Pratiloma marriage were in vague. This was essential to absorb foreigners to Indian social system. Joint family system was prevalent in the society where father dominated the family and property was owned by males. Since a pre-puberty marriage was common, the girls consent was taken. Polygamy was common. Public life was not closed to women. They could sing and dance. Women were allowed to ride horses. Vegetarianism was a common practice. People used to take meat at festivals. Entertainment included dice playing, sports, archery, drama, music and dance. In order to know time people used to watch the movement of the sun.

(ii) Economic Life

During the Gupta rule, the people were economically prosperous. Agriculture and trade were the main sources of earning. There were other professions like carpentry, smothery, cobbler, stone cutter, weaver, potter and oil man, etc. Traders guilds were organizing the activities of groups of professionals and artisans. Some people were also engaged in small scale industries. Most of the people were engaged in excavating, caves, sculpting, navigation, arm making, furniture and chariot making and ship-building, etc.

Apart from market places in villages or in a town, there were ports and industrial centres, mining and melting areas where large number of people congregated for work and job. Ports were doing overseas trading activities with Greek, Roman and Arab traders. The periplus of the Erythrean sea gives a vivid account of India's sea borne trade. There was enough evidence to prove that India had trade relationship with neighbouring countries and the balance of trade was in favour of India.

(iii) Religious Life

Religion was the guiding factor of all cultural activities of the Gupta period. The Gupta rulers encouraged religious freedom. Among several prevailing religions beliefs, social harmony existed. Jainism and Buddhism existed with Brahmanical faiths. The rulers respected all religions. They were liberal and secular. Under royal patronage, temples and shrines were being built and maintained. Large number of images of Jain tirthankars and Budhisattvas were made as the object of worship. Monasteries and vihars were being built by wealthy persons. They also used to distribute food and clothes as charity. Fa-Hien, the Chinese pilgrim has vividly described about public generosity and catholic attitudes towards religion. The Gupta emperors were liberal in granting land and endowments for Brahmans and temples. There was the practice of worshipping Hindu Gods like Vishnu, Surya and Siva. The Gupta rulers used to perform asvamedh, vajapeye, agnistome and atiratra sacrifices and issued gold coins on the occasion of celebration. These sacrifices had political and religious significance.

The tremendous achievements in the Gupta period reached the highest watermark. The cultural achievements reached its climax. The period evolved on All India norm or traditions which come to be known as classical tradition. Its achievements can be compared with Periclean age of Greece and Augustan age of Rome. The liberal patronage of Gupta rulers, a strung feeling of nationalism and love of learning helped to build up the prosperity of the Guptas. Aurobindo has rightly remarked, "Never in her history has India seen such a many sided blossom of her force in life."

4.7 Cultural Expansion: Overseas Trade and Commerce and its Impact on South East Asia

Indian culture is very old. From time immemorial the people of India had been maintaining free and intimate intercourse with the outside world. It had made in-roads to foreign lands more particularly in central Asia, Far East and South East Asia. India was a civilizing force in most of the backward countries of Asia. Assimilation was the keynote of Hindu cultural expansion. Indian culture went abroad not to destroy but to awaken wherever the Indians went they spread their own culture but at the same time absorbing the native cultural trades. Historical evidence reveals that Greeks knew about India since the days of Plato and Homer. It is a fact that Alexander's invasion of India bequeathed the resultant bonding of India's relationship with the western world. Further, the Gandhar School of art is a vital testimony of the cultural impact of India and the west. Religion had played an important role in stabilizing this relationship. Buddhism was a medium for this cultural tie. The Theravada Buddhists acted as cultural and commercial ambassadors of India in the west and even set up their own schools there.

So far trade and commerce are concerned it is found that India had contacts with the regions such as Far East and South East Asia. Iconographic representations of India are found in remote areas like Korea, Cambodia, Thailand, Laos, Myanmar, Sri Lanka, Malaysia and Indonesia. The social life and culture of these regions bear the indelible imprints of Indian impact. Literary sources also substantiate the fact. Among these, mention can be made of the Buddhist Jatakas, Brihat Katha Manjari, Katha Sarit Sagar, Katha Sarit Samagrah, Katha Kosh and the like. These speak of India's expeditions to and dominance over the region in general and subarna bhumi in particular. A sense of adventure, motives for material progress through external trade, the pan Indian missionary zeal of Indian ambassadors to these regions constituted the basis for Indian hegemony over South East and South East Asia.

The trade, commerce and cultural relationship of India with China, Sri Lanka, Myanmar and South East Asia are discussed below.

4.7.1 India and China

The ancient name of China was Champa. It was a Hindu kingdom having close cultural relationship with India. Amaravati was its Capital. History reveals that fact that the rulers of this Kingdom were patrons of Shaivism and they constructed Shiva temples. One of the Shiva lingham named Bhadreswar Swami still exists their. The rulers of Champa were very much fascinated by the Hindu philosophy of India. Apart from Hindu temples, there are some Buddhist shrines. The sea route to China from India was via Sri Lanka and Java. Fa-Hien returned to China by this route. I-tzing came to India by this route and reached Tamralipti in 673 A.D. This route was considered straighter than the route through Central Asia. The influence of Hindu (India) is much in evidence in the culture and language of China. The trade relationship between India and China was very much stable. In 745 A.D. Wang-Ta-Yuan wrote that the cost of living in India, particularly in Orissa was so less that Chinese traders preferred to settle down in Orissa rather than to return to China. Rice was sold very cheap at the rate of 46 baskets per cowrie in

Orissa. Ptolemy of the 2nd century states that there was an active trade between India and China. China imported precious stones, ivory, pepper, drugs, betel nuts and the textile fabrics of the then Kalinga. The China Silk called Chinam Suna was in heavy demand in Indian market. Thus the socio-economic and cultural bond between India and China was very strong.

4.7.2 India and Sri Lanka

Information revealed from Ramayan says that India had certain relationship with Sri Lanka. There was a close and cordial relationship between India and Sri Lanka during the ancient period. According to Mahavamsa, Vijay was the first king of Sri Lanka. He was the son of Simhala after whom the island country has been named. Emperor Ashok, with view to spread Buddhism there at Sri Lanka deputed his son Mahendra and daughter Sanghamitra to Sri Lanka along with eight families of Kalinga. Dathavamsa mentions the transfer of Buddha's tooth relic from Orissa to Sri Lanka by Hemalata and Danta Kumar. Mahendra IV, King of Sri Lanka married a Kalingan princess. Further king Vijay Bahu of Sri Lanka married the Kalingan princess Trilok Sundari. In 6th century, the royal couple of Kalinga paid a state visit to Sri Lanka. The Kalingan sailors had frequent voyages to Sri Lanka which signifies the strategic trade relationship between two countries.

4.7.3 India and Burma or Myanmar

The relationship between India and Myanmar was very close and rewarding. On account of its close proximity to Bengal and prevailing land route through Kohima, large numbers of Indians have been visiting the land in the early days of history. Ashok's son Sona and daughter Uttara were the first to cross Kohima and enter Myanmar for the spread of Buddhism. Buddhaghose, another great Buddhist scholar also visited Myanmar to promote Buddhism there. In course of time, Myanmar emerged as a stronghold of Hinayana Buddhism. Sri Lanka's Buddhist preachers also visited Myanmar because of the frequent contact through the sea route. Indian thought, art and culture made rapid headway in Myanmar. Hindu influences over Myanmar can be seen through archaeological remains there as well as the names of royal dignitaries that are Kalingan and South Indian in nature. These are found at Thatun, Pegu and Prome. Some raigned stupas have been found there. A manuscript written in Telugu script was found in lower Myanmar. The kings used the Indian names like Barman and Kisram. A number of pagodas, temples, bells and huge gongs, images of Buddha, sculptural representation of Buddhist Jataka stories and the life story of Buddha are found there. The royal garden in Rangoon, the capital of Burma (Myanmar) was named Srikshetra. Further the prevailing Buddhism and monks wearing yellow robes remind us the deep cultural contact between India and Myanmar over several centuries.

4.7.4 India and South East Asia

India's cultural and political relationship with the region of South East Asia is an interesting saga of relations dating back to pre-Christian times. The sailors and traders of India laid the foundation of this which was later cemented by cultural and political connections. A Japanese legend reveals that the Kalingan kings sent 2000 families of Java to settle there. Java's other name is Holiny which is derived from Kalinga. According to a Chinese record immigrants from Kalinga went to Java and established there a principality called Kalinga in western Java. The existence of Indianized Kingdom in Java and Borneo is attested by inscriptions from the 5th century onwards. Hindu colonies were established in Java. Various inscriptions found there exhibit that the Hindu culture was predominant in Java. By the beginning of the 2nd century A.D. a Hindu kingdom was established in Java and its king Dev Barman sent an embassy to China in 132 A.D. Fa-Hien, the great Chinese piligrim who was in India returned to China by the sea route and stayed in Java for five months. He described the country as a stronghold of a Brahmanical religion. It is also revealed that Ramayan and Mahabharat are found most popular among Javanese.

Borneo also gives a vivid testimony of the cultural relationship of India. The island of Borneo is situated in the East of Sumatra. The oldest inscriptions and antiquities, pointing the Hindu cultural influence in Borneo were discovered at Muara Kaman. Two standing Buddha images of the Gupta style have been discovered at Sambas. The archaeological remnants on the bank of the river Kapuas indicated that the Hindus from India colonized west Borneo. The discovery of the stone images of the Brahmanical Gods in a cave exhibits the flourshing state of Hindu religion in Borneo.

Similarly, history rewards the establishment of a Hindu kingdom in Bali in the 4th century A.D. The people of Bali are very much proud of their Hindu ancestral. The Kaundinya Kshatriyas were instrumental in establishing a rich, prosperous and vibrant Hindu kingdom there. It is evident from the rituals performed by the people of Bali that there was a strong cultural and socio-economic bond between India and Bali.

It is also revealed that in the 2nd or 3rd century A.D. in the central region of Siam (Thailand) on Indian kingdom named Dvara Vati was founded by the mons. In course of time it flourished as a gigantic Indian colony. Indian culture spread through this kingdom and to the neighbouring kingdoms. Buddhism spread to this kingdom by the Sri Lankan Buddhists and Hinduism entered into it through the missitionaries. Therefore both Hinduism and Buddhism made their impact on the Siamese life. The Brahmanical and Buddhist religious literature and art considerably influenced the Thai language, literature, art and social institutions. Many of the Hindu rituals, have become a part and parcel of the Thai customs and rituals. Siamese language bears the influence of Pali and the script was borrowed from South India. There are images of Buddha, ruins of stupas and monasteries in various parts of Siam. Siamese people are found to use Indian names. The Siamese literature also reflects the stories from Indian epics and puranas more particularly Ramayan and Mahabharat. They have adopted Hindu customs and Sanskaras. They also observe Dasserah festival to commemorate Ram's victory over Ravan, the Demon king of Sri Lanka.

Thus, the period from pre-Christian times till 15th century A.D. is highly significant not only for the growth of economic and political influence of India in regions of the South and South East Asia but also for the spread of culture through art, epics, social life and tradition and through Hindu, Buddhist pan

Indianism. The expansion of Hindu civilizations speaks for its once dynamic vigour which traversed oceans, cleared swamps and jungles and established its own culture and civilization. Thus, a greater India was established by a gentle fusion of races, by richly endowing the original inhabitants with the spiritual heritage of India. As R.C. Majumdar states, "In the early centuries of the Christian era, the Indians built an extensive cultural empire in Central and South Eastern Asia and within a few succeeding centuries, it flourished luxuriantly and existed for nearly a thousand years.

4.8 Hellenistic Impact on Art and Architecture

Hellenism means Greek culture. The word has been derived from the island of Hellas referring to Greece. The people of Hellas and their culture was known as Hellenism. The people of Greece came to know about India first through Persia. The story is as such Indus valley was a part of Darius is empire. He deputed a mercenary named skylax to explore the mouth of river Indus. Skylax was the first Greek to visit India and to make a sea voyage through Red Sea. Thereafter, Indus valley was annexed to the Persian Empire and Darius I made it his 29th province from which he got an annual tribute of 360 talents of gold dust and in return supplied some soldiers. The cost of gold dust could be equivalent of nine crores of rupees. After Persia was destroyed by Alexander in 370 B.C. (Battle of Arbela), traffic between India and the west slowed down. Punjab gained independence. But two centuries of Persian rule over Punjab and the adjacent region had a tremendous impact. India adopted the Kharosti script (witting from the right to left) and introduced it in the official records. As per the description of Maghasthenes, the Mauryas lived in Persian style. They lived in seclusion protected by guards. Their public appearance was rare. Chandragupta Maurya had adopted the Persian hair washing ceremony. The Ashokan pillars the lion capital, the loti form design at the top were initiations from Persia. Stone was used for building instead of wood. Ashok's system of propagating Rajadharma through royal edicts or inscription was a Persian method.

According to Historians, ancient Greece was the fountain head of European civilization. Alexander, the mighty king of Macedonia in Greece was the first to make the orient and occident meet. The invasion of Alexander was a high watermark in the cultural history of India, but it left very little impact on Indian civilization. Alexander was a conqueror but he was never a propagator of culture. The downfall of the Maurya empire led to this advent of the foreign invaders (Indo Bactrian) through the northwestern gateway of Northern India. This second Greek conquest of India was more important for India this the first one made by Alexander. The year long rule of the Greeks offered ample opportunities for cultural exchanges. Hence, the empire of Alexander vanished but its legacy was carried on by a civilization (Indo Bacterian or Greek) on the Model of the ancient Greek civilization which is known as Hellenistic civilization. The Greeks called themselves Hellens, and the civilization that marked the glorious age of Greece is called Hellenic civilization. But the civilization which grew around the empire of Alexander particularly Asia Minor and Persia, etc. and embodied the elements of oriental culture is called the Hellenistic civilization. The penetration of the Indo Greeks influence the art and culture of ancient India to a great extent. The impact of Greek culture on Indian culture is an interesting story. The nature and degree of the impact of Greek culture on Indian culture need not be over-emphasized, one school of thought suggests that Greek impact on Indian culture was quite insignificant. Indians learnt from Greek how to make coins and the Gandhar School of Art was very much the outcome of Greek tradition.

4.8.1 Gandhar School of Art

The invasion of Alexander to India in 326 B.C. bequeathed legacy to the Indo greeks, Indo Scythians and the Kushan Kings to rule over its north eastern parts. It was under their patronage that a remarkable style of sculpture emerged which is popularly known as Greco-Buddhist or Gandhar School of Art. This school was the product of the synthesis of Hellenistic, west Asiatic and native techniques. Greek and Roman ideas were skillfully employed. In restructuring the Gandhar sculpture which represented Indian culture in western garb. The theme is overwhelmingly Buddhist which was extended over a vast area from Taxila to Swat valley now in Pakistan and covered a large area in Afghanistan. The Gandhar artists specialized in patraying the Buddha in three different postures—the Sthanka or standing Buddha, the asan or seated Buddha and the sayan or recumbent Buddha describing the mahapari nirvana. The buddhas are seen in different Mudras. The Gandhar School of Art not only accupied a significant place in the history of Indian Art, but also achieved a greater success by becoming the progenitor of the Buddhist Art of Chinese, Turkestan, Mangolia, Korea and Japan. Gandhar is located in the north western part of the Indian subcontinent on the banks of the river Indus. It was ruled by the Achaemenids of Iran in the 6th century B.C. Later it was occupied by the Greeks, Mauryas, Sakas, Pellavas and Kushans. As a result, this place produced a mixed culture. Its art which was mainly Buddhist was profoundly influenced by Hellenistic art. The Gandhar movement was described as Greco-Buddhist. The Greek architecture also influenced existing Indian architecture. The artists working in the Gandhar region made the statue of Buddha in the model of Greek God Apollo. The image of Yaksha Kuvera was an imitation of Greek God Zeus. Large Boddhisattva images were made in the Kusan period and afterwords. Kaniska took keen interest in the art of architecture. In important cities of his kingdom he constructed many beautiful buildings, lofty towers, splendid monasteries and attractive stupas. He laid the foundation of the towns of Purushapura, and Kanshikapura, etc. He erected a great relic tower at Purushapura, his capital city, the superstructure of carved wood in 13 satyrs to a height of at least 400 feet. It was surrounded by a mighty iron pinnacle. He built a magnificent monastery by the side of the tower which becomes famous throughout the Buddhist world. The Gandhar Art is found in the reigns of Taxila, Bamiyan, etc. They consist mainly of Buddha images and reliefs. They are either of stone or stucco. Most of the remains have been preserved in the museum at Peshawar and Lahore. In Afghanistan, all the vestiges of Gandhar Art have been destroyed by Taliban Government.

The important of Gandhar Art is the anthropomorphic representation of Buddha. In Hinayan Buddhism, Buddha was not worshipped in human form, but it stated with the Gandhar School of Art. Several experiments were made to make the realistic image of Buddha, but the physical defails and the ornamentations did not tally with the philosophical concept of Buddhism. So, the Gandhar Buddha did not receive wide acceptance. It was a Greek tradition not in consonance with Indian ideal. In spite of the technical skill and love for the details, the Gandhar tradition was rejected as of foreign origin. Instead of Gandhara Buddha, the product of Mathura school of Art was found suitable to Indian Buddhists.

4.8.2 Mathura School of Art

During the region of Kaniska, the Mathura School of Art emerged as a new school of Art. The sculptures during this period were very much inspired by Mahayana sect of Buddhism and deserve fulsome praise for creating the new representation of Buddha. The fabric chosen by the Mathura artists for making images and statues was the sported red Sikri sandstone. The artists of this school not only constructed the image of Lord Buddha but also excelled in making the statues of Jain tirthankars along with Brahmanical Gods and Goddesses. They also handled secular subjects with dexterity.

The fragmented portraits of an enthroned king Vima Kadphises and a standing king Kaniska were the two most important creations of the Mathura School of Art. The massive Vima Kadphises is headless completely shattered across the knees and broken through the waist. Evident is the regal presence manifested by a majestic left arm streched to the waist and a right arm resting on the upper chest. The high boots upto the knees and the long flowing tunic clearly indicate the figure of Kaniska. The two lions flanking the thrown and an elevated foot rest confirm the image's royal authority. The towering and the headless figure of Kaniska carved of the distinctive red sandstone is also imbued with stylistic characteristics. The statue of Kaniska is identified by an inscription in Kharostha that was cut across the bottom of the mantle which reads, the great king, the king of kings, the son of God, Kaniska. The figure shows the great monarch. Apart from this many other royal Kushan figures were found in and around Mathura. The masterpiece of Kushan sculpture at Mathura was to be witnessed in the seated figure of the Buddha of the mid-2nd century, carved from the local red sandstone, the figure is seated on a lion throne and is an excellent example of an entirely Indian Buddha. Unlike the Gandhar Buddha having the Greco-Roman influence on their drapery and countenance, the Mathura Buddha is off not presented with togalike sanghatt. Dressed as a true Indian, in a transparent muslin garment that covers only one shoulder and gathers in small ringed folds along the upper left arm, the Mathuras Buddha appears truly in Indian disposition. This is definitely a distinctive feature of Mathura Art.

In spite of Somany upheavals all down the ages the Mathura school of Art has survived and its inherent Indianness has reached its culminating expression in the supreme development of the Buddha image during the classical period of imperial Guptas.

4.9 Impact of Islam on Indian Life

Prophet Mohammad propagated Islam in the 7th century A.D. in Arabia. Mecca and Medina were the two holy cities where Islam was first proclaimed. It was a monotheistic religion where Allah is considered as the all powerful God. The religion was called Islam and its followers were called the Muslims. Islam came to India in three waves. The first wave of Islamic surge into India was 712 A.D., when the Arab Moslot of lems invaded the Sind region near the mouth of the Indus, but the Arabs failed to push far inland and their influence in India was very much negligible. The second Islamic wave came in about 1000 A.D. when the Turkish Moslems attacked India from their bases in Afghanistan. This raid continued unabated for four centuries causing great loss to lives and property of people. The result was the establishment of numerous Muslim kingdoms in northern India. The third Muslim were struck in 1500 A.D. with the advent of the Moughals.

In the initial stage, the Muslim had to face a lot of challenge which this never expected. They had to put of with a population having altogether a different religion and a different culture. The Hindus in India were not in a position to accept all that the Muslims had brought with them and Muslims were not willing to this their identify. They were strong and stubborn to establish Islam in India. In this context E.B. Havella says, Islam seized her political capitals, controlled her military force and appropriated her revenues but India caring what she cherished most—her intellectual empire and her soul was never subdued. The Muslim conquerors who invaded India were highly civilized. They had own distinct culture and religion. Their conquest of India was bound tô affect Hindu culture and religion. As Tarachand remarks, "Not only did Hindu religion, Hindu Art, Hindu literature and Hindu science absorbed Muslim elements, but the very spirit of Hindu culture and the very stuff of Hindu mind were altered, and the Muslims reciprocated by responding to the changes in every department of life."

As the Islam grew as a dominant political power in India, the country was confronted with a new religion and a new culture. It is a fact that the civilization of India is very old and is based on the principle of unity in diversity. Indian civilization has absorbed the culture and civilization of all races invading India and they have settled here losing their identity. They include Greeks, Sakes, Kushans and Huns. But the Muslims invading India had a zeal and commitment to spread their religion and establish themselves here. They were culturally so advanced that Indian culture could not absorb them. Though the Muslims had conquered wide parts of India, they failed to convert large number of Hindus. Both Hindus and Muslims lived together. There developed a spirit of harmony, fellow feeling and cooperation between the two communities. In course of time, Islamic culture and tradition intermingled freely with the ancient Indian or Hindu culture and had become acceptable to the Indian society. Islam as a socio-cultural force had become deep-seated on the Indian soil, for it had undergone a thorough idealization. The regional Moslem monarchs and the aristocracy were by and large Indian in blood, thought and attitude and they considered themselves Indian Moslems, forgetting their origin. Thus a rich tradition initiated by the Moslem rulers was the patronizing zeal for scholars, artists and intellectuals without religious discrimination and this had a far-flung and large term impact on the future development of Indian life. The spirit of harmony, toleration and cooperation were found expression in the attempts of some Moslems to assimilate Hindu customs, religions beliefs and observances while living in Hindu environment. As Tarachand writes "the concept of the unity of God is a gift of the Islam. Hindu philosophy, Nyaya, the doctrine of karma and transmigration of soul influenced many Muslim scholars." There was a linguistic synthesis resulting out of Hindu Muslim contact.

4.9.1 Impact of Islam on Hindu Society

Islam had its compact on Hinduism in two fields. It made the Hindus more orthodox and conservative and the Hindu caste rules became more rigid for fear of conversion. It also gave an impetus to liberal reformatory movement in Hinduism. The Hindus and Muslims came in contact with each other by sheer necessity and these influenced each other irrespective of difference of their religions faith. In brought about certain favourable changes in the style of living of the people. The impact of Islam brought changes in the social custom of Hindus, which was quite contrary to the Hindu way of life. The Purdah system, seclusion of women unknown to the Hindus was introduced into the Hindu society. Child marriage was introduced in the society. Early marriages (Pre-puberty marriage) of the Hindu girls become the fashion of the day in view of avoiding their kidnapping by the Muslims. The condition of the Hindu women deteriorated considerably. They safeguarded their honour against the Muslims, the custom of Jauhar and sati were prevalent. The missionary zeal of Islam aiming at converting the Hindus forced them to be orthodox in outlook. Hindu nobles and rulers adopted the Muslim etiquette.

The impact of Islam on Indian life may be discussed as under:

(a) Language and Literature

The history of India during 711–1526 A.D. is witnessed great literary activities in almost all the languages of India.

A number of books and religion, philosophy and dramas were produced during this period. One of the most important aspects of the period was the preparation of historical texts which was not given due attentions. The Muslim contribution to Indian literature was not in considerable. The most impressionable influence of Islam on Indian life was the growth and development of regional language and concomitantly healthy literature. While Sanskrit was still in vague, Arabic and Persian were patronized by the Islamic rulers of Delhi. Persian was made the court language by the Turko Afghan rulers. Though Arabic was the religious language of the Muslims, the Muslim rulers in India preferred Persian language. It was considered as the language of aristocracy. Amir Khusrav, Amir Hasan Dehivi and Badr-Uddin were the most famous Persian poets. Amir Khusrav was a versatile genius. He was called Tuti-i-Hind or the PARROT OF INDIA. He was proficient in Persian literature. He was the first Muslim poet who wrote verse in Hindi. He called it Hindivi. *Mulla-ul-Anwar, Laila Majunu, Tarikh-i-Alahi* and *Khazainul-Futuh* were his important works. As Iswari Prasad states, "He was a gifted bard and singer. The variety of subjects and the marvelous ease and grace with which he describes human passions and emotions and senses of love and war place him among the greatest poets of all time."

Equally efficient and prolific was Amir Hasan Dehivi. He was called the Saadi of India. Badr-Uddin, Maulana, Umrav and Sahib-ud-din were great poets under the Tugluk rulers. Minhaj-us-siraj, Ml-Beruni, Hazam Nizami, Zia-uddin Barani and Tarikb-i-Firoksahi were great historians of the time.

One of the most significant outcome of Hindu Muslim coexistence was the synthesis of language. There was a curious admixture of Arabic, Turkish words with words of Indian origin. Urdu was the most volatile and typical language. There was a cultural exchange between Hindus and Muslims and both influenced one another. Amir Khusrav, Malik Muhammad Jayasi and Kutuban wrote an Hindu culture and Hindu writer Rai Bhanmal wrote on Persian language. The Muslim rulers of Bengal and Lucknow were great patrons of Bengali and Hindi. Muslim influence on Hindi language, grammar, Simoles and styles was an acknowledged fact. The grammatical structure of Urdu was essentially that of Hindu. The Muslim rule also saw the advancement of Sanskrit literature. Ramanuja wrote his commentaries on *Brahma Sutra, Jayadev, Gita Govinda, Rajatarangini*, etc.

(b) Food and Dress

After the advent of Muslims to India, the food habit and dress pattern underwent a radical transformation. Though non-vegetarian food was common and popular in India, delicacies like Pulau, biriyani, and kebab were introduced by Muslims in India and the Hindus accepted them without any hesitation. A general attitudinal change is observed when one analyses the change in the dress pattern of Indians. The Muslims in India introduced dresses like, Kurta, Salwar, Pajama and Lungi. These dresses replaced the traditional dhoti, chaddar, saree and choli.

(c) Dance and Music

Indian Classical Music and Dance underwent great changes through the contact of Muslim singers and musicians. With the merger of Indian Veena with the Iranian Tambra emerged one the sweetest and melodious string instrument, the Sitar. The Hindu mridanga was replaced by the Dugi and Tabla introduced by Muslims. These become very much popular among Indian dancer and musicians. Dugi and Tabla assume much prominence today. Today no music whether vocal or string or dance is complete without the 'Taal and Laya' of the dugi and tabla. Different Rags and classical vocal music underwent subtle and intricate changes by coming into contact with Muslim rulers. The ragas malhar and Todi, with fine changes by Tansen were termed Mian-ki-malhar and Mian-ki-Todi and today they assume the status of original ragas. The Kathak dance become the recognized dance in the courts and it acquired popularity among the common people. The dance from underwent a bifurcation by developing into the Lucknow style and the Jainpuri style. Thumari, Tarun, Ghazal and Geet were great contributions of Muslims to Indian classical music. Muslim exponents of music were highly influenced by the Indian Dhrupad, Dhanmor, Tuppa, Kajri and Bhajans. The Quwwalis song by the quwwals in the mazhars of the sufi saints acquired a great popularity in India. Several saints of Bhakti cult and Sufis also heaped the promotion of music. Sarangder wrote the sangit Ratnakar which is regarded as the encyclopedia of Indian music.

(d) Development of Secularism

Most of the rulers strongly felt that mutual harmony, respect and cooperation can make life worth living in India. Secularist like Akbar tried to promote the secular spirit. Some Muslim schools made serious attempt to translate Indian scriptures and to understand them well. Islamic saints made a deep study of yoga and Vedanta. Hindu astronomers borrowed some technical terms from Muslim astronomers. They adopted Muslim calculation of longitude and latitude and accepted some items of Islamic calendar.

(e) Art and Architecture

In the field of Art and Architecture, a structural change was brought in through the exchange of idea between two communities. When the Muslim empire was established formally they wanted to spread their culture which was reflected in their Art and architecture. The rulers imported experienced builders and craftsmen to India from Persia. The tradition that they brought was based on their accumulated experience of centuries. The two traditions were brought together and were destined to build as a new type of Islamic architecture. The Muslims introduced massive and extensive buildings and masques spherical domes, arches, tall minarets, open courtyards, pillared caves, huge wall sets. The Muslim rulers used materials of destroyed Hindu temples and places, etc. They employed Indian craftsmen of high caliber and excellent craftsmanship. As a result, there was a synthesis of Hindu and Muslim system of architecture. The styles of architecture assumed three forms—Imperial or Delhi style, provincial style and Hindu architecture. The Muslim rulers introduced the arch, dome, minaret, and window. The Muslim rulers introduced the arch, dome, minaret, window screws and imposing facades. The Muslims adopted the Hindu technique to make their structure superb and strong.

The fort of Kumbal Garh, Jai Stambha and the Victory Pillar of Chittor in Rajasthan are examples of their craftsmanship and architectural skill. The significant impression of the Islamic style of architecture is also found from Tajmahal, the Red Fort of Delhi and the palace at Fatehpur Sikri. The saracenic architecture laid emphasis on splendor and form. Indians tried to have a synthesis between the two powerful traditions of blending Muslim structure with Hindu decoration. As Tarachand says, the craftsmanship, ornamental richness and general design remained largely Hindu, the arcuted form, plain domes, smooth faced walls and spacious interiors were Muslim super impositions. Such synthesis can be seen not only in palaces, gateways, and other great monuments, but also in houses, bathing ghats and places of worship and religions. In the field of art and architecture, the sultanate period, has its own significance for which it is described as the period of transitional changes in the Indian art.

4.10 Socio-Religious Reform Movement

The advent of Islam and its aggressive policy of conversions was a great shock to Hinduism. It shattered the supremacy of Brahmans. From Multan to Bengal, from Bihar to Tamil Nadu hundreds of Hindus temples were destroyed. The Hindu idols were desecrated and places of worship were plundered ruthlessly. With the destruction of Hindu kingdom there was no patron to rebuild the temples or restore the damaged ones. Consequently, Hinduism adopted two paths for its survival. First was to withdraw to its own cell for self-preservation. It was a policy of withdrawal for conservation. Secondly, Hinduism started a process of introspections in order to rebuild itself. Many Hindu saints and reformers appeared in the scene to reform Hinduism from some of its dross. It was a positive step to face the challenges posed by Islam by reforming the Hindu faith. The reformers appeared in different parts of India, not at one time but over two to three centuries from 12th century A.D. They gave new life to Hinduism through their teachings. This is known as reform movement.

The reformers were saintly persons. They spoke to the people in their folk language to explain the message of God in a language which was easily understandable to the common men. The reform movement in Hinduism was the result of a reaction to defend itself against the onslaught of Islam. The reformers were exponents of Bhakti. The religious movement ushered by them is known as Bhakti movement. The saints of Bhakti movement denounced ritualism, sacrifices, fasting, etc., enjoined by the Brahmins. They believed in the equality of all men and the unity of God. They held that through love and devotion one could attain God. Though devotional songs one could reach the state of ecstasy and feel the presence of almighty. Many doctrines of Bhakti cult are found in the *Bhagwat Gita* from the cycle of birth and rebirth.

4.10.1 Evolution of the Concept of Bhakti

The word 'Bhakti' has been derived from the root 'Bhaj' which means to love, to adore, to serve and to honour. The philosophical base of Bhakti is as old as Vedas and finds mention in the *Rig Veda, Sambita* and *Bribadaranyaka*, *Chhanagyan Katha* and *Upanishads*. The concept Bhakti may be defined as that state of mind when all the energies of mind and all the organs of knowledge and action in one unified mental code are directed to supreme being, spontaneous like an instinct and devoid of any extraneous motives. Vedic scriptures prescribe four main paths for attaining salvation such as Bhaktiyoga, Karmayoga, Jnana Yoga and Rajyayoga. Pure Bhakti is not at all easy. It comes only when devotion is deep-rooted and the minds leaves towards God.

Islam propagated a significant message in to India which conveyed the idea of monotheism or oneness to God, social equality and no caste system, community prayer and no idol worship. It also taught a sense of pride in one's own religion. The Muslims held Prophet Mohammad and the Koran with highest veneration. A Muslim had to believe in his own religion and in no other religion. He looks at an utter contempt the followers of other religion. The Muslims believed in one common brotherhood. Some of these lessons had a salutary effect on Indian mind. He now looked towards his religion, God and community in a different way. In bringing this change in outlook the saints of

Bhakti cult were most successful. Thus Bhakti cult emerged as the consequence of the contact with Islam.

The Bhakti movement was a new approach to Hinduism. It was beset with many liberal ideas such as love and faith in one God, no caste restriction, complete equality, community prayer through Bhajan and no supremacy of the Brahmans, no superficial ceremony and direct communion between the God and his devotee. The oneness of God was there in the Philosophy of Upanishad. But it was not practiced in reality. Hindus believed God as one, the Parambrahma. He is the source of life. In the later part of the Vedic period and during Gupta period, polytheism was very much in practice. Many Gods and Goddesses were accepted to accommodate the ideas and concepts of many. The process of assimilation created scope for polytheism. But after the association with Islam, Hindu faith as monotheism was revived. Hence, this process is called religious revival or revival of the concept of monotheism.

4.10.2 Factors Responsible for the Evolution of Bhakti Movement

The following factors are responsible for the evolution and growth of Bhakti movement in India:

(a) Social inequality like rigid caste system and untouchability, exploitation and torture of the low caste people came to a breaking point. The condition of Hindu women deteriorated considerable. Due to Muslim rule slavery crept into the Hindu society. The system of slavery had always been prevalent in India, but under the influence of Islam, the system degenerated further and become inhuman. The condition of female slaves was worse. Female slaves were offered in dowry as domestic help, they were also bought by the upper strata for their pleasure in the harems. Women were treated as inferior species. The increased rigidity of the caste system produced far-reaching consequences in the society. There was a social unrest every where demanding attitudinal change in religion. Bhakti cult, during this transition assured equality before God and equal accessibility; so that social need of the time was a reform movement.

(b) People were fed up with the highly philosophical exposition of Hinduism as given by Shankaracharya and they were looking for a system which could be easily comprehended by all. Bhakti movement was a purifying movement to make Hinduism more suitable for the masses.

(c) Islam was gaining popularity for its simplicity, absence of rituals and priests. In the competition with Islam Hinduism had to change its internal structure with new impetus of purity and simplicity.

(d) Bhakti philosophy was not new to Hinduism. It was preached earlier as Bhakti Yoga. It created a new concentrated energy through group activities. The group represented the community which in a chorus sought for salvation in monotheism. The Bhakti saints were theist. They spoke of God as essentially one and eternal.

(e) Emergence of saints like Ramanuja, Ramananda, Madhava, Vallabhacharya, Kabir, Sri Chaitanya and Nanak was a positive help to promote Bhakti cult.

4.10.3 Some Great Reformers of Bhakti Cult

Ramanuja—(1060-1118)

Ramanuja was the most prominent propagator of Bhakti movement. He gave a philosophic basis to the teachings of Baishnavism. His philosophy was reaction against the Advaita philosophy of Shankaracharya. In his exposition he has given much emphasis to Srilaxmi, the consort of Vishnu. He composed Vedanta Samgraha, the Bhasya on Bhadrayans Vedanta sutras and *Bhagawat Gita*. He traveled all over India to propagate the Bhakti philosophy. After wandering a lot he settled down at Srirangam till he breathed his last in 1118. He was a great Vaishnav saint and a master on Vedanta philosophy. He refuted Shankar's absolute monism (*mayabad*). He established Bhakti within the philosophy of Vedanta. According to him, Brahma is the one supreme reality. Soul can reach God through Bhakti. He did not accept Nirguna Isvara and said that love of God is the only way to salvation. God is saguna because he is endowed with many qualities and virtues. The philosophy of Ramanuja is known as visisthadvita.

Nimbarka

Nimbarka was a great exponent of the Bhakti movement. He was the contemporary of Ramanuja. He wrote Vedanta Parijat Saurava, a commentary on Brahma Sutra. He advised men to surrender themselves to the mercy of God with absolute devotion to him. He propounded the Radhakrishna cult. His philosophy and teachings maintained a balance between Dvaita and Advaita.

Madhava

Madhava was a devotee of Bishnu. He hailed from South. He sang the praises of Vishnu as narrated in the Bhagabat Purana. He was not in favour of monism propagated by Ramanuja. He was of the view that salvation was not achieved without knowledge. Knowledge leads to Bhakti which is the ultimate path to moksha.

Ramananda

Ramananda was a foremost propagator of the Bhakti movement. He pioneered Vaishnavism in Northern India. His missionary zeal dragged him to all the holy places of India. He was a staunch devotee of Rama and Sita. His approach was secular. He was opposed to caste system and had free social relation with people of the lower caste. His door was open for everybody irrespective of caste. One cobbler named Raidas, one barber named Saindas and one weaver named Kabir were his loyal disciples. As R.K. Mukharjee puts it, "From him sprang the three great mystical schools—the major branch was Ramaili another was Krishnaili and the third under the leadership of Kabir. According to Ramananda, all men are equal before God. He preached in Hindi, the language of the people which made him extremely popular and accessible. His life was dedicated for the abolition of caste prejudices. He democratized the Bhakti movement.

Vallabhacharya

Vallabhacharya was an exponent of Krishna cult. He hailed from the Telegu Brahman family. He was the founder of Pushtimarga or the path of divine grace. He propagated for pure non dualism devoid of the concept of the maya. He insisted on complete identity of both soul and body with the supermen spirit. Mirabai and Narsi Mehta were very much influenced by him.

Narsi Mehta

Narsi Mehta was a poet saint from Saurashtra. His Bhajan "Vaishnava Jana to tene Kahige Je peer parayee Jane re" touched every Indian heart. Mahatma Gandhi was very much influenced by this song.

Janeswar

Janeswar was a contemporary of Namadeva. He made tremendous contribution to the Bhakti movement in Maharashtra. He was against caste system and a propagator of secularism.

Kabir

Kabir was the most famous disciple of Ramananda and he kindled the light of Bhakti movement through his dedication and effort. According to him no one can reach god by leading a family life. He was an exponent of monotheism. His religious sermons are contained in a book called *Vijak*.

His birth and growth are shrouded in mystery. It is said that his mother being Brahman widow left him near a pond. He was taken by the wife of a Muslim weaver and brought him up. He adopted the profession of weaver. Being a weaver, he suffered persecution by orthodox Muslims. He believed in honestly pursuing the family profession to earn livelihood. He managed with scanty earning and showed no greed. He did not believe in asceticism. Being a Muslim he had some knowledge about Hindu philosophy. Like his Guru, he was against idol worship, caste system and rituals. He tried his best to bring harmony and synthesis between Hinduism and Islam. According to him every one was equal before God and all were equal. He accepted both Hindu and Muslim disciples without any bitterness. His philosophical tenants were very simple. He preached Bhakti or devotion through the medium of his Dohas. His Dohas touched everyone's heart and everybody liked him. He preached a religion of love and aimed at the promotion of unity among all seats and creeds. He was the first saint who tried to reconcile

Hinduism and Islam. He was not in favour of ceremonial formalities. Anybody can attain God through the path of Bhakti. He emphasized much on soul. He considered it as the creator and destroyer of all things. Soul is life, soul is breath and soul is knowledge. Soul was the greatest innovation of the almighty. According to him salvation would not be achieved by singing devotional songs and worship. Soul must be free from all meanness cruelty, hypocrisy, dishonesty and in sincerity. His philosophy was influenced by Sufism. He said that Bhakti is the only means to achieve salvation. He taught I through small poems which have been collected and compiled as Kabir panthis. He also said that one need not go to the temple or mosque to attain purity of the self.

He was a versatile genius. He was not only a saint but also a social reformer.

Nanak

Guru Nanak was one of the most important exponent of Bhakti movement. He initiated a religious reform movement to bring about a balance between Hindus and Muslim. As Srinivas writes, "Nanak's mission was to reform the Hindu religion on the basis of unity of Godhead and to bring about friendly relations between the Hindus and the Muslims." His followers were known as Sikhs and his hymns have been preserved in *Adi Granth*. He was a vibrant propagator who traveled for and wide to preach his philosophy of universal toleration of uniformity of Godhead. He disbelieved in idol worship. He was a staunch defender of caste restriction.

According to him, God is formless. Through love, devotion and dedication one can get the grace of God. He emphasized on purity of deeds and believed that all religious acts and austerities practiced by different sects were useless. He said that God is truth, Ek Onkar, Sat Naam. He is the sole supreme being of eternal manifestation, creator, immanent reality, without fear and without rancour. He was neither born nor will he die. He is karta purukh, sat kartar, the creator. He is nirankar, formless.

He believed in the existence of the soul. Regarding soul he has said many things. He said that man is bonded to the cycle of birth and death because of his sins and evil deeds. Sin is maximized through evil deeds. When evil deeds increase, the soul cannot contain the burden of the sin. Soul cannot rise to higher planes because it is engulfed by darkness on all sides. Only the name of God can pierce this darkness with his divine light and could help the soul in its upward journey. Hence good deeds are essential to maximize virtue and to attain the grace of God. For attaining Godhood, he suggested for total submission before God.

His preachings and ideals opened a new avenue in the Bhakti movement.

Sri Chaitanya

Sri Chaitanya played a significant role in the Bhakti movement. He was born in a Brahmin family at Nava Dweep in East Bengal in 1486 A.D. His childhood name was Vishwambar or Nimai. After completing his formal education he was married to Laxmi. In course of time, he developed a sense of remarks towards worldly affairs. At the age of 22, while he had been to Gaya to offer homage to his deceased father he came in contact with a hermit named Iswarpuri and he was initiated by him through Krishnamantra. After initiation his life was changed completely. He was so devoted to Krishna that he started chanting Krishna's name continuously. Once, while chanting his name he could lose his sense. He felt that through devotional music and dance one can lose himself and experience the presence of God. In 1510, he renounced the world and accepted the life of a hermit. Hereafter he was known as Chaitanya. He believed in one supreme God whom he called Krishna or Hari. He was of the view that the presence of the God could be realized through love, devotion, song and dance. He stressed on perfection of a disciple. A disciple can achieve perfection of a disciple. A disciple can achieve perfection through Guru only. He denounced caste system and proclaimed the universal brotherhood of man. He did not believe in karma. He preached the praise of Hari through devotional songs called Bhajan. According to him one can attain salvation only through Hari Nama Japa and Kirtan. Through love and devotion, song and dance, a state of ecstasy could be reached in which the devotee can realize the presence of God. Regarding Bhakti, he demonstrated the glories of madhurya bhava, the transcendental love of the Gopis for Krishna as the highest perfection of the soul. His exposition of madhurya bhava and of the Raslila is the most magnificent gift to Indian philosophy. Kirtan was an integral part of his philosophy. According to him, true worship of God largely depended on love, devotion, music and dance. A blending of all these can make one feel the presence of God.

4.11 The Reform Movements

India witnessed a period of renaissance in the 19th century. It was the outcome of the impact of western education. India's contact with modern civilization of the west taught them the significance of humanism and rationalism. Humanism means sense of social equality between man and man, man and woman, one nation with another nation and one race with another. On the other hand, rationalism means scientific mind and scientific temperament.

Like the reform movements of 13th and 14th centuries which was in defence of Hinduism, the reform movement of the 19th century was also started in the same direction, i.e. to deferred Hinduism and Indian cultural heritage. The reform movement assumed two forms. Reformist movement like the Brahmo Samaj, Prarthana Samaj and Aligarh movement and the revivalist movements like the Arya Samaj, the Ramakrishna Mission and the Deoband movement. The difference between them was very thin and marginal. If the first group ushered reforms from the viewpoint of humanism and rationalism defined by the west, the second group viewed reforms from the viewpoint of rationalism in Indian tradition and culture. The first was an approach with eastern look and the second from Indian point of view. Both laid stress on socio-religions reforms because in India, all social activities have a deep religious root. No social reform in India was possible without touching religion. The prophet of modern India—Raja Rammohan Roy had rightly understood that religious reform would precede social reforms. This gave birth to Brahmo Samaj.

4.11.1 Reforms of Raja Rammohan Roy

Raja Rammohan Roy was one of the greatest socio-religious reformers of the 19th century. He is regarded as the father of modern India. Before he entered into the social service measures, he found that Indian society was suffering from several social structural rigidities. He tried his best to put an end to these. He raised his voice against the prevailing sati system. As a result, along prevailing ugly practice of the Hindus was uprooted. He protested against idolatry. He criticized idol worship by the Hindus. He rejected polytheism, idol worship and rituals of different regions. He advocated monotheism or unity among Gods. He inspired men to cultivate rationality. Since he was an outstanding scholar, he formed Atmiya Sabha to carry on discussion among scholars on religion and philosophy. He advocated the liberty of women and raised voice against child marriage and polygamy. He was the champion of women education. He opposed the ugly caste system prevailing in Indian society. He possessed sharp intellect in the Vedas, Upanishads, *Quran, Bible* and other holy scriptures. He very well realized the importance of English education and visualized the need of a scientific rational and progressive education for the Indians. He was the father of Indian journalism. He believed in the freedom of the press. He was the founder of a newspaper in Bengali named *SAMBAD KAUMUDI*. In his editorials, he used to write about important social, political, economic religious and other problems for arousing awareness among public. His economic ideas were tinged with literalism. He was of the view that the universal religion of mankind could be established by combining the best elements of all religions. He attempted a spiritual synthesis, stressing the unity of all religious experience. He was a complete monotheist.

4.11.2 The Brahmo Samaj

The Brahmo Samaj was the first Reform movement in the 19th century. It was influenced by western ideas. Raja Rammohan Roy was its founder. He was a polygot who knew several languages. Arabic, Persian, Sanskrit, English, French, Latin, Greek, and Hebrew which helped him to study extensively without cherishing an ill feeling or prejudice against any concept or philosophy. He was a versatile genius.

Raja Rammohan Roy was a staunch Hindu and a true Indian. He never intended to establish a religious. He only wanted to purify Hinduism from some of the evil practices prevailing in it. All through his life he wore the sacred thread and remained a Hindu. From very young age, he was opposed to idol worship. He was a thorough researcher who studied the Hindu scriptures extensively and with vertic knowledge defended his theory against idolatry. He condemned the prevailing caste system and unethical social practices like polygamy and concubinage. He wanted to establish a culture synthesis between east and west. He was a monotheist. For him God had no shape or form. He was invisible, omnipresent and omnipotent. He was the guiding spirit of the universes with these ideology he established the Brahmo Samaj in August 1828. According to the trust deed its object was "the worship and adoration of the eternal, unsearchable, immutable being who is the Author and preserver of the Universe". The first temple of the Samaj was opened in Calcutta in 1830. The ultimate objective of the Samaj was to revive monotheism or the concept of one true God on the basis of Vedanta.

The Brahmo Samaj was opposed to idol worship and no image, statue, sculpture, carving, painting, picture, portrait or anything of that sort was allowed in the Samaj building. Only form of worship was through prayer and meditation. Adequate emphasis was laid on charity, morality, virtue, benevolence and bonds of union between men of all religious beliefs and creeds.

The scope of Brahmo Samaj was too narrow initially as it was confined to the urban areas with members from educationally enlightened Bengalis. As opposed to the Brahmo Samaj a counter organization named Dharma Sabha was set up by one Raja Radhakanta Deb. The death of Raja Rammohan Roy in 1833 was a great setback to the reform movement initiated by him. After his death, the Brahmo Samaj lost much of its momentum. The leadership of the Samaj was vested upon Debendra Nath Tagore who infused new life and gave it a theistic touch and guidance. In 1839, he established the Tattvabodhini Sabha to carry on Raja Rammohan's ideal. It advocated the development of vedantism. Further great intellectual named Keshab Chandra Sen was associated with the Brahmo Samaj in 1858. He tried his utmost to popularize the ideals of the Samaj. He took some radical steps such as breaking caste barrier in marriages and introducing the practice of reading out religious scriptures of all religions like Islam, and Christianity in the prayer meeting, etc., which was not accepted by Devendra Nath Tagore who dismissed him Acharya of the Samaj in 1885.

The role of Brahmo Samaj cannot be underestimated as it was the starting point for all reform movements in the British period. It discarded the faith in divine avatars, denied the infallibility of Vedas, criticized the caste system and did not take any definite strand on the doctrine of karma and the transmigration of soul. Thus the social reform measures of Brahmo Samaj ushered a new era by attacking upon existing social evils. Really speaking Raja Rammohan Roy laid the foundation stone of a reform movement in the British India which germinated and grew big in the later stage. He was the pioneer of the reform movement. As Collect writes, "He stands in history as the living bridge over which India marches from her unmeasured past to her incalculable future. He was the arch which spanned the gulf between ancient caste and modern humanity, between superstition and science...." He was really the morning start of the great renaissance of India.

4.12. Swami Dayanand Saraswati and Arya Samaj

Dayananda Saraswati was born in a Brahmin family in Morvi state in Gujarat. In his childhood he was very much influenced by his father, who was a great Vedic scholar. He was proficient in Vedic lore, logic, philosophy and ethic. He left home to learn yoga. He was wandering ascetic who traveled throughout India for long 15 years to learn yogabhayas. From his very childhood, he had no faith in idol worship. In 1860, he found a guru in Swami Virajananda, who was blind from infancy, but was a man of great learning. Having imbibed the teachings of Virajananda, Dayanand went out into the world taking his stand on the Vedas. His interpretation of the Vedas, the primeval scripture of humanity has given a new orientation to the Hindu faith. He propagated his philosophy not as a defender but as an offender. He believed that Hinduism was superior to any other religion. According to him, "I believe in a religion based in universal and all embracing principles which has always been accepted as true by mankind and will continue to command the allegiance of mankind in the ages to come." His thoughts are contained in the *Satyarth Prakash* which is known as the Bible of Arya Samaj. In this he extolled the virtues of Hinduism. Dayanand founded the first Arya Samaj at Bombay in 1875 and another at Lahore in 1877.

Principles of Arya Samaj

The principles of Arya Samaj are as follows:

(i) God is the primary source of all true knowledge.

(ii) God is almighty, all truth, all knowledge. He is the immovable creator of the universe and alone is worthy of worship.

(iii) The Vedas are the books of true knowledge.

(iv) An Arya should always be ready to accept truth and abandon untruth.

(v) All actions must conform to Dharma.

(vi) The principal aim of the Samaj is to promote the well-being of the world, material, social and spiritual.

(vii) All persons should be treated with love and justice.

(viii) Ignorance should be removed and knowledge increased.

(ix) Everybody should consider his own progress to depend upon the upliftment of all others.

(x) Social well-being of mankind should be given utmost priority over individual well-being.

4.12.1 Reforms of Dayanand Saraswati

Dayanand Saraswati was the champion of oriental knowledge and was a great social reformer. He put emphasis on Veda. He was so fascinated with the contents of the Vedas that he said that the Vedas as the only authority of correct interpretation and exposition of Hinduism. Vedas carry the message of equality, purity and morality. Vedic practices can help in reconstructing and reforming the society. Though he was a perfect exponent of Vedas, he opposed idol worship and raised his voice against ritualistic religious practices. He appeared as a saviour of Hinduism and initiated a movement called 'SUDDHI MOVEMENT' through which he was able to bring back the converted Hindus from Christianity or Islam to the field of Hindus again.

He championed the cause of women. He protested against the existing evils in the society such as child marriage, purdah system and widow marriage, etc. He asserted the right of women over property and laid stress on women education. He condemned polygamy and polyandry. His reforms gave a moral boost for the social safety of women and helped them for their upliftment. He also put greater emphasis on the spread of Vedic education. He was an ardent supporter of nationalism. He fought for national unity. He injected a sense of pride and dignity in every Indian by unfolding the glories of cultural heritage. He watered to get rid of western influence.

He stressed on the development from bottom. He said that villages should be involved in the system of administration. Nation's prosperity lies with the prosperity of the villages. Virtually he was a nation builder. He felt the necessity of a common language for fostering national unity. He was modern and progressive in his outlook who laid stress on the revival of Vedic learning. He uttered the word swaraj and put emphasis on Swadeshi on self-reliance. The reforms of Swami Dayanand Saraswati through the establishment of Arya Samaj inspired the Indians to a considerable extent. Among major ideals, the Samaj spoke about the fatherhood of God, brotherhood of man, equality between man and woman, justice and fair play for all, etc. The Samaj laid stress on the spread of Vedic education by setting up Dayanand Anglo Vedic institution. In 1886, the DAV movement was launched and in due course it gained momentum and popularity. The new education system gave the Hindus profound self-confidence. The Arya Samaj movement was a breeding ground of Indian nationalists.

4.12.2 Swami Vivekananda and His Reforms

Vivekananda was born on 12th January 1863 at Calcutta in West Bengal. His childhood name was Narendranath Dutta. He was the son of advocate Viswanath Dutta and Ragini Devi. He learnt his first lessons from his mother who taught him *Ramayana* and *Mahabharat*. In the later stage, he was educated at various educational institutions of repute and accepted Ramakrishna as his Guru. By his blessings, he got Nirvi Kalpa Samadhi. Then he became famous as Swami Vivekananda. As per guru's instruction he had traveled from Kashmir to Kanyakumari. He preached the message of Vedanta in the nook and corner of India.

As a Vedantist, he preached the gospel of universal religion and as a reformist he tried his best to remove superstition from religion. He wanted to make religion very simple and practical and carried on his crusade against the prevailing social dogmas. His spiritualism, free from dogmas kindled the lamp of hope in the inner hearts of millions of downtrodden Indians and paved the way for their upliftment.

4.12.3 Message and Reforms of Swami Vivekananda

Swami Vivekananda was a saint reformer. His message had far-reaching effect and tremendous impact on the people of India. He considered Hinduism as the mother of all religions. He established it through historical sequences. He told that all the religions of the world have the same values and importance. He attached great importance to the unity of all religions and their fusion into one universal religion.

He was a socialist par excellence, who wanted to bring positive changes in the pattern of living of the Indian masses belonging to the lower strata of society. He supported the varna system as described in the Vedas. Unfolding the advantage of the caste system, he said that division of labour can lead to specialization which would ultimately lead to the excellence in any field.

He was a feminist. He raised his voice for the cause of women. He glorified the role of women. He considered women's Shakti—the creating force. They are to be given proper education because they are the mother first and mother last. Educated women will educate children and in a chain like process the whole nation will be educated. He says that one should see God and feel the presence divinity through men. His motto was "Servicve to mankind is service to God". It is the duty of every human being to work for the upliftment of the poor and down-trodden. Keeping this in view, he established Rama Krishna Mission. Through it, he desired to render continuous service to the poor, the destitute and needy persons.

Swami Vivekananda was a hardcore nationalist who emphasized on the virtues like manliness and patriotism. He wanted everybody to be free from the bondage of other. Giving a clarion call to the youth of India he repeated the Upanishad doctrine:

> Arise, awake and stop
> Not till the goal is reached.

He was a crusader against superstitions. He opposed the dominance of Brahmans and the in-equality existing in the society. He gave a strategic blow to all the existing prejudices and advised people to be united for a common cause—the cause of the motherland.

Through Ramakrishna Mission he tried to serve the mankind. This mission preached the Vedantic philosophy and created new spiritual awakening in the hearts of the people. Apart from this, the mission carried on philanthropic works at the time of natural disasters occurring in the country such as flood, cyclone, earthquake, epidemics, etc. His sharp intellect coupled with reformative attitude made Hinduism a progressive force in the world.

Growth of Nationalism

5

5.1 Growth of Nationalism

Nationalism is a feeling of territorial patriotism on a sense of identifications of the individual with the entire people of the land. This consciousness is fostered by a common language, expansion of education and means of communications and transport, growth of political parties, democratic institutions and a free press and by the active participation of the people in government and other public affairs.

The term nationalism has been variously understand and defined. It is described as a state of mind in which the supreme loyalty of the individual is due to the nation state. It implies the identification of the state or nation with the people or at least desirability of determining the extent of the state according to ethnographic principles. It is a state or condition of mind. Characteristic of certain people with a homogenous culture, living together enclose association or given territory and sharing a belief in a distinctive existence and a common destiny.

Nationalism in India can be interpreted in two senses—colonial nationalism and anti colonial nationalism. The nationalism in India belongs to the category of anti colonial nationalism. It signifies a common political consciousness or patroatism which the people of an independent country share among themselves for the purpose having the self rule. It represents the consciousness of a society at an advantaged stage of material development. It also implies an integrated political system on the countrywide basis.

5.2 Historical Preview

Indian history goes back to many centuries before the Christian era. Very often the country was exposed to foreign invaders. During the fag end of the 18th century India was conquered by a trading corporation named East India Company. Along with the consolidation of British political hegemony in India, there followed the colonization of its economy. The British rule in India gradually squandered away India's resources and saved the seeds of poverty and misery of the masses. People expressed resentment over the British administration. A powerful national struggle against British imperialism developed in India in the later half of the 19th century. The struggle was the outcome of the clash of interest between the British rulers and Indian people. Political nationalism emerged out of this conflict. As a result of British rule, India was transformed into a classic colony. The colonial character of the British rule and its harmful impact on the lives of Indian people led to rise and development of a powerful anti imperialist movement in India. The intellectual resurgence of India during the 19th century provided a great fillip to the growth of modern Indian nationalism. The bourgeoisie (middle class) intelligentia which took leading part in modern Indian regeneration had been mainly nurtured on ideas derived from the west. Besides, the glorious struggle waged by the Sikh, Marathas and the leaders of the sepiy muting revolt in 1857 had nurtured the patriotic thinkers. As the British extended their sway over India, the people of India started expressing resentment. They felt that they were being looked down upon their own country. The intensity of discontent against British rule becomes visible through different uprisings. The need to use Swadeshi goods was given priority. Bankim Chandra Chatterjee's *Anandmath* highlighted the tyranny of the rulers. The year 1885 marked the beginning of a new approach, because in that year in December, the Indian National Congress organization was set up in Bombay to discuss the political situation in the country.

The establishment of Indian National Congress in 1885 was a harbinger of a new age of nationalism. It was the result of the growing consciousness of India's political positions. But the National Congress had no political vision at that time of its birth. Its objectives were not earmarked. It might be wrong to say that it was national because in reality only a few western educated elites had formed this association. They were the educated middle class intelligentsia. They drew inspirations from the western school of liberalism. They were aware of the growth of Nationalism in Italy and Germany which had culminated in the foundation of two nation states in Europe. They had no such end in view. Attainment of constitutional progress by peaceful means through 3 P's (Protest, Petition and Prayer) was the goal of the Indian National Congress during 1885 to 1905. They heavily relied upon the grace of the crown.

Thereafter (1905-1918), the Congress aimed at uplifting the social, cultural, economic and political condition of the people through various reforms. Swaraj or self Government dawned at their mental horizon. They came another phase of Indian nationalism. The political platform reverberated with the demand of purna swaraj or complete independence. This time Mahatma Gandhi was the undisputed leader of the National Congress. He adopted the policy of non violence to wage the freedom struggle for liberating India from the British rule. Along with non violence, he also adopted the non cooperation and civil disobedience to paralyze the British Government. He ultimately succeeded in his efforts through a mass movement and India achieved Independence in 1947.

5.3 Factors Leading to Indian Nationalism

The following factors are responsible for the emergence of Nationalism in India:

(a) British Rule

The British rule over India had some beneficial effects. Though they did not want to promote nationalism in India, their liberal policy was instrumental in promoting nationalism in India. They disseminated liberal education in the schools and colleges and created new opportunities for merit and talent. They encouraged intellectual freedom and scholarship through discussion, debate and free thinking which created conducive atmosphere for the growth of nationalism.

(b) International Scenario

The French revolution in 1789 the American war of Independence in 1774, the rise of Japan, the unification of Italy and Germany had deep impact on the people of India. Further, the British had initiated the process of renaissance which generated such forces like nationalism in India.

(c) Political Unity of India

Under the British rule India achieved political unity. India came under one authority, and one type of administration. This created a sense of national unity which generated nationalism.

(d) Peace and Tranquility

The British rule gave India peace and tranquility. Peace generated creative urge tantamount to national consciousness. The people could find time to consider their problems and remedies. This engineered the spirit of Indian nationalism. Linguistic hegemony, pan Indianism, communal harmony created an opportunity to ponder over national issue. This was the spirit of nationalism.

(e) Development of Transport and Communication System

During the Governor Generalship of Lord Dalhousie several measures of modernization had been undertaken by the British Government in India. The aim was administrative convenience and easy deployment of troops. The measures included planned development of modern means of transport network of roads connecting the metropolitan cities and provinces, introduction of railways and telegraphs, etc. The new postal system introduced in 1850 not only earned revenue for the state, but also provided the benefit of cheap postal service to the people. This made communication easy. It helped in bringing newsletters and published materials at hand. The convenience in maintaining contact gave an impetus to the growth of nationalism.

(f) Modern Education

The most powerful factor which paved the way for the growth of nationalism was western education introduced by the Government and Christian missionaries. The English language served as a bond of unity throughout India. English became a common medium to communicate each other for unity. Educated Indians were highly inspired to read the success of foreign freedom movement and the strong current of nationalist ideas passed over the whole of Europe stimulated growth of nationalism in India.

(g) Emergence of Modern Press

The press, the newspapers, periodicals and bulletins such as the Bengali, Indian Mirror, Amrit Bazar Patrika, Bombay Chronicle, the Indu Patriot, the Maratha, Keshari, the Hindu and Kohinoor, etc., started coming in large number circulating new ideas among educated people. Not only press in English, but also vernacular press played a significant role in influencing opinion on national issues. The problems of India were projected. The demand for constitutional and economic benefits were projected to draw the attention of Government on all major and minor issues, the press aroused a strong national consciousness and gave a strong incentive for the growth of Indian nationalism.

(h) Influence of History

In the 19th century, there was a fresh attempt to write the history of India projecting its past glory. The past glory inspired the Indians. The role of Asiatic Society of Bengal was very significant. Maxmuller, William Jones and Rath, etc., spoke about the cultural heritage. Excavations of Alexander Cunningham made new impact or historians and nationalism. Their discoveries were highly inspiring. Got recognition throughout the world. It inspired nationalism.

(i) Racial Consciousness

The great revolt of 1857 had created a bitter race consciousness between the Indians and the British. In the British press Indian cartoons appeared very offending to the Indian people. They were painted as half Guerilla and half Negro. It was insulting to the Indians. The British considered themselves as a superior race. The legal code was written accordingly. They were superior to law and for the same offence received, light punishment that the Indians. The Indians well ill treated. Such unfair approach provoked national consciousness among Indian people. The educated Indians reacted strongly.

(j) Drain of Wealth

The colonial rule was thoroughly exploitative. Indian wealth was drained out of the country in several ways. The railways, telegraphs, educational institutions had an exploitative aim. British army thrived at the cost of the Indian people. British industries grew on Indian raw materials. British capital took away interest and profit from India. These facts were brought to the notice of the public through debates and discussions. The cause of growing poverty was disturbing to the educated mass. They decided to agitate against the foreign government and its colonial policy.

(k) Growth of Political Parties

Lord Macualay was a thoroughbread imperialist. His aim was to exploit the colony for the good of the imperial power. His attitude was very high hands. Though he advocated the introduction of western liberal ideas of democracy and equality, liberty and political rights were fascinating concepts. These political concepts surcharged the young educated mind as never before. They expressed a strong desire to form political association and cultural association for the progress of the members. These associations brought unity among Indian professionals like languages, landholders, zamindars, castes and communities like Muslims, Christians, Brahmans, Karanas and students, etc., such associations created new tradition by meetings, discussions and criticisms of government policies.

(l) Lord Lytton's Reaching Measures

The reactionary measures of Lord Lytton ignited the fire of nationalism burning on the hearts of Indians. During his tenure, the age limit for appearing the ICS examination was reduced from 21 to 19 years. In 1878 he promulgated the vernacular press Act by which it was stipulated that the editor of an Indian newspaper was to be oath bound before the magistrate that nothing derogatory or detrimental to British interests could be published in papers. Similarly, an ammunition Act was passed whereby an Indian had to spend money to obtain a license for possessing arms and ammounitions for self-protection. These retrograde steps of Lord Lytton gave a best to the awakening of national consciousness.

(m) Lord Ripon and the Libert Bill

Lord Ripon was a liberal viceroy. Duing his tenure Lord Libert introduced a bill by which an Indian magistrate could prosecute a guilty European. The Libert bill created a tremendous furore among the Britishers. Lord Rippon was criticized vehemently on the ground that no Indian lawyer should be given such power to presecute an Europoean. Under heavy pressure he had to bring an amendment to the bill. As per the amended bill it was stated that though an Indian magistrate could prosecute an European, it was mandatory that another European had to give an evidence as a witness to the allegations brought against the convicted European. Thus, a mockery of the British Judicial impartiality was made by this bill and it exposed British hypocrisy. The bill created a sense of hatred in the Indians for British.

(n) Social Reform of the 19th Century

The socio-religions reforms of the 19th century gave the Indians an opportunity to strengthen their morality and self-confidence. They were not to suffer from any inferiority complex after competing the reform measures. Hinduism had everything to be proud of. They reformed their religions and society. The success inculcated a sense of self-respect and patriotism. They derived great strength from India's past heritage. This feeling promoted an all India pride and sense of nationalism.

These were the factors which created a conducive atmosphere for the growth of Nationalism.

5.4 Indian National Congress and Its Objectives

The struggle for India's freedom struggle began with the establishment of the Indian National Congress in 1885. It was possible due to the whole hearted supported an untiring effort of Allan Activean Hume, a British servant, who wanted to see the Indian public opinion to be well organized. He wanted that there should be a responsible public forum which the British Government would consult as and when necessary to study. Indian public sentiment and views on various issues of national interest. His aim was to combine the provincial associations to a national one.

The story behind the formation of Indian National Congress is like this. Surendranath Banarjee of Calcutta had organized the Indian Association of Calcutta and the Indian National Conference. In 1883, he had invited representatives from major Indian towns to a meeting in Calcutta. But it was replaced by the Indian National Congress in December 1885. Thus the Indian National Congress created by W.C. Banarjee now merged with the INC. For the first time notable national leaders like Dadabhai Naraoji, Mahadev Govinda Ranade, Feroz Shah Mehta, K.T. Telang and several others joined the meeting of the INC. The proposals formulated in this session influenced the freedom struggle later on.

The objectives of Indian National Congress were as follows:

(a) To cultivate a deep bond among the workers living in different parts of the country.

(b) To awaken national consciousness by removing caste, religious and parochial feelings.

(c) To prepare a general list of the demands of the people and present it to the British Government.

(d) To arouse public consciousness and to give direction to it.

5.5 Indian National Congress (Pre-Gandhian Period)

The History of Indian National Congress from 1885-1991 before the advent of Mahatma Gandhi into the arena of freedom struggle may be divided into two phases:

(a) First phase (1885-1905)

(b) Second phase (1906-11)

First phase (1885-1906)—This phase is known as the period of moderates or period of protest, petition and prayer. This was also known as the period of political mendicancy. The leaders of this period were Dadabhai Naraoji, P.M. Mehta, D.E. Walth, W.C. Banarjee and S.N. Banarjee, etc. These moderates or constitutionalists worked for the development and consolidation of the feeling of national unity irrespective of region, religion or caste.

The moderates through their unified efforts achieved something marginal which may be discussed under the following heads.

(i) Economic Reforms

The poverty of Indians deeply hurt the feelings of the moderates. Dadabhai Naraoji had expressed the policy of exploitation pursued by the British in India. These leaders put pressure upon the government for laying the foundation of a modern industrial infrastructure in India. They also recommended the British Government to provide economic assistance to these industries. A request was made for the reduction of land revenue and provision of easy loan to farmers. The moderates advised the government for a revolution of the salt tax and demanded an improvement in the living condition of workers in the tea plantations. An effort was made to stop the drain of wealth from India to England.

(ii) Constitutional Reforms

Moderate leaders made a definite effort to bring about changes in the administrative system. They advised the government for an increase in the membership of the legislative councils and also wanted elected representatives of the people to become members of the body. The moderates prevailed over the government for an accretion of power of these bodies. The government was bent down to accept the demand of the moderates and passed the Indian Council Act in 1892. As a result, the membership of the imperial legislative council and the provincial legislative council was increased. It was also stipulated that these councils could now debate on the annual budget. However, the members did not have the voting rights on this issue. This naturally enraged the moderates for they wanted Indians to have control over the national finance. The moderates adopted the American maxim, "No taxation without representation" and this confrontationist attitude startled the British government.

(iii) Administrative Reforms

In the administrative sphere the moderates brought about multifaceted reforms. They wanted an idealization on the top positions in the administrative hierarchy. From the economic point of view there was a graze discrepancy between Europeans and Indians. The Europeans were paid a high salary. The resultant drain of wealth impoverished India. Politically the moderates put forth the argument that Indians ought to be employed in higher posts of the Government. They also demanded that the British Government in India should look to the welfare of the Indians, provide them health and police facilities, etc. There should be complete separation of judiciary from the administrative wing of the Government. For the moral and intellectual progress of the Indians provision for establishment of schools should be made in all parts of India.

5.6 The Activities and Achievements of Moderates

The moderates were moderates. Their approach to British government was very much mild. They always requested the British Government. It was something like mendicants prayer. The leaders of the moderate groups failed to unite the Indians to make a common cause against the British. Therefore the achievement was not very spectacular. The moderate leaders were called the old guards. They had to face upspring criticism for their loyalty and submissive attitude to the crown. The only achievement of the period was the appointment of public service commission in 1886 for which there was a great demand and the ICS examination was being conducted in England previously. The leaders of the moderate group succeeded in bringing out a resolution in the House of the Commons in 1893 for simultaneous Civil Service Examination in London and India. Another achievement was their assessment of the economic impact of British rule in India. They felt that India's poverty was due to the policy of exploitation of India's economic resources. Dadabhai Naraoji formulated the Drain theory to criticize the policies of the British Government in India.

5.7 Second Phase (1906–1911): Age of Extremists

The second phase of the Indian National Congress extending from 1906 to 1911 witnessed the rise of extremism or radical nationalism. The movement saw the involvement of angry young men who did not like the policy of mendicancy and prayer. They were an impatient and prostrated group who demanded change in leadership. People like Lala Lajpat Rai, Bal Gangadhar Tilak, Bipin Chandra Pal, Aurobindo Ghosh were the leaders who personified new outlook. The rise of extremism was the reaction against the attempts of western reformist's to reconstruct India in the image of the west. They were also influenced by the growth of spiritual nationalism in India. The period from 1906-1919 marked the age of extremists.

5.8 Factors Leading to the Rise of Extremists

The following factors are responsible for the rise of extremists in India.

(a) Realization of the Intentions of the British

Several factors were responsible for the rise of the extremists. There was dissatisfaction with the working of the Indian National Congress. The approach of the congress was disgusting. Criticisms against the government grew more and more strident. The people realized the true nature of the British Government. It was exploitative and undemocratic. The extravagant expenditure in civil, military and other affairs was appalling. People were very much vigilant in coming through the book *Poverty* and *Un British Rule in India* by Dadabhai Naraoji and *Economic History of India* by R.C. Dutta.

(b) Reaction Against Westernization

The leaders in the Congress came to know the western influence on Indian society was becoming more and more pronounced. Along with the spread of Christianity western culture was gradually spreading. The Brahmo Samaj was an imitation of western civilization. Most of the leaders did not like the philosophy of Brahmo Samaj. Bal Gangadhar Tilak resented against the anti Cow killing society. He popularized Ganapati festival in Maharashtra which also caused reaction among certain sections. The extremist leaders in this critical juncture appeared on the political horizon as a reaction against westernization of Indian culture.

(c) Growth of Self-Confidence

There was a gradual rise in the self-esteem and self-confidence among Indians. Bipin Chandra Pal and Bal Gangadhar Tilak laid great emphasis on the growth of self-confidence among Indians and to evolve an inherent trust in their own capabilities. People started uniting to drive the British out of India.

(d) Growth of Education and Rise of Unemployment

The growth of education was brought about by the Britishers. Indians were influenced by western education. The Britishers failed to provide suitable jobs to the Indians. The educated Indians become highly critical to the government and his trend encouraged the extremists.

(e) Influence of the World Politics

Some very significant events took place in the area of world politics. The Indians in South Africa were ill treated by the whites. It aroused anti British sentiment, Nationalist movement in Egypt, Persia, Turkey and Russia were gaining momentum. Thus the world politics very much influenced Indians to unit against the British.

(f) Curzon's Anti Indian Attitude

Viceroy Lord Curzon was a thorough bred imperialist. He was despising the National Congress and held a very uncompromising view on agitational politics. He used insulting words against Indian intelligentsia and talked very low of Indian people. Such statements were highly provocative. Further in 1903, curzon partitioned Bengal. The Bengalis' got agitated. It gave way for Swadeshi movement. Curzon's decision failed to divide the Bengalis. They became united against the British Government's policy Divide and Rule.

5.9 Achievements of Extremists

Achievements of the extremists may be discussed under the following heads:

(a) Swadeshi Movement

After the partition of Bengal the Swadeshi movement was intensified throughout the country by the extremist leaders. This movement was a reaction against the British economic policies. Bal Gangadhar Tilak took the lead role for the movement in Maharashtra, followed by Subaramanium Aiyyar in Madras and Swami Sradhananda in Punjab. They also took steps to activate the progress and development of Indian industries.

(b) The Boycott Movement

The extremist leaders initiated the Boycott campaign along with the Swadeshi movement. The very objective of the movement was to ban the use of foreign goods. Heaps and piles of foreign cloths were dumped on the road side and a bonfire was made of them.

(c) Non-Cooperation Movement

Bal Gangadhar Tilak preached non-cooperation in 1902. The extremists talked of democracy, constitutionalism and progress and talked of making national movement broad-based. They highlighted the negative aspects of British colonial policy. They spoke of passive resistance against injustice by mass agitation. They spoke of Hindu nation and protection of Hindu political interests.

(d) Home Rule Movement

Bal Gangadhar Tilak started the Home rule or Swaraj movement. Prior to this, in 1916, Annie Besant had formed the Home rule league in Madras. The same year in December, Tilak established the All India Home Rule league. Under the leadership of Tilak and Annie Besant, the Swaraj movement gathered a strong momentum. Its purpose was self-rule and attaining democracy for Indians.

All these movement made by the extremists shocked the British administration. The partition of Bengal was annulled in 1911. The Indian got new confidence for their success. The demand for Swaraj entered into political agenda as a priority claim. The British Government had to yield constitutional privileges to the Indian people from time to time in the shape of reform acts.

5.10 Third Phase (1919-1947): The Gandhian Era

With the advent of Mahatma Gandhi, the history of Indian struggle for freedom entered into the third and final phase in 1919. In this phase, the revolutionary character of the freedom struggle along with the nature of the Indian National Congress underwent drastic changes. The very objective of this struggle was to attain Swaraj by all legitimate means.

5.10.1 Mahatma Gandhi, His Roles and Ideas

Mahatma Gandhi was the first national leader who recognized the role of the masses. He converted the national movement into a revolutionary movement. Under his leadership, the people of India become heroic, patriotic and intrepid fighters for national emancipation. He was born on 2nd October 1869. He had spent twenty-one years of his life (1893-1904) in South Africa. He was very much inspired by the writings of Tolstoy, Thoreau and Ruksin, etc. While in South Africa, he started his political career by joining a protest movement against racial discrimination policy for which Indians and Asiatics were victims. He succeeded in getting the obnoxious racial laws repealed in 1914. His success was made his famous in his home country to which he returned in 1915. He is highly revered as an immortal personality of modern India for having played the role of the father of the nation. His severe but strong personality was a source of attraction for multi trade of Indians. He dominated the national political scene from 1919 to 1947 and almost all political events during this period took place under his directions. His ideals and personality were so overwhelmingly superior to contemporary leaders that this crucial phase in the freedom movement is rightly referred to as the Gandhian era or the age of Gandhi.

5.10.2 His Philosophy

Gandhi was a humanist. He believed in human freedom, which is related to violence, greed, passion and ambition. He was determined to achieve freedom for India through non violence and non cooperation. He urged upon the path of Satyagraha or persistence of truth. Satyagraha means fearlessness. The basic philosophy of Satyagraha is that mind must be free from fear. He adopted the path of non violence and non cooperation. These two notions are complementary. Gandhi directed the force of Satyagraha against exploitation by British imperialism in India. He believed in the essential goodness of men and its ultimate victory over tyranny.

5.10.3 Programme of Social Reconstruction

The basic objective of Gandhi was to attain India's freedom. He included certain constructive ideas in the programme of

India's national congress. He thought of achieving social, material and moral welfare of his countrymen. So he initiated the programme of village reconstruction and basic education. He emphasized on the promotion of cottage industries and made Khadi the symbol of economic freedom and self-sufficiency. He desired for the abolition of social inequalities like caste, creed and wealth for the promotion of social welfare of the masses. He also desired for the welfare of the horizons, condemned the evils of drinking and removal of inequality among women, etc. He was an avowed champion of Hindu Muslim unity. He was a social reformer. He adopted the policy of disobedience against the government for which his critics called him an anarchist. He pursued the path of truth and remained honest and sincere. Their major policy decisions determined the path of Indian National Congress. These were (a) The Non Cooperation movement, (b) The Civil Disobedience movement, and (c) The Quit India movement.

5.10.4 The Non-Cooperation Movement and Its Objective

The freedom movement in India got a new thrust with the entry of Gandhi into the political mainstreams of India. He was quite frustrated with two dreadful events caused by the British Government. The first one was Jallianwalabagh tragedy which took away the lives of eleven hundred innocent people and the second one as the passing of Rowlatt Act which entrusted move power to the executive to arrest and try political offenders by curtailing freedom of the individual. Hence, he adopted the method of Non cooperation to paralyze the administration of British Government in India.

5.10.5 Objectives of Non Cooperation Movement

When Gandhi lost all hopes of getting any fair treatment from the British Government, he planned to wreck the administration of the country by withdrawing the country's cooperations from the governance. A special session of the all India Congress Committee was held at Calcutta. The Congress cooperated Gandhi's plan for non cooperation till the Punjab and the Khilafat wings were removed and Swaraj established. Finally, it was ratified at the annual session of the Congress at

Nagpur, in December 1920. The movement was to be directed in two distinct phases.

The first phase of the movement contained the following principles:

(i) To give up all titles conferred by the British and to resign from all government posts.

(ii) To boycott the elections to be conducted under the Government of India Act of 1919.

(iii) Non-participation in any function arranged by the British.

(iv) To quit government educational institutions.

(v) Barristers were to quit courts.

(vi) Indian members of the Vidhan Parishad (Legislative Council) were not to participate in its proceedings.

(vii) Discarding of foreign goods.

(viii) To pursue the non cooperation movement through non violent means.

(ix) Not to cooperate the Government in any activity.

The second phase of the movement took up certain constructive measures which included the following:

(i) To set up Gram Panchayats in villages to try suits.

(ii) To set up national schools and colleges for the growth of education.

(iii) To develop cottage industries.

(iv) To use only home-made goods.

(v) To build up communal harmony.

(vi) To abolish untouchability and caste system.

(vii) To set up a fund known as the Tilak Swaraj fund and deposit at least ₹ 1 crore to be utilized during the non cooperation movement.

5.10.6 Progress of the Movement

The response to the non cooperation programme was quite encouraging. Gandhi along with other leaders mobilized public opinion in favour of the movement. The voters abstained from taking part in the elections to the council. The response from the students and women was very much effective. In the course of the movement, the National Muslim University of Aligarh, the Gujarat and Kashi Vidyapeeth, the Bengal National University and a large number of National schools were started in all parts of the country. Women gave up purdah and offered their ornaments for the Tilak fund. Lawyers abstained from their usual legal practice. Students left schools and colleges. Women took active part in picketing before the shops selling foreign clothes and liquor. Distinguished persons such as Rabindranath Tagore and other renounced these titles. Foreign cloths were burnt in bonfires in market places. Subash Chandra Bose who was qualified in the ICS examination gave up his posts. It was a mass movement Gandhi along with his followers started his movement from Bardili. Seeing the nature and magnitude of this movement, the Prince of Wales came to India in 1921. The people boycotted his visit and observed hartal. When there was great ferment and commotion throughout the country, the British Government was determined to take drastic steps to suppress the movement. The British Government arrested all the top leaders like Motilal Nehru, Lala Lajpat Rai, Maulana Abul Kalam Azad, etc. Thousands of volunteers were put into jail without trial. The firing on peaceful demonstrations during the visit of the Prince of Wales to India created a strong revolution against the Government. This helped in the spreading of the movement to all parts of India. The Government was forced to adopt stern measures and arrested people in discriminately.

5.10.7 Chauri Chaura Incident

The non cooperation movement, in spite of several suppressive measures taken by the British Government got people's support. Though the leaders of the movement were put into bars, the movement was getting momentum as people had a strong feeling of unity and nationalism. During this period, an undesirable incident took place at Chauri Chaura in the Gorakhpur district of Uttar Pradesh on 5th February 1922 when police fired at a procession 3000 farmers. The angry mass set fire to the police station and 22 police personnel were burnt alive. This inhuman act deeply heart Gandhiji. Without any consultation with other leaders he called a halt to the movement. So other fellow leaders were perturbed. Though the movement was called off. Gandhiji was arrested and sentenced for six years of imprisonment. Later on health ground, he was released in 1924.

5.10.8 Impact of the Non Cooperation Movement

The non cooperation movement, in spite of several upheavals shocked the British administration. Due to the dynamic leadership of Gandhiji a nationalist movement was transformed to a mass movement. The impact of the movement may be discussed as under:

(i) It demonstrated to a remarkable degree the willingness of the masses to sacrifice for the cause of national independence.

(ii) It brought Hindu Muslim Unity.

(iii) People realized the importance of self-respect and self-government.

(iv) It created an awareness among common people.

(v) It brought stability in the congress.

(vi) There was economic revival through the adoption of Charkha and involvement in the village reconstruction programme.

(vii) The movement also stressed on the removal of social evils such as casteism and untouchability, etc.

(viii) The principle of Satyagraha enunciated by Mahatma Gandhi was found unique a weapon to drive out Britishers from Indian soil.

(ix) This movement passed the way for creation of nationalism among people.

5.10.9 The Civil Disobedience Movement

Though the non cooperation movement did not achieve the expected degree of success, it sowed the seeds of a greater success in the future and Gandhi was regarded the undisputed leader of the masses. After a short break, Gandhiji rejoined national freedom struggle. In 1928, he decided to organize the civil disobedience movement. The proposed movement was planned differently and aimed to create a deadlock in the British administration. For this he wanted to break the salt laws.

The occurrence of the civil disobedience movement was due to the following reasons:

(a) Appointment of Simon Commission

In 1927, the British Government appointed the Simon Commission to supervise the functioning of Government of India Act. As the commission lacked Indian representation, the leaders protested with demonstrations, 'Simon, Go back'. Throughout the country there were strikes and demonstrations.

(b) Nehru Report

In 1928, different political parties in India made a joint effort to frame a constitution of India. A committee was constituted under the captainship of Motilal Nehru. The committee submitted its report demanding a dominion status of India. It is popularly known as Nehru Report. The new labour Government of Ramsay MC Donald declared that the Government would consider the proposal for granting dominion status to India, but it was rejected by the British Parliament.

(c) Lahore Congress and the Demand for Purna Swaraj

As the Government did not accept the demand of the Congress for dominion status to India, the Lahore session of the Congress held in December 1929 demanded for complete independence or Purna Swaraj. Meanwhile, Gandhi came back to active politics and began to consolidated the nationalist ranks. At mid night of 31 December 1929, Jawaharlal Nehru, the President of the Congress raised the National Flag of India in Lahore. Independence day was celebrated on 26th January 1930 and it was decided to hold similar celebrations every year on that day.

(d) Gandhiji's Proposal to the Viceroy

Gandhiji presented a consolidated 11-point administrative reform proposal to Government before lunching the civil disobedience movement. Gandhiji wrote a letter to the Viceroy Lord Irwin with warning that if his proposals were rejected he would be forced to launch the civil disobedience movement campaign. Lord Irwin rejected his proposal and the civil disobedience movement was started in 1930.

leaders of the congress were released from jail. The Government agreed to withdraw all ordinances and release all political prisoners, except those guilty of violence. The Congress also agreed to suspend the civil disobedience movement. Since the pact did not reflect anything regarding Purna Swaraj demand, some of the leaders like Subash Chandra Bose and Jawaharlal Nehru criticized the pact vehemently. Gandhiji was bold enough to tackle the situation tactfully and got the pact ratified in the Karachi session of the Congress.

5.10.14 Second Round Table Conference (1931)

The Karachi session of the Congress paved the way for the second session of the Round table conference by ratifying the Gandhi Irwin pact. Gandhi represented the congress to participate in the second round conference. In December 1931, the conference was held under the presidentship of Ramsay Macdonald, the then British Prime Minister. Winston Churchil criticized Gandhiji as half naked fakir. The British monarch George-V threatened that if his majesty's Government was not supported by Indians he would blow them up with machine guns and bonnets. To him Gandhi replied, "my countrymen consider your bonnets as mere fire crackers". As the British betrayed the Indians, the conference ended disastrously. With a view to strengthen the British rule in India, the British Government deliberately implemented the divide and rule policy. It was decided to have separate electoral constituencies for Hindus, Muslims and Harijans. Being severely humiliated Gandhiji came back to India and resumed the civil disobedience movement for which he was put in Jail. The Congress passed a resolution for the renewal of the civil disobedience movement. Government resorted to repression. The Congress once again was declared illegal. Finally the movement was called off in 1934. Gandhiji kept himself aloof from politics for a year.

5.10.15 Communal Award

The British Government started a foul play to continue its administration here in India by tantalizing Indians. While the civil disobedience movement was in full swing in India, the British Government declared the communal Award in 1932. This was intended to create a gulf among different religious groups in India. This award was intended as an attempt to disrupt national unity. Accordingly to this award, the Muslims, Sikhs, Anglo Indians and Harizans were given the right to elect their representatives through separate electorates.

5.10.16 Poona Pact

The declaration of communal award greatly hurt Gandhiji for which he went on a fast. A compromise formula was put forward by B.R. Ambedkar, the leader of the depressed class. Poona pact was its outcome through which the system of separate electorates for Harizans was replaced by reservation of seals for them.

5.10.17 The Third Round Table Conference 1932

The third round table conference was convened in November 1932. None of the members of Indian National Congress participated in conference. At the end of the sitting a white paper on developments in India was produced. It was sent to the British parliament for an indepth discussion in the House of Commons. There was a difference of opinion among Indian leaders regarding the communal award. Hence, the Indian National Congress called a halt to the movement in 1933 and 1934, it withdrew the movement. The civil disobedience movement gave a boost to the national freedom struggle. Undoubtedly it made the British think about their future course of action in India. The Indians were not afraid of beatings and firings. The magical personality of Gandhiji enchanted the whole nation. He started his individual civil disobedience in 1940, but in view of the occurrence of the Second World War, he withdrew it.

5.10.18 The August Offer 1940

In August 1940, the then Viceroy announced that after the war there would be expansion of victories executive council and he promised to devise the framework of a new constitution for India. This is popularly known as August offer. This offer was rejected by the Congress as unsatisfactory. Some provocative statements made by Prime Minister Churchill annoyed Indian public opinion. At this critical juncture, Japan entered into the Second World War by launching a surprise attack on the USA at

Pearl Harbour. The Japanese army also occupied a major portion in the Far East and South East Asia. That became an eye opener both to the West and East. Japanese progress in war posed a threat to the defence of India. That forced England to have a new attitude. In March 1942, Sir Stafford Cripps gave a proposal offering Indian people a constituent assembly. He promised representation of British India and Indian states in it. He also gave the option to Muslim majority states to put out of the Indian federation. The proposal of Cripps was for late to mend. Since, the Indian nationalist were frustrated time and again by the British Government, the offer was rejected by all the Indian parties and the mission failed to satisfy the Indians.

5.10.19 Quit India Movement

The failure of the Cripps Mission, invasion of Japan in the Far East and South East Asia, oppressive attitude of the British Government, price rise, internal disturbance and bad governance caused widespread discontent among the Indian public. Since the British Empire was at critical situations, Gandhiji adopted a very stern attitude to pressurize the British Government to quit India. The Congress working committee adopted a resolution calling for complete non violent non cooperation with any foreign forces invading India. On 14th July 1942, the Congress working committee at Wardha declared that British rule in India must end immediately. This resolution is known as Quit India resolution. The Congress pleaded that India's freedom was essential not only to India but to the security of the world. The working committee resolutions of July 1942 was ratified and endorsed by the Bombay resolutions of the All India Congress Committee held on 7th and 8th August 1942. The Committee was of the view that there should be an immediate end of the British rule in India. Addressing the National Congress, a day before Gandhiji said, "I therefore want freedom immediately this very night before dawn, if it can be had. Fraud and untruth today are stalking the world. You may take if from me that I am not going to strike a bargain with the Viceroy for ministries and the like. I am not going to be satisfied with anything short of complete freedom. Have is a mantra, a short one, that I give you. You may imprint it on your hearts and let every breath of yours give expression to it. The mantra is 'Do or Die'. We shall either free India or die in the attempt. We shall not live to see the perpetuation of our slavery."

He asked the government to leave India to God or if that was too much leave her to anarchy. The Quit India movement or August revolution marks a turning point in the history of India. It was a revolt of the mass against tyranny and oppression. This movement is no way less than the French revolution. Its sustaining impulse was hatred of the British as rulers of the land. Its basic objective was to remove Britishers from India. Initially the movement was based on the principle of non violence, but the repressive policy of the British government made people violent. The Gandhian message of non violent struggle was pushed into the background and people devised their own methods of struggle. The movement started its beginning from Maharashtra. Government institutions were attacked, rail lines were dislocated and a wireless centre was set up at Bombay to propagate the names of those taking active part in the progress of the movement to the mass from time to time. In Karnataka, the movement was conducted with great skill, many people duped the police, continued the movement with great zeal and destroyed many government buildings. Gujarat observed Hartal and schools and colleges were closed down. Employees of Ahmedabad Municipality set on a Dharna protest. At Patna in Bihar students hoisted the national flag on the eastern gate of Patna secretariat in defiance to the police atrocities. At Katra in Muzaffarpur, people snatched away guns and weapons from the police. In North Bhagalpur, a parallel government was set up under the leadership of Siyaram Singh. The Bihar police station was attacked. The movement spread fast in Uttar Pradesh. People hoisted national flag in many places. Administration in the Benaras University was brought to a standstill. At Nagpur in Madhya Pradesh, all the police stations were captured by the people. The Government treasury was looted. In Calcutta the movement was widespread. People did not allow some trains to run. In the Tamluk subdivision, there was open rebellion against the British. In Orissa, people burnt past officers and besieged police stations. In reaction the Government took some stringent actions. All the front line leaders were arrested. This resulted in violent public reaction. The Government started drastic repressive measures. Several thousand people were killed and many more got wounded. The Quit India resolutions was withdrawn in 1944 after the release of Gandhiji. In June 1945, the Viceroy Lord Wavell initiated the Simla conference by inviting the representatives of the Congress and the Muslim League. The very objective of this conference was to break the deadlock through an understanding. But he failed to control the situation. After the Second World War was over, the new Government in London was headed by Sir Clement Attlee of the labour party. He assured India full independence and appointed the cabinet mission to visit India to chalk out the structure of the constitution. The mission comprising of Lord Pethick Lawrence, Sir Strafford Cripps and A.V. Alexander visited India in 1946 to discuss the matter with the Congress and the Muslim League on granting Independence to India. While the Muslim League proposed the creation of Pakistan, the Congress remained firm on the unity and integrity of the country on 16th May, 1946, the cabinet mission plan was prepared.

The mission contained the following proposals:

(i) The Indian federations would comprise the British ruled states and the native provinces.

(ii) Representatives of the British ruled states and of the provincial governments shall be in charge of the administration of the federation.

(iii) The federal government shall be in charge of external affairs, defence and communication.

(iv) The other departments and residency powers shall be in charge of the provincial government.

(v) There would be three categories of provinces. Madras, Bombay, Bihar and Madhya Pradesh would be united provinces. Bihar, Orissa and the Hindu dominating states shall be regarded as Hindu provinces. There should be creation of Sind, Baluchistan and North West Frontier provinces.

(vi) A constituent assembly would be set up.

(vii) There should be separate constituent for very province.

(viii) Leaders of different political parties would join together to form interim government and would take over the administrative from the Britisher.

(ix) Any state opting for withdrawal from the freedom can do so.

The cabinet mission also proposed for a separate state Pakistan. Since there was no special provision for the Muslim people, the Muslim League did not agree to this provisions of the cabinet mission. Being dissatisfied with the mission objective, the Muslim League threatened to observe 16th August 1946 on Direct action day. In protest of the proposal of cabinet mission, communal riots started in Bengal and other places. Gandhiji's vision based on communal harmony was shattered. However, an interim national government with Jawaharlal Nehru as the Prime Minister and Licquat Ali Khan as the finance minister was formed at the centre. The proposed constituent assembly held its inaugural sessions on 9th December 1946.

On 20th February 1947, the British Prime Minister Attlee declared to transfer the power to the people of India by 20th June 1948, people did not accept this a happy news for maintaining integrity and harmony among themselves. There were communal riots every where. Gandhi tried his best to cool down the situations but no pay did pay any heed to him. There was violence and hatred among people. In March 1947 Lord Mountbatten was appointed as the viceroy to India by replacing Lord Wavell. He thought it desirable to give freedom to India instantly in order to restore peace and communal harmony. He discussed with the leaders of two leading parties such as the Congress and the Muslim League. Realizing the tense situation, Mountbatten thought it desirable to divide India before granting freedom. The nationalist leader agreed the proposal of partition. They did not agree with M.A. Jinnah's two nation theory and refused to concede one-third of India to the Muslim League. That was the demand of the Muslim League. The long-standing band between the two communities was ransacked. The British Government succeeded in its mission of divide and rule. By an Act passed in the British parliament the administrations of India was handed over to the Indians with effect from 15th August 1947. The Indian Independence Act 1947 provided for the setting up of two independent states—India and Pakistan. Thus, the two sovereign independent states came into existence on 15th August 1947 in formity with the declaration made by Lord Mountbatten on 3rd June 1947. As a result of the declaration, the British Government ceased to exist and power was transferred to Indian leaders in the constituent Assembly of India.

The princely states were given the choice to whichever side they would like to merge with. There was some problem with the Nawab of Junagarh, Nizam of Hyderabad and Maharaja of Jammu and Kashmir. In Junagarh, the people wanted to join with India, whereas the Nawab wanted to join with Pakistan. In a swift action Indian troops marched into Junagarh and plebiscite was held to obtain the endorsement of the people in its union with India. The Nizam of Hyderabad wanted to remain independent. But he was forced to accede to Indian union. In case of Jammu and Kashmir, the Maharaja's delay in cession to India gave an opportunity to Pakistan to launch a full-fledged attack. The national conference party wanted to join with India. Finally in October 1947, the Maharaja signed the instrument of accession and Jammu and Kashmir became an integral part of India. On the midnight of 14th August 1947 at the Zero hour when the new India was emerging from the world of history offer a long period of travail in the shape of struggle for freedom, Jawaharlal Nehru made a speech for the nation as, "Long years ago we made a tryst with destiny and now time cames when we shall redeem our pledge, not wholly or in full measure, but very substantially. At the stroke of midnight hour, when the world sleeps, India will awake to life and freedom."

Thus, India achieved her freedom from foreign rule. She overcame the obstacle to join the country of nations. She was to overcome many more hurdles before making her people free from hunger and sufferings. India looked forward to a new age of socio-economic development.

5.10.20 An Assessment of Mahatma Gandhi

Mahatma Gandhi was a universal and undisputed leader of India's freedom. He was a national leader and the epitome of Indian nationalism. His personality was molded by Indian tradition and heritage. He respected Indian values and made a balance between modernation and extremism. His life was a programme of social reconstruction. He loved Indian village life and culture. His concept of Swaraj was identical with Ramrajya. He was not only a political leader but also a social reformer. He was a saint politician who believed in the philosophy of Satyagraha, a moral force. He urged upon social equality. His way of economic development had roots in Indian culture. He was a role model, a nationalist, a social reformer, a prophet and a common man. He was the apostle of secularism and cooperation. He is rightly regarded as the father of Indian nation.

Paying tribute to Gandhiji, the Indian parliament had passed a resolution which says,

> That the house pays its respectful tribute to the father of the nation, lead the country to Swaraj by non violent means who infused a new spirit into the masses, who uplifted the teeming million of the apprised and down-trodden, who awakened the national conscience of the people and who inspired the people with a spirit of dedication and service. Places on record its deep gratitude to that apostle of Ahimsa who crusade for peace, justice and equality and gave the strife-ridden world the message of universal brotherhood and humanism and rededicates itself to promote the high ideals of truth, nonviolence and service to the nation and to humanity for which the Mahatma lived and sacrificed his life.

The tragic end of Mahatma's life is a great loss to the nation and mankind.

5.11 Rabindranath Tagore

Rabindranath Tagore, the son of Debendranath Tagore and the younger brother of Satyendranath Tagore, was born in Calcutta on 7th May 1861. He was born in a family which was an adherent of the ideals of Brahmo Samaj. The Tagore family has gained fame by supporting the Renaissance in Bengal. The members were liberal in attitude and as such were great proponents of the reform movement initiated by Raja Rammohan Roy. Though they favoured western education, they had great love for Indian tradition and culture. Rabindranath Tagore was a widely traveled person who gained experience and knowledge about people living in other parts of the world. He was a humanist par excellence and an outstanding gonium. He was an ardent advocate of nationalism. He made India proud by winning the Nobel Prize in Literature for his immortal work *Gitanjali*. He was influenced by the ideals of Mahatma Gandhi.

5.11.1 His Political Philosophy

Rabindranath Tagore had a superb philosophy. He always responded to the call of the country. He was a humanist and internationalist. The India of his dreams is reflected in our national anthem "Jana Gana Mana" composed by him and in his other famous poem "where the mind is without fear". To bring unity and harmony among people he introduced the Rakhi celebrations against the partition of Bengal. As a protest against the partition of Bengal, he called for boycutt of Calcutta University examinations of 1906. His political ideas were for a find meeting of East and West on an equal footing. He stood for the society rather than for the state for the promotion of individual talent. He was a democratic socialist and he opposed fascism of Italy, Nazism of Germany and the socialism of Soviet model. He advocated communal harmony among Hindus and Muslims.

In his 'Swadeshi Samay' published in Banga Darshana, he pleaded that provincial representative assembly should have its branches in districts and villages. Tagore very much opposed the impersonal rule of England in India. He always pleaded for Liberty of thought and action and liberty of conscience. He had a spiritual cooperation of freedom. He was a prophet of individuality and not of domination. He accepted the idea of comprehensive social and cultural growth of India. He was a champion of the political freedom of India. He pleaded for self-Government in India and believed in the regeneration of the spirit of the people of India. He sponsored a moral approach of politics. As a champion of Swadeshi movement he came in close contact with Gandhiji. He was against colonial oppression and was a strong critic of British imperialism. His views were presented in the book *Crisis in Civilization*.

He was an admirer and critic of Gandhi, whom he called the 'Mahatma'. He condemned the authority for arresting the leader of the salt Satyagraha. He used to uphold Gandhiji because when he undertook fast against the communal award 1932. Tagore denounced in a mass rally in Calcutta the brutal police firing on the political prisoners. He believed in the multi religions, multiracial nationalism in India. His political philosophy proceeds from his deep spiritual humanism.

The difference of opinion between Tagore and Gandhi was somewhat striking but was almost inevitable. Tagore represented the aesthetic instinct of India as Gandhi represented her religious ascetic instinct. Tagore was the poet and Gandhi was the political crusader. Tagore believed in Art and Gandhi believed in action. Both of them represented two different aspects of India, but they also complemented each other.

Tagore believed in Indian unity transcending the diversity not only of creeds, but also to castes. He denounced the caste ideas. He pointed out that it was the love of reason and liberty that had led to the development of science and free society in modern Europe. He wanted a synthesis of East and West. He believed that the problems of modern civilization could be solved through changes in social and political institutions alone. He put his faith not only on any new institution but in individuals all over the world, who would think clearly, feel nobly and act in the right manner. His lifelong crusade for social equality and economic reforms are outstanding. He was a visionary who wanted far-reaching changes in the society. He preached an ethic of active social service. He wanted to establish that this emphasis on ethical activity and social service was a continuation of old Indian thought. The national anthem written by him conveys the noble message of unity amidst diversity singing the eulogy of the various regions and the people who constitute Indian republic.

5.11.2 His Contribution to Education, Literature and Music

Rabindranath Tagore was an avowed champion of education. He was determined to promote mother tongue by making it the medium of instruction. According to him education should encourage freedom and individual personality. In December

1910, he established a school at Shantiniketan, a Brahmacharya Ashram on the pattern of ancient forest hermitages. In course of time, he developed it into Vishva Bharati, and International University for the different culture in the world.

Rabindranath Tagore was an important figure of the Bengali literary renaissance that constituted the background for political awakening. He made outstanding constitutions for enriching modern Bengali literature. As a creative writer, he excelled in every literary form. His works included *Kadi O Kamala* (1886), *Manasi* (1890), *Naivedya* (1901), *Khoga* (1906), *Gitanjali* (1910), *Balaka* (1916), *Puravi* (1925), *Mahuya* (1929), *Pratika* (1938), *Nabajatak* (1940), and *Janadin* (1941). He also wrote children's literature *Sisu* (1903) and *Sisu Bhalanath* (1922). He wrote about two hundred songs which have been translated in many languages of the world and earned him high reputation. He was the first Indian to receive the Nobel Prize in 1913.

He had tremendous contribution to the Bengali Drama. Chitargada, Sahyama and Chandalika were his famous works. His serious plays included, "Raja O Rani" (1889), "Visarjana" (1890), "Malini" (1895) and "Bansari" (1933). His light plays included, "Godya Galad" (1892), "Vaikunthir Khata" (1897), and "Kumar Sabha" (1901). His symbolic plays were, "Raja" (1910), "Achalayatane" (1911), "Dakghar" (1912), "Muktadhara" (1922), "Raktakaravi" (1924) and "Tasre desa" (1933). He wrote several essays covering various aspects like literary, religions, biographical, historical, political and humorous. He also wrote his autobiography. He dominated the field of Bengali literature till he breathed his last in 1941. Bengali literature was flourished by him.

Rabindranath Tagore was fortunate enough to be born in a family of Music lovers. His brother Jyotindra Mohan Tagore made commendable efforts for the revival of Indian music. Rabindranath also followed his footsteps to popularize Bengali music. He provided a new direction to Indian music which is recognized as Rabindra Sangeet. It provided a curious synthesis of sweetness, simplicity and instrumental music.

5.12 Jawaharlal Nehru, His Political Career and Philosophy

Jawaharlal Nehru, the first Prime Minister of free India was born on 14th November 1889 at Allahabad. He was the son of an illustrious personality Motilal Nehru, the lawyer politician. Jawaharlal Nehru, from his very childhood was dynamic. He was educated in England. After completing Bar at Law he came back to India in 1912 and joined politics.

When he was a student in England, he had toyed with Fabian socialism. He was a staunch nationalist. In his autobiography he has vividly described his position, "I was a pure nationalist. My vague socialist ideas of college days having sunk into the background". He began his political activities by his association with Home Rule league. In 1916, he met Gandhi. He was a vehement critic of the Britishraj following the Jallianwalabagh massacre in 1919. In 1920, he visited some villages in the U.P. and the deplorable condition of the peasant had a deep impact on him. The non cooperation movement brought Gandhi and Nehru close to each other. In 1923, he was appointed as the general secretary of the Congress. He was the participant in the congress of oppressed Nationalists at Brussels in 1927. In 1929, he was elected president of All India Trade Union Congress. In the same year he succeeded his father as the Congress president at Lahore. He had the unique distinction of presiding the Congress five times. In 1931, he introduced and carried the resolution of fundamental rights. In 1945, he attended the Simla conference, held parleys with the British Cabinet Mission in 1946. Forming the interim Government of 1946-47 he negotiated for the final transfer of power in India.

Nehru was a well bred personality. He was very much influenced by the writings of Bernard Shaw and Betrand Russel. He subscribed the general philosophical ethos propounded by Mill, Gladstone and merely. He was a man of ideas. He was an westernized aristocrat who used to hate the inequality prevailing in the caste system. He accepted the moral and ethical aspect of Gandhian movement. He attempted to spiritualize politics. His life and philosophy was influenced by Buddhism. He was a staunch supporter of Buddhist concept of Panchasheel. His Internationalism was not in disharmony with nationalism.

He was a great lover of mankind who dedicated his life for the cause of democracy and human freedom. He gave moral support to the freedom movement in many countries of Asia, Africa and South America. He was the champion of world peace and supporter of the UNO. He played the role of the peace maker when world peace was threatened in Korea, Suez Canal, Laos, the Congo, Vietnam, West Asia and other places. He said Internationalism can develop only in a free country. He was an exponent of peace. He was a firm believer in the principles of United Nations and was opposed to the bipolarization of world politics. He pursued the policy of non alignment which forms the basis of India's foreign policy.

He had a strong belief in the fundamental unity of India based on its cultural foundations. He was greatly influenced by the idea of synthetic universalism propounded by Tagore. He believed the concept of self-determination. He was against national arrogance of the British rulers. He adopted a secular approach and had his faith on national integration. He had a scientific outlook. He advocated the growth of science and technology for the welfare of human beings. He popularized science and technology in India and wanted to make India technologically vibrant. He was a secularist who urged upon the people to develop commercial harmony for national integration. He presided over the destiny of India for long 17 years as her prime minister. For the quick progress of Indian economy, he introduced economic planning. As chairman of the Planning Commission he tried to make India self-sufficient in food production and industrial output. During his teenure as prime minister he laid emphasis on the development of Agriculture and heavy industries. He exercised his innovative ideas to import the technology of USA, Great Britain, Germany and Russia for implementing the five-year plan projects. He evolved a socialistic pattern of society which envisaged harmony between Marxism and capitalism.

As an avowed champion of world peace and non violence, he preached the value of Panchasheel and encouraged the non alignment movement by holdings periodic meetings among neutral countries. He organized Afro-Asian conferences and conferences of commonwealth countries. To achieve this he gave the call "Hindi Chini Bhai Bhai". He accepted the role of peace maker in Korean conflict and Vietnam worse. He had no ideological bias. He wanted to strengthen the UNO as a peace maker in the world.

He was a humanist throughout. He strove tirelessly against war and for total disarmament. He was the first head of the Government to support the partial test ban pact signed by three nuclear power in 1983. He set his face against all political and military blocks as the greatest impediment of world peace. He was opposed to casteism, untouchability and gender discrimination. He supported the cause of women education and growth of education among scheduled caste, scheduled tribe and other backward castes. He wanted to build a classless society. He strongly urged for national unity and solidarity. He fought against divisive forces like caste, religion, language and strove for the upliftment of the less privileged.

5.12.1 An Estimate of Jawaharlal Nehru

Jawaharlal Nehru was a good writer and orator. He wrote several books such as *Discovery of India*, *Glimpses of World History*, *Letters of a Father to His Daughter*, etc. These books had great social relevance. These are excellent works on Literature. These writings have immortalized him. He symbolized the emergence of a new India. His aim was to make India politically stable, socially strong and economically developed. He was a great leader of man. He was out and out a pacifist and democrat. He was the architect of modern India. Pandit Radhakrishnan paid him glorious tributes, "As a fighter of freedom he was illustrious, as a maker of modern India and his services were unparalleled. His life and work had a profound influence on our mental makeup, social structure and intellectual's development. According to S. Gopal, his biographer, Nehru played a decisive role in the history of the 20th century, as a leader of the Indian people, as representative of a new mood of Asia and as a spokesman of the International conscience. All said and done, Nehru should be judged against the time in which he lived and worked, the purity of his public life his honesty and his aversion to corruption. He had made India what she is today. He gave India an ideology for which he is proud of today.

5.13 Subash Chandra Bose

Subash Chandra Bose, the son of Janakinath Bose an advocate of Cuttack was born on 23rd January 1897 in Oriya Bazar at Cuttack in Orissa. After completion of his early school training at the Protestant European School in Cuttack, he took his higher studies at Ravenshaw Collegiate School, under the inspiring guidance of Beni Madhav Das, the then Headmaster who taught him many interesting things about glorious past of India. Later on Subash Chandra Bose studied in the Presidency College, Calcutta while studying there, he was deeply attracted by the fiery writing of Aurobindo Ghosh. On 15th September 1919 he left for England to appear at the Indian Civil Service Examination. There he spent all the time in his studies with intense concentration and came out with flying colours in the examination. He had no inclinations to join Government service. So he resigned Civil Service and returned to India in 1921 to take a plunge in the struggle for freedom. His dynamic leadership attracted masses. In 1924, he became the Commissioner of Calcutta Municipality. He went against the accepted norms of inviting Englishmen to deliver the welcome address and instead called upon leaders like Mahatma Gandhi and Pandit Madan Mohan Malaviya to do this honours. Hence he was arrested by the British. Between 1933-36 makings a pretext of illness he traveled to Europe and widely exposed to barbaric atrocities of the British in India.

5.13.1 His Political Career

Subash Chandra was a political disciple of C.R. Das who brought him into Indian politics. C.R. Das, in those days was bringing out a paper and also running a national college so as to give a prop to national awakening. He entrusted Subash to edit the paper. Subhas sponsored an organized demonstration in the city of Calcutta to protest against the visit of Prince of Wales. He was arrested. This is the first time that Subash went to jail after which he was arrested at least eleven times till he left India. He secretly established his contact with the Indian revolutionary group like the Anu Shilam Samiti, the Yuganter Group, the Hindustan Republican Armed Force who accepted him as their patron and Adviser. Because of his associations with revolutionaries, he became a thorn in the flesh of the Government.

Subash had very high regard for Gandhiji as a man but he regarded him very poorly as a politician and statesmen. He did not like Gandhi's approach of non violence. As a student of history, he knew very well that the British interest remained in exploiting India's manpower and material resources for the benefit of British economy. During the Lahore session of Congress in 1929 Subash Bose said, "I take this opportunity of conveying my cordial and hearty thanks to Gandhiji for coming forward to move a resolution which declares Swaraj to mean complete Independence. But I move this amendment because I believe that this programme laid down by his resolution is not such as to carry us towards the goal of complete Independence. My amendment is consistent with the goal and in keeping with the spirit of the time—let us be for complete boycott or none at all. I am an extremist and my principle is all or none." In 1938, he become the president of Haripur Congress. He raised the slogan of complete independence but his extremist views did not find favour with Gandhiji. He was re-elected President of INC in 1939 in spite of the opposition of Gandhiji. Later on he resigned from the Presidentship of Congress and organized a separate political party under the name of Forward Block. He activated the freedom struggle. He made the clarion call—"Give me blood, I will give you freedom." During the Second World War Bose was under house arrest in Calcutta. He was considering the prospect of joining the fascist powers like Germany, Italy and Japan to wage a war against the British for liberation of India. In a surprise move he escaped from house arrest in January 1941 via Kobul to reach Germany through Russia. From there he traveled in a submarine to Japan where arrangements had been made for him to lead a liberation army towards India. Japan and promised help. The whole world knew about his next move. He called upon his countrymen to revolt against the British and to throw them out of India.

5.13.2 Formation of INA

There were many Indian revolutionaries working abroad for the cause of India. An Indian revolutionary named Rasbehari Bose had formed the Azad Hind Fauj or the INA in Japan. He seized the opportunity offered by the war to mobilize for an armed struggle against the British. There were a number of Indian soldiers fighting on behalf of the British. The Japanese after defeating the British in South East Asia took a number of Indian soldiers as prisoners of war. Major Fuziwara a Japanese Army officer persuaded Captain Mohan Singh, a prisoner of war to work in collaboration with the Japanese for India's freedom. In March 1942, a conference of Indians was held in Tokyo where they formed the Indian Independence League. This was followed by a conference in Bangkok in June 1942, where Rasbehari Bose was elected President of the league and decision was taken to raise the Indian National Army. Captain Mohan Singh was appointed as the Commander of INA. This conference invited Subash Bose to led the movement. After landing in Tokyo Subash Bose declared in his first statement "The opportunity which this Great War has offered may not recur in a hundred years to come. It is our resolve to avail fully of this opportune movement for the liberation of Bharat. It is our duty to offer blood as the price for freedom—our fight is against all types of imperialism—comrades, let your one slogan be 'Chalo Delhi' (March on to Delhi). Whatever befall you in sun shine and dark hours, in grief or joy, I assure you will always remain with you. But today I cannot offer you anything except hunger, thirst, hardship, travails and death itself. It is no matter who of us lives or dies. Let us sacrifice everything and make India free." Subash Bose was received by Toji, the Japanese premier. When Bose arrived at Singapore, on 2nd July 1943, he was welcomed with enthusiasm by an immense surging crowd who felt that at last new blood was infused INA which could lead them on as victors to liberate their own motherland. Subash Bose proclaimed the inauguration of provisional government of free India on 21st October 1943 at Singapore. He and his ministers took an oath in the name of God as "I take this sacred oath that to liberate India and thirty-eight crores of my countrymen—after winning freedom, I will always be prepared to shed even the last drop of my blood for the preservation of India's freedom". The provisional government was recognized by nine world powers—on 28th October 1943 he flew to Tokyo. He was received an honoured by the emperor of Japan. He attended the greater East Asia conference as the head of the Azad Hind Government. General Tojo announced that Japan decided to handover the Andaman and Nicobar Islands to the Azad Hind Government. Netaji visited the Andaman Island on 31st December 1943 and named the two Islands as Shaheed and Swaraj Islands.

The aim of Subash Chandra Bose was to march up to Delhi to throw out the British Government in coordination's with Japan. The INA launched the liberation war of India in March 1944. He reached Kohima on the Indian boarder where the Tricolour Indian Flag was unfurled. It was in Assam border. But there was a sudden change of fortune. Japanese army could not proceed further and the dropping of atom bombs on 5th and 8th August 1945 led to the Surrender of Japan. The war suddenly came to an end. It was separated that Bose, while escaping from Singapore towards Japan died in a plane crash on 18th August 1945.

The soldiers of INA surrendered to the British Army and they were to be tried as prisoners of war as accused of treason. A military court was to conduct the trial at the Red fort in New Delhi. There was nationwide protest and agitation against the trial of INA soldiers. The accused persons were regarded as National heroes from Indian viewpoint. All political parties including the Muslim League and the Congress joined together for the defence of the accused. The Indian National Congress set up the INA defence committee to defend the INA soldiers. Great nationalists like Tej Bahadur Sapru, Bhulabhai Desai, Nehru, etc., come to Red fort trial as defence lawyers.

There was popular resentment in the country. Though the military court convicted the accused, the Government of India set them free respecting the public demand. The British Government now realized their foolishness to depend upon the Indian army. The Indian Navy recruits in Bombay also were on the war path. Once rebellion spread to the Army and Navy, there was no power to retain India as a port of the empire. The world public opinion was in support of granting the right of self determination to India. India's demand for freedom received support of the Government of USA. President Roosevelt advised the British Government to grant freedom to Indian people. Then came the famous Attlee declaration of making India free. It was high time for the imperial British Government to Quit India.

Though Subhas Chandra Bose was not alive to see for himself the final result of the struggle, his contribution to the cause of freedom did not go unrecorded and unrecognized. His courage and patriotism made him immortal in the history of India's struggle for freedom.

5.14 Mohammad Ali Jinnah

Mohammad Ali Jinnah, son of Jinnab Poonja, an ordinary hide merchant was born at Karachi, on 25th Dec. 1876. He belonged to the Khoja Muslim Community who represented Agha Khan. He received his education at Karachi and Bombay. In 1896, he passed the Bar-at-law examination in England. His married life was not all satisfactory as his first wife died early and his second wife was divorced. These unhappy events made him a bitter person making himself centred and introvert.

5.14.1 His Public Career

The public career of M.A. Jinnah may be classified into four periods:

(a) 1906-1920—During this period, he was a culture nationalist, a leader of the Indian National Congress Party. His outlook was secular. He worked for national unity. He never wanted to mix up religion with politics.

(b) 1920-1928—During this period he alienated himself from the Congress organization; but his faith on Indian unity was remained intact.

(c) 1928-1937—During this period he came under the influence of the Muslim League and its ideology. He becomes the undisputed leader of the Muslim League.

(d) 1937-1947—He emerged as the Chief Speaks person of the Muslim community and advocated the two-nation theory and demanded a separate homeland for the Muslim.

5.14.2 His Political Career

Initially Jinnah was not interested in politics, but later on he came in close contact with the moderates. He was very much influenced by liberal nationalists such as Dadabhai Naraoji, Surendranath Banarjee, G.K. Gokhale, and Feroz Shah Mehta. He also worked as the private secretary of Naraoji for some time. He writes, "I learnt my first lesson in politics at the feet of Surendranath Banarjee. To Gokhale he had obligations as political disciple. He had won great admiration when he defended B.G. Tilak in the sedition cases against him in 1908 and 1916."

In 1910, Jinnah was elected to the imperial legislative council by the Muslim electorate of Bombay. He was re-elected to the council in 1916 but in 1919 when the Rowlatt Act was passed, he resigned from the council in protest of the Act. In 1916, when the Home Rule leagues were founded, he did not join at first. But after the internment of Mrs. Annie Besant he joined the Home Rule league. First he had been opposed to communal electorate, later he declared that separate electorate was a matter of interest to the Muslims. He pleaded for harmony and understanding among various communities for the sake of national unity. It there was an understanding between the Congress and Muslim League it was his handiwork. This culminated in the Lucknow pact of 1919. For constitutional reform only he supported the Congress League joint venture. In 1919 he criticized the Rowlatt Act as Block Act. During 1920-28, he withdrew himself from active politics. He was very much sentimental and developed an aristocratic temperament. He was not in favour of the popularity of Mahatma Gandhi and the non cooperation movement launched by him. He thought of haring the topmost position as the leader of the Muslim League. Since he was quite junior to Maulana Mohammad Ali he did not find favour. After the death of Mohammad Ali in 1931 he spread his intellectual acumen and organized people in his favour. He emerged as the only choice to be the undisputed leader of the Muslim League. The election of 1937 crowned him as the leader, but the Muslim League was not given the chance in the formation of ministry. When Congress refused the cooperation of the Muslim League, Jinnah was violent. His attitude changed abruptly. He described the Congress as anti Muslim. He alleged that the Congress was planning to have a Hindu Raj. The Muslims expressed apprehension of Hindu tyranny and observed a day of deliverance and thank giving when the Congress ministries resigned in October 1939 over the issue of joining the Second World War.

5.14.3 His Two Nation Theory

Jinnah formulated a two nation theory in which he stated that the Hindus and Muslims represented two nations not two communities. This concept first came from political thinker Mohammad Iqbal. He gave the idea of separate state for the Indian Muslims. In 1930, he declared at the Allahabad session of the Muslim League that Indian Muslims deserve a homeland for their culture and identity. That would give a permanent communal settlement. Punjab, North West Frontier province, Sind and Baluchistan should together form a state. This North West Indian Muslim state would be the final destiny of Indian Muslims. That this province would be named Pakistan was the idea of Rahmat Ali a student of the Cambridge University of England—P for Punjab, A for Afghanistan, K for Kashmir, I for India or Sind province and stan was in reference to Baluchistan. He said that Hindus and Muslims were fundamentally different nations. He wrote "our religion, culture, history, tradition, literature, economic system and laws of inheritance are fundamentally different from those of the Hindus. These differences extend to the minute details of our lives. We Muslims and Hindus do not interline, do not inter marry, our national customs, even our diet and dress are different."

Jinnah was a staunch Muslim. He became restless for the creations of Pakistan. He also demanded the North West Frontier provinces and large areas from Bengal and Assam. Leaders of the Congress bitterly opposed Jinnah. They criticized Jinnah saying he could segregate the Hindus in Punjab, Bengal and Assam and then form Pakistan with the remaining areas. Gandhiji opposed to partition at any cost and declared, "If India would ever be partitioned, it could only be over my dead body." Jinnah refused to oblige Mahatma Gandhi. He was opposed to Gandhi for two reasons—First, Gandhiji's too much emphasis on religion and satyagraha and second, Gandhiji was his political rival in the Congress. So he changed over to communal politics.

Jinnah went on repeating every where his two nation theory pleading for the creation of Pakistan. He took the most rigid and inflexible stand on which there was no negotiation, no compromise. He gave the ideological justification to the Muslim demand for a separate homeland. He gave the slogan (Leke

Rehange Pakistan) "we must win Pakistan". This appealed to the Indian Muslim who gave whole-hearted support to Jinnah. Jinnah's diplomacy destroyed the success of Simla conference of 1945 and the cabinet mission plan of 1946. Further he threatened direct action or communal riots if the demand would not be conceded. Under the holocaust of communal disturbance and mass killing by fanatics, the Congress leaders and the British Government finally accepted partition of India as a 'fait accompli'. Pakistan was created on 14th August 1947 and Jinnah became the first governor general of Pakistan. He died in 1948 after making Pakistan a reality.

5.14.4 An Estimate of Mohammad Ali Jinnah

Jinnah was the epitome of Muslim separatism. In the early part of his life, he was a liberal politician, but he changed his attitude and objective later on. Born in a lower middle class he became rich and developed an aristocratic temperament. He was Indian by birth, but English in taste and manner, morals and opinions. Though he had no personal respect for Islam, he proved to be a fundamentalist in identifying the interests of Indian Muslims. He did not know Urdu, yet became the charismatic leader of the Muslim. He combined religion with politics to achieve his political goals in the form of Muslim state called Pakistan.

He was a shrewd politician. He could far surpass Gandhi, Nehru and other Congress leaders in the art of political charisma and diplomacy. He used to visualize his own plan and course of action. It is said that he won Pakistan for the Muslim with the help of a type writer alone. Though he used religion for political gains, he did not want Pakistan to be an Islamic state. His aim was to give Indian Muslims a political identity and succeeded in partitioning India justifying his two nation theory.

Bibliography

Avasti Amareswar, *Public Administration*, Laxmi Narain Agarwal, Agra, 1982.

Bailey, F.G., *Political and Social Change*, Orissa, 1951.

Buxi, V. and Patrice, *Crisis and Change in Contemporary India* (Ed.), SAGE Publications, New Delhi, 1955.

Brahmananda, P.R. and Panchamukhi, V.R. Himalaya, *The Development Process of the Indian Economy* (Ed.), Publishing House, Bombay, 1987.

Chattarjee, Partha, *The Nation and Its Fragments*, Princeton University Press, Princeton, 1993.

Devi, S., *Caste System in India*, Pointer Publishers, Jaipur, 1999.

Dhal, P.C., *Democracy in India, Constraints and Opportunities*, Aaviskar Publishers and Distributors, Jaipur, 2002.

Dube, S.C. (Ed.), *India Since Independence: Social Report on India*, Vikash Publishers, New Delhi, 1977.

Dass and Deulkar, *Caste and Social Reality*. Dominant Publishers, New Delhi, 2005.

Kansal, Jairam, *Sociology and Social Change*, Dominant Publishers, New Delhi, 2004.

Gajendragadkar, P.B., *Indian democracy: its major imperatives*, B.I. Publication, Bombay, 1975.

Ghurye, G.S., *India Recreats Democracy*, Popular Prakashan, Bombay, 1978.

Ghurye, G.S., *Caste and Class in India*, Popular Prakashan, Bombay, 1950.

Joshi, N.C., *Democracy and Social Values*, Sterling Publishers, New Delhi, 1979.

Kothari, Rajani, *Democratic Polity and Social Changes of India*, 1979.

Khan, M.A., *Issues in Religion and Sociology*, Mittal Publiclation, New Delhi, 2005.

Nehru, J., *The Discovery of India*, Gardencity, New York, 1960.

Oster, Akas, *Culture and Power*, SAGE Publications, Delhi, 1984.

Pemberton, R.B., *The Eastern Frontier of India*, Mittal Publications, New Delhi, 2005.

Prulthi, R., *Social and Cultural History of Modern India*, Pointer Publishers, Jaipur, 1999.

Prulthi, R., *History of Indian Culture*, Pointer Publishers, Jaipur, 2007.

Reddy, K. Venugopal. *Class, Colonialism and Nationalism*, Mittal Publications, 2002.

Saberwal, Satish, *The Roots of Crisis*, Oxford University Press, Delhi, 1986.

Srinivas, M.N., *Social Change in Modern India*, Berkeery, 1966.

Sitaramaya, B.P., *The History of Indian National Congress*, Bombay, 1046.

Sharma, V., *Society, Culture and Religion—An Assessment*, Mittal Publishers, New Delhi, 2006.

Singh, V., *Indian Society—Ancient to Modern*, Mittal Publiclations, New Delhi, 2006.

Sirohi, Anand, *Fundamentals of Sociology*, Dominant Publishers, New Delhi, 2007.

Thomas, Santosh, *Studies in Religious Mysticism Christianity and Buddhism*, Mittal Publications, 2005.

Tiwari, K.P., *Foundation of Indian Culture*, Pointer Publishers, Jaipur, 2007.

Weber, A. *History of Philosophy*, Mittal Publishers, New Delhi, 2007.